Lyric Personhood

*opera*LAB

Explorations in History, Technology, and Performance

A series edited by David J. Levin and Mary Ann Smart

ADVISORY BOARD

Carolyn Abbate
Gundula Kreuzer
Emanuele Senici
Benjamin Walton
Emily Wilbourne

ALSO PUBLISHED IN THE SERIES

Music in the Present Tense: Rossini's Italian Operas in Their Time
Emanuele Senici

*Singing Sappho: Improvisation and Authority
in Nineteenth-Century Italian Opera*
Melina Esse

Networking Operatic Italy
Francesca Vella

"Don Giovanni" Captured: Performance, Media, Myth
Richard Will

New Orleans and the Creation of Transatlantic Opera, 1819–1859
Charlotte Bentley

Screening the Operatic Stage: Television and Beyond
Christopher Morris

Lyric Personhood

ON THE AESTHETICS OF BEING
SOMEONE IN THE WEST

Dan Wang

The University of Chicago Press   CHICAGO AND LONDON

The University of Chicago Press, Chicago 60637
The University of Chicago Press, Ltd., London
© 2025 by The University of Chicago
All rights reserved. No part of this book may be used or reproduced in any manner whatsoever without written permission, except in the case of brief quotations in critical articles and reviews. For more information, contact the University of Chicago Press, 1427 E. 60th St., Chicago, IL 60637.
Published 2025

34 33 32 31 30 29 28 27 26 25   1 2 3 4 5

ISBN-13: 978-0-226-84355-1 (cloth)
ISBN-13: 978-0-226-84357-5 (paper)
ISBN-13: 978-0-226-84356-8 (ebook)
DOI: https://doi.org/10.7208/chicago/9780226843568.001.0001

This book has been supported by the AMS 75 PAYS Fund of the American Musicological Society.

Library of Congress Cataloging-in-Publication Data

Names: Wang, Dan (Musicologist) author
Title: Lyric personhood : on the aesthetics of being someone in the West / Dan Wang.
 Other titles: Opera lab
Description: Chicago : The University of Chicago Press, 2025. | Series: Opera lab: explorations in history, technology, and performance | Includes bibliographical references and index.
Identifiers: LCCN 2025004416 | ISBN 9780226843551 cloth | ISBN 9780226843575 paperback | ISBN 9780226843568 ebook
Subjects: LCSH: Motion pictures—Philosophy | Opera | Persons—Philosophy | Personalism | Narration (Rhetoric) | LCGFT: Film criticism
Classification: LCC PN1995 .W3525 2025 | DDC 791.4301—dc23/eng/20250407
LC record available at https://lccn.loc.gov/2025004416

Authorized Representative for EU General Product Safety Regulation (GPSR) queries: **Easy Access System Europe**—Mustamäe tee 50, 10621 Tallinn, Estonia, gpsr.requests@easproject.com
Any other queries: https://press.uchicago.edu/press/contact.html

Contents

INTRODUCTION: Self-Evident — 1

1. THREE SPEECHES DELIVERED BY COLIN FIRTH — 24

2. WHITE LOVE: ROMANTIC COMEDY, THE '90S, AND GENRE IN THE BACKGROUND — 46
   Three Punch Lines (What's Comedy Doing in Romantic Comedy?) — 50
   Musical Montage, or Heterosexual Aesthetics — 67
   Revelations of Form: A Reading of *You've Got Mail* — 77

3. METARHYTHMS OF THE ADDICT: *TANNHÄUSER* IN THE COMPULSION ARCHIVE — 95
   Get Better — 95
   Two Concepts of Tragedy — 100
   Addiction and the Event of Thought — 108
   Silence and World — 115
   Coda: Audiovisual Aesthetics and the Problem of the Whole — 122

4. THE SOUNDTRACK IS SO CLICHÉ: AMBIENT WESTERNNESS AFTER 9/11 — 128
   Zooming Out, Fading In — 128
   USA, the Backstage Musical: *The West Wing* — 132
   Event Without Content: *The Happening* — 135
   Personhood and the Cliché: *Non-Stop* — 148
   Race After the "Postracial" Terrorist Film — 156
   Hold Music, General Forms, and the Lyric Ordinary: *Kajillionaire* — 163

EPILOGUE: Where Nothing Happens   168

Acknowledgments   175
Notes   177
Bibliography   191
Index   199

INTRODUCTION
Self-Evident

When it begins, the audience grasps immediately the kind of pleasure that is expected of them. The singer in Leonard Bernstein's *I Hate Music!*—a "cycle of five kid songs for soprano"—appears in the guise of a ten-year-old named Barbara, and the first few numbers enact familiar kinds of unknowing that mark the child's anteriority to the world of adults: Barbara puzzles over where babies come from ("My mother said that babies come in bottles; but last week she said they grew on special baby bushes") and fantasizes about outer space after learning that Jupiter has seven moons ("or is it nine?").[1] Meanwhile, behind the scene of the performance, Bernstein instructs the singer in a note that "coyness is to be assiduously avoided," which is to say that what would threaten this particular artifice is the appearance of any sign—a look, a pause, a slightly knowing enunciation, a twitch of muscle—that exposes the presence of an adult consciousness housed within the child. If the mind of the singer were to make an appearance here, winking across the stage to the other adults in the hall, the child would suddenly become the performance's referent rather than the persona that supposedly enacts it. The soprano's primary expressive task, therefore, is to suppress any trace of irony that might reveal the child to be a mirage made entirely by adults; only then could the "natural, unforced sweetness of child expressions" produce the effect of a real and present thing.

If there is something that feels familiar about the child's relation to its audience, it may be because a theatrical tendency already tends to arise in ordinary interactions between children and adults.[2] That is, when interacting with children, the adult will sometimes find themselves becoming a scene partner to a foreign rationality, playing along in its reality while, perhaps, continuing conversations in offstage asides to nearby adults or signaling through the bad acting of artificially heightened tone and gesture their awareness that they are currently *in a scene*. The aesthetic intensification of reality into pantomime allows the adult to remain both within and outside the scene, as both its performer and spectator, while the child becomes a spectacle unaware of the fact of the spectacle—a secret that the adult, even while relating, must keep. The categorical distinction between children and adults is an ordinary part of a culture's ideology, of course, but it is sustained in everyday practice through aesthetic rituals and gestural repertoires that continually distinguish the spectacle from the spectator, the stage from the hall, and theatrical from ordinary speech.

But something disturbs these conventional arrangements at the start of the cycle's last song. "I just found out today that I'm a person too, like you," Barbara sings. When personhood dawns for Barbara, it does so as the discovery of similarity between her and her interlocutors, which suddenly complicates the matter of her difference and its relegation of her to an epistemic subclass. Barbara discovers that her taste is no different from anyone else's ("I like things that ev'ryone likes: I like soft things and movies and horses and warm things and red things: don't you?"), nor her capacity for thinking and philosophy ("I have lots of thoughts; like what's behind the sky; and what's behind what's behind the sky"). That the tone of these passages seems both bemused and frustrated—as if she's trying to puzzle something out, but has also puzzled out enough to sense the contour of an injustice—seems to be out of a sense that her descriptive similarity to the unspecified "you" who occupies the formal position of personhood should not only mean something, it should mean the most decisive thing: ultimately, it is this formal sameness, and not the differences of embodiment and experience, that should determine her equal and proper moral status. Personhood is the theory that the accidents of historical, political, and embodied difference obscure a deeper, more morally resonant, more politically insightful, and ultimately mimetic truth: that, at the end of the day, I'm a person too, like you.

But Barbara's invocation of personhood fails to produce the recognition she seems to hope for. Instead, far from dissipating the logics of her objectification, the appeal to personhood ends up producing a fresh set of problems:

> I like balloons; lots of people like balloons:
> But ev'ryone says: "Isn't she cute? She likes balloons!"
>
> I have lots of thoughts; like what's behind the sky;
>   and what's behind what's behind the sky
> But ev'ryone says, "Isn't she sweet? She wants to know ev'rything!"
>   Don't you?

In other words, when Barbara tries to insist that she is actually the same, the discovery of this similarity somehow gets translated back into a mark of difference. Even the drive toward empirical knowing somehow looks precious and feminized on her. Every time Barbara attempts a reading of similarity, she finds that similarity *looks different* on her than on others. The problem, it seems, is not exactly that her difference from the normative and implicit embodiment of the public causes her to be relegated to a different moral status; it is that the *same* traits produce general knowledge about her but only incidental knowledge about them. It turns out that Barbara is ensnared not only by the qualities that are read in her, but also by an architecture of address that has already contained her as the scene's third person. When she attempts to address her audience directly with the second-person pronoun ("Don't you?"), the response that comes is a rhetorical question that bypasses her, finding instead another consumer of her aesthetic presence ("Isn't she cute?").

When Barbara attempts to use the universalizing category of personhood to leverage a recognition that might lead to justice, it is in the register of *general* knowledge that the attempt seems to malfunction. As she tries to emphasize, the stain of stereotype is not necessarily that it's false, but rather that it names a sensuous material that becomes a certain kind of knowledge, predicting and predictable, only when it encounters the low atmosphere of your kind of body. And yet, in the attempt to make this known, Barbara discovers that her otherness had already been predetermined on some discursive plane prior to the plane of content, even though her objectification makes it seem as if it has to do with content. If there is an atmosphere of frustration in the phrase "I'm a person, too," as if it should be too evident or obvious a fact even to argue, this frustration seems to register a double bind in which the one who argues for their personhood has already, in needing to argue it, conceded the opposite of what the phrase claims. "I'm a person, too," then, is a claim that wishes it were articulated in a different zone of knowledge than the one in which it actually is articulated, language; it wishes, rather, for the kind of knowledge that precedes language, the zone of self-evident and incontrovertible things. And yet the nascent political ambition that might be excavated from this frustration is met with the hopelessness of ever making her audience see the truth of their investment in her, as a material in what Hortense Spillers has called the "national treasury of rhetorical wealth."[3] In fact, the voice of the other hasn't even been present during this exchange, since it is already fully embedded in her rationality: she has been staging the argument all by herself, playing both parts.

The cycle closes without the other ever recognizing what Barbara wants them to recognize. In the end, her insight remains trapped within her.

And yet there is one external place, one register of figuration and sense, that does seem to corroborate what Barbara is trying to say about the conditions that predetermine her appearance in advance, and to which she could point as both sedimentation and evidence of the truth she is trying to impress. This is the aesthetic architecture of the performance itself, in which her appearance on a stage and her interlocutors' location in the audience predetermine the conventions of speech, silence, pleasure, visibility, and use within which her acts and utterances appear. And it is also the strange inconsistencies that appear in the activity of genre, which seems to precipitate its categories unevenly in relation to normative and other embodiments. That is, it is in aesthetics, in the trail of disturbances recorded by medium and genre, that the optimism for and disappointments of personhood as a political horizon have left the residue of a form.

Lyric Personhood argues that, in the last two hundred years of European culture, a person has become an affectively and aesthetically apprehended concept, and not just a legal, moral, political, or philosophical one. A person is not just a recipient of certain legal or moral rights (as in bioethics and political science) or the bearer of specific qualities or distinguishing aspects (as in metaphysics and philosophy). Instead, it is key to the contemporary and contemporizing West that to imagine the *person* or the *human*—the concept's individual and collective valences—is also to invoke a felt truth that requires no further elaboration. The felt component of personhood is the emphatic part in the delivery of a line like "I'm a person, too!", which seems to want to convey a *something* there through the force of insistence alone. In its modern use—the focus of this book—personhood would not be personhood without this quality of self-evidence. This is why it can feel dispiriting or self-defeating to argue for one's personhood in an environment of its denial: even to concede the necessity of argument and evidence would be to concede the very quality that seems to matter the most.

Any concept that seems both to call irresistibly for evidence and yet would also be defeated or disappointed by the evidentiary as such—common domains include love and faith—is liable to produce a rich tradition of metaphysical thought. When Immanuel Kant begins to ground the specialness of personhood in the fact of its self-authorization—"For as a person (*homo noumenon*) he is not to be valued merely as a means to the ends of others or even to his own ends, but as an end in himself, that is, he possesses a *dignity* (an absolute inner worth) by which he exacts *respect* for himself from all other rational beings in the world. He can measure himself with every other being of this kind and value himself on a footing of equality with them"[4]—the formulation seemingly cannot be completed without exposing itself to further questions. What, for example, if one fails to exact respect "from all other rational beings in the world"? It is as if one cannot claim personhood's immanent dignity without being able to refer to others—that is, without making it a social description, and without leaving open the possibility of a political one. Stanley Cavell brings out this latency in Kant's metaphysics when he writes that our failure at times to respond to other people's suffering is not, as it is commonly framed in philosophy, a result of the fact that we don't know other people's pain in the same way that we know our own—as if access to inner and inexpressible experience were the origin of moral responsiveness. Instead, Cavell shifts his discipline from the problem of knowledge to the performativity of acknowledgment: we know other people's pain, and their pain becomes real in the world, through our acknowledgment of it, in the same way that we regularly acknowledge and fail to acknowledge—and thereby create and fail to create—the reality of our own pain.[5] In Lauren Berlant's work, these facing and interpersonal scenarios of acknowledgment expand to the collective recognitions of politics. Writing that subordinated groups who ground their claims for justice in the fact or experience of pain are also forced continually to re-represent this pain in order to secure an ongoing political legitimacy, Berlant suggests short-circuiting the self-evident collapse between suffering and identity by relocating the incandescent truth of political pain to the discursively constituted arena of ideology.[6]

These dispersed yet continuous entries in the theorization of personhood in the West expose the presence of a central and structuring undecidability. This undecidability can be expressed as follows: is there something intrinsic to personhood that radiates a moral demand, which would then frame ethics as a practice of response, or is personhood an effect of gestures, some normative and some requiring commitment, around the recipients of its recognizing acts? It is perhaps unsurprising that pain, and in particular the pain of others, became a key material for working through the question of one's responsibility to near and distant others amid the losses, during the shifts collectively called the Enlightenment, of the certainties of social obligation and status that birth had once at least partially or divinely offered, and as these were gradually replaced in practice and thought by liberalism's deracination and focalization of the individual in European culture.[7] One place where the ongoing effects of this metaphysical tradition can be traced is in the necessity, in the politically pragmatic zones of contemporary bioethics, of framing one's arguments about personhood as a double performative. That is, in order to argue for or against the inclusion of fetuses and other liminal cases within personhood's "moral community," one must propose a set of conditions that adjudicates the proper application of the designation "person" while also acting—for this designation to have the immanent and ontologically transcendent quality it needs to move the law—as though what one confers in one's recognition were not granted but merely observed.[8]

The subtle operation by which personhood's socially enacted significance becomes an immanent and a priori one has been a focus of the postcolonial critique of Western humanism, which sees an enabling relation between the West's colonial expansions and a metaphysical system in which a social distinction of inside/outside is suppressed to produce a pure inside as a transhistorical category. For example, Sylvia Wynter writes that "race . . . was [the] construct that would enable the now globally expanding West to replace the earlier mortal/immortal, natural/supernatural, human/the ancestors, the gods/God distinction as the one on whose basis all human groups had millennially 'grounded' their descriptive statement/prescriptive statements of what it is to be human, and to reground its secularizing own on a newly projected human/subhuman distinction instead."[9] In the shift to rational and secular modernity, the transparent horizon of the "human" as a universal signifier could only be sustained by incorporating generic processes of sensuous and corporeal typification. These processes involved, first, polarizing the field of available qualities into oppositions—such as rational/irrational, mind/body, innerness/ornament, civility/savagery, love/hate, compassion/cruelty, beauty/ugliness, adult/child, the distinct individual/the undifferentiated mass—and then "assigning" each negative term to representative embodied populations, such that their sacrificial expulsion from the human category would also purge the qualities they were now seen to originate from humanity's symbolic. At the same time, for this symbolic to become a "prescriptive" rather than a "descriptive" category—for the human to name an innate and transhistorical truth rather than a historically created and contingent one—it had also to be expunged of the memory that these aesthetic processes ever took place, of the historical and political distributions of the sensible.[10] Personhood can only claim to transcend the ravaging accidents of history and embodiment by effacing its own historical itinerary. Protecting the human as a political aspiration, then, is its apparent lack of forms and descriptive qualities; in fact, it is more commonly the sense that it is so powerfully obvious as a good that it does not need, and would even be cheapened by, definition.

This book's political interest, then, takes form as an interest in description. It aims to rematerialize the transparent reference of personhood by tracing its trail of aesthetic effects, focusing on diffuse and interrelated moments of audiovisual mediation in opera, film, and video. Its central contention is that to be encultured in the modern West is to learn, on top of everything else, a kind of unspoken and mostly felt sense of what it would mean or feel like to be someone, a sense transmitted not only discursively but also through encounters with aesthetic form. If the word "person" or "human" or "love" seems to conjure an innate meaningfulness when spoken or thought of, the book is interested in how and where this meaningfulness became a collective possession by tracing sensory and formal legacies that might have accrued, over time, to their internal and unspoken sense. Thus, while much existing work argues that to be encultured in the West means to absorb a great deal of ideology and language about what it means to be a person—for example, to possess a voice, to have the capacity for love, to be self-determined and agentive—this book makes a further claim: part of the reason for these concepts' enduring force is that they do not only exist as language or ideas, but are also encoded in the textual structure and audiovisual fabric of Western storytelling.[11] When someone takes in an opera or a film about romantic love, for example, they are absorbing not only arguments or ideas about love and its place in a life worth living, but also configurations of space and time, sonic phrasings of foreground and background, and other aesthetic patterns that produce a felt sense of what awaits when one finally achieves the fullness promised in human experience.

At the same time, writing about personhood that only aims to produce the epistemic fade-in from *that which need not be said* to the explicitness of scholarly argument will be incomplete without a sense of how this formal passage itself—of what it's like to sense the atmosphere shift from opacity to transparency around the wanted object of knowledge—is central to personhood's promise and figural enactment. As a result, the book's argument will not be a reflectively formalist one in which descriptions or accounts of Western personhood are first given and then sought in the codifications of aesthetic texts. Instead, the chapters ahead often track moments in which modern personhood first occurs to someone in the form of an idea, a dreamlike image, a montage, or a nagging vision of injustice, as it does for Barbara. When it occurs, it seems to confer a sense of clarity in the place of a former muddiness, and often seems to indicate a path for thought and action to follow. The chapters' case studies collectively suggest that when one lives in relation to a concept like personhood, one generally doesn't experience it as an encompassing and sedimented historical concept, but rather in specific situations in which one needs it to help articulate or mediate a feeling that something is missing in the rightness of self, other, or world. Personhood appears to its experiencing subject in shimmers of opacity and exposure, in shifts between, say, despondency and indignation as modes of relating to powerlessness, in the decision between the separating impulse of difference and the sentimental one of similarity, and in the sensation of being picked up by a coalescing concept as it conveys you out of the mire of the present.

The book is interested, then, less in what personhood is or has been than in the question of what, exactly, personhood manages to do. Where does it tend to show up in mediated accounts that seem to say something about ordinary life, and what effects does it produce when it does? I learned this method of deriving a concept by attending to its affective experience from politically interested writers working in affect theory and, in somewhat different ways, from ordinary language philosophy, especially in the modes of reading I found in J. L. Austin, Stanley Cavell, and Eve Kosofsky Sedgwick.[12] Both of these traditions are founded nonidentically on the idea that attention to the ordinary and the everyday can produce insights of a startlingly different mood and epistemic register from what tends to count professionally as historical or philosophical knowledge. In affect theory and in the Marxist tradition of aesthetic criticism that it inherits, genre becomes a particularly potent term for tracking the gaps between the particularities of historical experience in a given moment and the symbolic resources that a culture possesses to make sense of them. In Fredric Jameson's work, for example, to write about genre is not just to catalog its formal features, its social uses, and its transformations over time—what he calls an "antiquarian relationship to the cultural past"—but also to be attentive to the sense that existing genres are always historically belated forms that are called upon to make sense of fresh cultural contradictions emerging in the present.[13] The language available in any historical moment to make sense of its own present is always, then, anachronistic, in the sense that its semantic clarities necessarily precede the emergence of formations of experience still too nascent to have accreted into concepts.[14]

The aim, then, is not only to use description and analysis to generate historical concepts of personhood and its surrounding culture, but also and explicitly to track how the details in the works discussed in this book gesture toward the historically variable sense-reference of personhood even as, at the level of the narrative and its enunciation, this reference must remain unarticulated and diffuse in order to deliver its transhistorical promise as an atmospheric one. To see something historical in felt atmospheres is to draw from affect theory's insight, as Lauren Berlant writes, that "affective atmospheres are shared, not solitary, and that bodies are continuously busy judging their environments and responding to the atmospheres in which they find themselves," responses that are not merely subjective but "may be said significantly to exemplify shared *historical time*."¹⁵ When people read the room—that is, judge their environments—they are often picking up, in ways that might not fully enter conscious thought, details of tone and comportment, impressions of style, and interpretations of body and gesture that a lifetime of being embedded in culture has enabled them to grasp efficiently. For affect theorists who are interested in the concept not only as a pure vibratory potential beyond the codifications of language, then, but also as a way of tracking how the historical enters into and shapes encounters in the present, "shared history" does not refer to the classical concept of an era's master code, now merely transmuted into a sensuous ether that permeates all historical experience.¹⁶ Rather, it is in what comes up for you when you enter a room that one can sense the histories, aesthetic and otherwise, that allow you and others to produce something like a reading of the room at all. In affect theory's interest in history as a lived and present effect, it connects in this place, in my reading, both to the psychoanalytic retemporalization of the past in the present and to ordinary language philosophy, in which the normative figurations of culture are understood not as the effect of an ideology imposed from a static height, but rather as carried within utterances and acts continuously done.

The interest in ordinary experience also shapes *Lyric Personhood*'s attraction to melodramatic and sentimental works, since these terms often index the commercial, the intensely affective, and the lowbrow registers of cultural aesthetic production. The book's case studies draw broadly from Hollywood romance, queer melodrama and comedy, the action-thriller, the amateur YouTube proposal video, and song and opera in some of their more explicitly theatrical and sensational moments. The project focuses primarily but not exclusively on lowbrow aesthetics because, unlike modernist or experimental genres, the lowbrow is where people go not to be improved but to be soothed, recalibrated, and reminded that as much as things change, they don't change all that much. This does not then lead the book to a critique of the mass entertainment object as politically regressive or indoctrinating, however. Rather, lowbrow popular forms are aesthetic texts whose purpose is to encode the forms of life to which people are affectively attached, rather than the ones to which they intellectually or morally aspire. They are thus a key political repertoire in which to listen for the quiet reproduction of normative forms in the background of people's better intentions.

Tracking the aesthetic experiences that people entrained in the valuation of personhood in the West have absorbed is significant, then, because the sensory tends to index the unconscious, unthought, and instinctive registers of historical knowledge. As I have suggested, it is crucial that personhood be not only secured socially or via papers, but also experienced lyrically as a self-evident and internally felt truth that would only be cheapened by evidence and explanation. The adverb *lyrically* gestures here to an ordinary ambivalence found in the root word's colloquial uses: the lyrics are the words, but lyricism also refers to a quality of phrasing and musicality that can exist outside of words. "Lyric," therefore, captures an undecidability between language and expressivity as human endowments, on one hand, and the transposition of these endowments into sheer sensation, movement, and figure, on the other—but only when the voice is conflated with its natural, melodically spontaneous, and smoothly contoured uses, and not, say, its mechanical, sharp, or guttural ones. Key to the concept of lyricism, then, is the transitivity of a quality identified especially with what is tender, precious, expressive, and humane about the human into a figure that can migrate beyond specifically human occasions, allowing the encounter with its presence in aesthetic texture and form.

In particular, scholars of music and literature have used the term "lyric" to name an emergent aesthetic and historical mode around and after the European Enlightenment, when, as Jonathan Culler writes, "a more vigorous and highly developed conception of the individual subject made it possible to conceive of lyric as mimetic: an imitation of the experience of the subject."[17] In Jessica Gabriel Peritz's study of the lyric voice in late eighteenth-century Italy, the exceptional metaphysics attributed to Italian vocality came to ground the emergence in that period of a broadly modern European political subjectivity.[18] This book shares with these studies, along with others in intimate domains such as sexuality and love, an interest in the broad material and historical shifts from the late eighteenth to the late nineteenth century that "made it possible for man to constitute himself as an object of knowledge," in Michel Foucault's phrasing.[19] Here, the commonplace gendering of humanity's noun archives the sleight of hand by which a historically contingent subject form came to offer the mirage of a universal one, proffering a beguiling yet always reticent horizon of perfect knowledge that would come to sustain the endless productivity of Western scientific methods and their disciplines.[20]

Though lyric as a poetic genre and as a metaphysical concept of the voice has often been traced to origins that significantly precede modernity, then, some have suggested that its focalization of poetic or vocal enunciation around the startlingly embedded singularity of the individual—a gesture that at once aggrandizes this ordinary point of view in the embedded claim that it can carry poetic or metaphysical enunciation while also sharply delimiting the scope of the enunciation's omniscience—aligns formally with the emergence, around the eighteenth century, of what are often considered to be modern formations of subjectivity.[21] At the same time, scholars of the more recent past have tended to emphasize the lyric's anachronism as a conduit of historical experience in the twentieth century.[22] Some recent engagements with the idea of the lyric seem to reach for the word because it indexes something unavailable or in tension with the systems of signification we currently possess to collectively narrate experience. In Claudia Rankine's *Citizen: An American Lyric*, for example, fragmentary evocations from the ordinary life of racism produce an intense innerness in part because their impressions often fail to circulate beyond the self into an apprehension that might be shared. The book's achievement of poetic enunciation is thus simultaneously an exhibit for the helplessness of communication, a paradox that seems to frame the lyric as one of the last and finest sieves for capturing impressions and sensations that might otherwise disappear from accounting.[23] In a different mood, Min Hyoung Song's *Climate Lyricism* reaches for the form ambitiously. Song suggests that the attentionally overwhelming effects that climate and other disasters can have on modern sensoria are due in part to frame disorder, and that the lyric provides an aesthetic interface that might mediate our perception and attention in ways that make sensation less overtaxed and agency less expensive in the midst of terminal and interminable crises.[24]

This book shares with these accounts the sense that something of the lyric's conceptual and formal figuration is useful in an account of the present. It is, however, much less ambitious than much work in the critical humanities that proposes aesthetics to be a site for the collective transformation of attention, interpretation, affective orientation, or energy. Instead, its formal interest is in seeing how the experience of sensation and movement that lyricism can be said to name is not just found in vocal or musical utterances, but also describes broader and more diffuse formations, less concretely locatable in a voice or a melody, that are nevertheless a part of how modern persons sense and affirm their own historicity. Lyricism, after all, is a word that seems to promise a certain kind of continuity between this moment and the next, and then between that one and the next one, unfolding a movement whose opening and closing are shaped, though not entirely determined, by inner senses of momentum and gravity. Because lyricism can be said to name this self-extension of a moment in time, it seems inevitably also to produce those nearby into an audience, framing their interjections largely as appreciations, additions, or interruptions until the lyric phrase draws to its close. That is, in attending to the formal components of lyric enunciation, one might see the outline of a figural container that is transposable into arenas of aesthetic and cultural symbolization beyond the concretely musical.

For example, in an early passage in *The Order of Things*, Foucault invokes the word to capture a mode of historical experience: "This is why utopias permit fables and discourse: they run with the very grain of language and are part of the fundamental dimension of the fabula; heterotopias (such as those to be found so often in Borges) desiccate speech, stop words in their tracks, contest the very possibility of grammar at its source; they dissolve our myths and sterilize the lyricism of our sentences."[25] Here, "lyricism" names something like the vectoral convergence of what is articulable in a given historical location with the rhetorical treasury of its founding myths and fantasies. Specifically, lyricism emerges where the convergence of language and myth renders both *transparent*, leaving behind, as they evaporate from view, only the frictionless sensation of thought and language's flow. Unlike the heterotopia, in which different social worlds with their own articulations of truth, value, and norm abut one another in space and expose the contingency of each of their languages, the unifying singularities that ground a culture's mythmaking instead occlude its subject from a historical view of itself. If ideology names the system of institutions and effects that governs the appearance of meaningfulness as such, lyric personhood is the experience of being in the groove of meaningfulness, of losing one's third-person view of oneself, for just a moment, as language and norm evanesce into the vapor of truth itself.[26]

Though the book traces moments across the audiovisual formulation of personhood in the last two centuries, then, its particular methods and interests have also been shaped in response to transparent codifications of what it means to know (something) in the present, which, at the time of its writing, circulate mostly as unspoken and common sense. One such codification has to do with what it means to know something politically, in both academic and mass-critical cultures; the second concerns what is sometimes called the turn to affect and emotion, primarily in the humanities and social sciences, in the last several decades.

The first kind of common sense to which the book responds is the widespread framing of experiences, embodiments, and affects deemed "political" as a kind of content, that is, as something to be represented. In the mass political theory crystallized in such phrases as "representation matters," what is said to matter—literally, to have substance—is located in the space of representation, where the signifier of the political is imagined to appear. And yet this vernacular distillation of aesthetics and politics stands in conspicuous contrast to the use of the word in aesthetic theory, where it has traditionally existed precisely to index the fact that the representation is never exactly the same as the thing to which it refers.[27] Hence the book's first premise: in any aesthetic-historical period in which the other of comportment, embodiment, language, and affect is primarily conceived as a content, the relation between content and form will represent a particularly occluded or disavowed component of political knowledge. This is not to deny the life-saving effects of less predictable representations of the classically subordinated on the sensorium of a mass public; nor is it the impatient view that a politics of representation is merely the naive counterpart to a politics of structure.[28] Rather, it is to argue that in such periods, the most sublimated and difficult-to-grasp elements of political and historical knowledge will likely not be found in already articulable zones of representation, but rather will be located or masked outside of the space of content and its positive appearance.

As an example of how the habitual production of knowledge might simultaneously foreclose other kinds of knowledge from appearing within the frame, consider a setting of knowledge's predictable consolidation and transmission: the film music classroom. There, a student may encounter a lesson like this one: "In *Behind Office Doors* (1931), for instance, Mary (Mary Astor) and her boss, Jim (James Duneen), return to her apartment after a giddy night of dancing. He makes sexual advances, which she declines, apparently reluctantly. Without music underscoring the scene, however, Mary's actions in this sequence are difficult to decipher with confidence, and the result is an intense unease over her response that would likely produce precisely the audience whispering and coughing mentioned above."[29] This passage, from James Buhler and David Neumeyer's "Music and the Ontology of the Sound Film: The Classical Hollywood System," explains why the musical underscore—and in particular those parts of it that don't exist in the world of the film, and which the characters can't hear—came to be naturalized as a convention in early sound film, even though some critics and practitioners worried that such unjustified additions would break the audience's immersion in the plot. What enabled the nondiegetic underscore's broad adoption, in this account, was the discovery that audiences found it unbearable to have access to sounds in the film world and yet not to know what the characters were thinking or feeling. With the further loss of silent film's live musical accompaniments, then, sound film needed a supplemental technical element whose task was to supply information that was unavailable or opaque in the fictional representation itself.

I turn to this example because it contains efficiencies that I recognize from my own teaching of film music, especially when compelled, in the peculiar interpellation toward both specialization and instrumentality that characterizes the undergraduate classroom, to produce a neat explanation that the student can carry away with them—proof that teaching has happened. I have given this explanation many times: the audience doesn't know but naturally wants to know what a character is thinking or feeling, and music provides that information. Often, when this explanation is given, there is a sense of satisfaction or at least closure in the room, as if the contract between the student and the teacher, or between the student and the idea of a college education, had been honored. But every lesson is double: the student is given something, but also grasps, from what didn't come up, the terrains of question and interest that must (they can only assume) be either too inconsequential or banal to have counted as knowledge within the class's frame.

In this case, is the lack of an interpreting soundtrack the only possible cause of the audience's epistemic tension during this scene? We might also consider the sexual advance itself. A sexual advance, we might say, is a performative gesture whose effects include putting someone on the spot. To be put on the spot means to enter the visual and temporal condition of being onstage, to become a kind of performer in relation to others, who now become one's audience. Notably, when on the spot, to do nothing is still to do something, because every gesture and decision one makes now takes part in the stage's conversion of being into performance. Even if one is nominally or actually free to respond how one wishes, then, what one cannot choose, what has been decided by the advance itself, is that some answer must be given now, in this time and place. Whether one likes or doesn't like the advance, then, or whether one takes it in, coasting in the wake of its disturbance, and perhaps only later quietly fills an entry in the column of desire—part of what one is reacting to is the sense, even if one had done nothing, that something had nevertheless been extracted from you, which is responsiveness itself.[30]

In other words, the epistemic relief that an interpreting soundtrack might provide is preceded, in this case, by the advance's framing of Mary's response as an epistemic mystery. When it comes to desire, after all, the question "What do you want?" can be an interested one, but it could also be exasperated (including playfully exasperated). If exasperated, what it says is: it is not the content of your desire but its inexplicitness, your failure to articulate a desire, that frustrates me; if only you knew or said what you wanted, we wouldn't be here. The problem of not knowing (another's) desire revolves not only around absences of transmitting mediums that might relay inner and already existent facts, but also around dramas of what is at stake in consolidating desire into something knowable and articulable in the first place. The clarity and relief of knowing definitively how to read someone's actions cannot simply be disinterested when this very clarification is a demand in the scene itself, as the space and time for one's feeling out of what one might want is pressured onstage by the performative that turns one into the subject of the performance.

It is not inaccurate to say that music will sometimes communicate characters' feelings, moods, and inner states and thereby modulate and guide an audience's response. But in taking the scene's interpretive discomfort to be solved by the addition of an interpreting musical element such as the soundtrack, the lesson locates the epistemic problem of otherness in the film's audiovisual apparatus and its capacity to represent the fiction adequately, and not as a condition or experience internal to sexuality itself; it turns an ordinary problem of relation into a technical problem of representation.[31] And in closing the mystery there, the lesson frames as complete an inquiry that has yet to begin into the range of interpersonal, political, and historical conditions that might be engaged in the significances of forming, articulating, interpreting, eliciting, or expressing a desire at all. This is especially the case in intimate registers like love and sexuality as central sites of self-definition—which is to say, of the management of one's interpretive openness—in modern subjectivity. The plots of romantic comedy are as much about the hero's quest for their own nonambivalence as they are about the quest for another, who is often just a formal catalyst within a journey of arriving in the land beyond questions.[32] Under such epistemic conditions, the wish to be after interpretation, to know definitively what one person or another thinks or wants, is as much a historical and cultural matter as it is a technical and audiovisual one.[33]

If I cite Buhler and Neumeyer's article as an example of the conventional ways in which the teaching of film music can foreclose a historically particular attention to feeling and its knowledge by taking these to be merely technical problems of efficient narration, I do so also because it raises an interpretive possibility that few others have suggested: namely, that there is a deeper and formally co-constitutive relation between love and sexuality as cultural forms and, on the other hand, the construction of the mass audiovisual form of sound cinema. Buhler and Neumeyer seem to suggest this relation in various places: "What seems to have forced the issue [of the need for musical underscore], as [film composer Max] Steiner astutely noted, was the need to reconcile the love scene with dramatic sound film"; "Thus, it was the love scene in particular that seemed to demand a return to music." But other than a sense that "dialogue scenes that had strong emotional components" seemed to drive the adoption of the musical underscore—and with it the spatioconceptual separation of sound-film worlds into "foreground (usually dialogue) and background"—the authors don't clarify why the problem of representing love in particular might have led to the codification of an audiovisual infrastructure that would remain conventional for the next century.[34]

Nevertheless, the suggestion remains—in the idea that the necessity of representing love in particular "forced" sound film into its now-conventional audiovisual form, or that the pressure of "strong emotional components" on film's representational system generated the formal and phenomenological separation of foreground and background—that love might not only be one of many kinds of cultural content represented within sound film's technical system, but that it emerged as a cultural form in part through its coarticulation with the technical form of audiovisual representation itself. If the former view sees love as a technically transcendent and ultimately "cultural" property that might find expression in various mediated contexts, the latter offers a different path: reading audiovisual material not for what seems to be represented within its frame, but rather for traces of form that might be revealed, as when peering into a lit window from the dark, in the momentary flash of the outline of the historical subject peering in.

The second formation of knowledge within which this book finds itself concerns the broad and interdisciplinary interest in writing histories and theories that take feeling as their object, particularly in the humanities and social sciences of the last several decades. I begin by collecting a few examples, taken out of context, and happened upon without a larger programmatic aim, in the interest of proposing a collective situation in which anyone interested in the production of knowledge centered on feeling today will find themselves:

> I've been gathering moments that leap out because they provide complex accounts of what it *feels* like for people of color to live in the context of racism.
>
> I wasn't seeking opinions or attitudes about social class or inequality, like those we might find on a survey, but rather investigating what it *felt like* to be wealthy in this historical moment.
>
> How does one *feel* when becoming-machine?[35]

Why is the verb "feel" italicized in each of these examples? Is there any theoretical significance to be derived from this small, collective detail?

If there were, then there would be a difference between asking "what does it *feel* like?" and "what does it feel like?" But what is this difference? Italics are a part not of grammar or syntax but rather of emphasis and insistence, as if the italicized form of a word were prefaced with an unspoken, "no, but really. . . ." To ask someone what it *felt* like, rather than what it felt like, is not just to ask for an explanation but also to imply that explanations have already been given, here or elsewhere; that accounts or descriptions of the experience already exist, are more or less adequate; but now I want to know what it *really felt* like (perhaps: for *you*). The italics, in other words, seem to acknowledge, as some of the passages in which they appear explicitly do, that this is not the first time an explanation of a subject has been ventured, while also implying that earlier passes had left out something vital. The italicized question performs a double movement of knowledge: it both acknowledges and dismisses what has been codified into discourse in order to gesture at (felt) truths as yet unrendered in language. By using italics, the writer seems to be both doing something and also pointing at the thing they are doing, fantasizing that something they mean might be pushed, with enough force, directly into the reader's brain. They are the closest a writer gets to touch.

In the context of writing about feeling, then, the italicized *feel* seems to point at once to a confidence and a skepticism that the crucial otherness of knowledge derived from feeling can ultimately be captured in language, an ambivalence that can be found both locally in academic production and more broadly in the word's popular and ordinary functions. Within the academic production of knowledge, we might note that the turn to the study of affect and emotion in the last few decades—the movement to codify all kinds of feeling-knowledges that were once deemed extraneous to the frames of their disciplines—is accompanied by a parallel wish to retain "feeling" as a name for the as-yet-uncodified parts of knowing that have not yet fully entered language. It may be that, in this now-belated moment of the affective turn, when the legitimacy of feeling as a site of historical and theoretical knowledge no longer needs to be argued for as such, the italicized *feel* now functions to recapture the original and elusive object of inquiry that the unitalicized "feel" no longer quite points to, having now drifted to index the bodies of writing and knowing that have accrued from its initial and irruptive ambition.

When, in the itinerary of disciplinary knowledge, a once-uncaptured phenomenon within objective discourse now finds itself to be a reliable site of knowledge's production—that is, when this phenomenon no longer bears any tension in relation to the positive appearance of knowledge as such—the work that follows, in order to engage the culturally and generically contingent object of "academic knowledge," will need to focus not only on producing more felt knowledges but also on the affective experience of this knowledge: on where this knowledge might be desired and what it seems to promise, as much for the writer's subjects as for the writer themselves. Though the book's chapters are replete with figures who seem to long for epistemic clarity within narratives of love, citizenship, health, and self-becoming, it turns out that merely to be given this clarity would constitute a disappointment. Instead—and in ways that echo the affect theorist's own orientation to knowledge—the satisfaction of genre hinges on the maintenance of an ambivalence toward the longed-for arrival of clarity, which must always be kept on a fulcrum between the desire to know and to spare what knowledge points to from dissolving entirely into the positive appearance of language. In the writing of this book, I have found that tracking these modern subjects' desires to be beyond the muddled middles and already at the point of retrospection from which spans of living cohere meaningfully in hindsight could not remain unentangled from a fantasy of writing and of knowledge that replicates the same arc. The theorist of love, for instance, cannot claim merely to write about the subject from a distance, since the very wish to offer clarity and arrival effects cannot help but entangle the theorist within the formal promise of love itself.

Lyric Personhood does not offer a comprehensive or consecutive account of personhood as it has shaped the particularities and generalities of experience across the modern West. Instead, it gathers a few moments across this broad horizon in which the work of audiovisual form and genre seems to expose something about the aesthetics that structure the very appearance of personhood's enigmatic referent. In doing so, its primary aim is to demonstrate modes of reading by which the latent aesthetic substrate that operates in the background of cultural production might be brought into articulation. In the sense that this describes a formal project concerned with the disappearance of forms, the book joins traditions of cultural analysis whose aim is to provincialize or relocalize forms of life that claim for themselves a nonspecific universality as their categorical privilege.[36] And yet I am often most interested not in pointing out the injustice and epistemic violence of these categorical sleights of hand, but also in describing the attractiveness and promise of the act of disappearance itself as a moment of passage from history to ahistoricity, from sharpness to fuzziness, as the sure anchors of place and time blur out to produce the intensity of merely being alive.

Some might argue that it has become less and less meaningful to hold on to the geographical and historical category of the West in a time of global capitalist competition, the wane of US superiority in ways more actual than symbolic, the broad and unfinished retractions of the European colonial moment, and the interpenetrations of cinema, the internet, and other global mass-cultural forms. Others might prefer to emphasize not the "West" as this book's conceptual horizon, but rather whiteness, or capitalism, or the Enlightenment, or heteropatriarchal structurings of time, space, and value, or liberalism as a philosophical and political formation. I hope that this ambivalence about naming is internal to the book, and that the reader will follow me in discovering when and where each of these imbricated concepts, along with others, rises to a particular discursive salience. For example, when the ordinary and unmarked US or (Western) European subject experiences, at the beginning of the twenty-first century, the threat of exogenous terrorism that emerges from the vague "thereness" of the Middle East, this subject becomes interpellated not only as a US or European subject, but also as a subject of the West. The threat of terrorism exposes the salience of an identity form that may not normally arise in the local encounters that make up ordinary experience, where other signifiers, such as those of class, gender, or race, might be more significantly operative.

At the same time, a descriptive project of the "West" is not meant to name a sharp contrast to something else, like the East. To say that experience as it forms in the West must differ from that which forms elsewhere is both banally obvious and also risks the kind of essentialism that, say, postulates nonwhite subjects both "within" and "outside" the West to be essentially unlike white subjects. It is more instructive to say that minoritarian experience in the West cannot but unfold within the frame of whiteness, in agon with whiteness, and therefore that the aim of its study should not be to elucidate its essential difference but to understand better what whiteness sets forth as a legible and promising form of life. There are a few places in the book where minoritarian life is read to offer alternatives to the dominants of the culture in which it necessarily unfolds, but these are exceptions within a broader interest in tracking the affective and formal lineaments of normativity itself.

If the broader arc of the book aims to show that there has been an aesthetic continuousness to the imagination of personhood in the West, the chapters each focus on a major system of signification that has become central to this imagination over the last two hundred years. Chapter 1, the book's briefest, serves as a kind of slideshow that introduces the concerns of the chapters ahead. Focusing on voice as a metonym for the self-realizations promised in romantic love, national belonging, and the metaphysical achievement of "presentness," the chapter traces the audiovisual figuration of this voice in three speeches delivered by the actor Colin Firth at the ends of three different films: *Love Actually*, *The King's Speech*, and *A Single Man*. In doing so, the chapter highlights a region of audiovisual form that operates below and through the differing articulations of genre: in this straight romantic comedy, this historical drama about a king's sovereignty, and this queer melodrama about the temporal displacements of trauma and their overcoming, the resolution comes in a scene in which Firth must deliver a speech, even though his capacity to speak has been hindered in some way by the plot (by a foreign language, a stammer, or death). While contemporary genre studies typically assume the historical frame of consumer capitalism, where aesthetic style articulates the difference of who you are, tracing this audiovisual figure in its shifting form across these three endings also points to broader aesthetic formations that underlie contemporary mass-cultural storytelling as a whole.

The three remaining chapters then each expand at length from one of the regions introduced in the first, focusing in turn on romantic love, the formal structure of health and recovery, and the ambience of national citizenship. Chapter 2 is a study of the formal and rhythmic components of romantic love as it is imagined in the West, which it explores mostly via close readings of commercial romantic comedies from the beginning of sound film to the present. Contrary to the colloquial claim that true love is ineffable and indescribable, the chapter argues instead that certain formal problems consistently emerge in the attempt to represent love in audiovisual form. These problems also inform the amateur aesthetics of the proposal video, in which the romantic subject becomes both director and editor in the attempt to render a feeling in audiovisual time. The chapter explores the techniques that these directors reach for in the attempt to represent love, such as the musical montage, in which the temporality of a song is laid over quick cuts of scenes from a couple's life, imbuing them with a formal coherence and momentum that otherwise fails to crystallize in the ordinary time of living.

Chapter 3 then moves from the couple form to the scene of therapy, asking what the proliferation of therapeutic discourse since the nineteenth century (along with the further postwar explosion of therapeutic styles, particularly in the United States) can tell us about how contemporary subjects learn to think about illness and health, but also about narrative, knowledge, and the proper affective arcs of a normal life. The chapter's interest in tracing the advent of a contemporary subject of health shifts the book's attention from screen cultures to operatic theater, and particularly to Richard Wagner's opera *Tannhäuser* as an aesthetic document from the middle of the nineteenth century that sits between older and newer discourses for making sense of debilitating repetition. In particular, the chapter engages moments from Carolyn Abbate's reading of the opera that seem to capture a sensory shift in the opera's audiovisual imagination from a tragic to an addicted subject, a shift that, at the same time, is difficult to capture in the objective language of music-theoretical description without producing lexical anomalies. I argue that the essay form is crucial for allowing the writer to move in the space between the musical object and the disciplinary languages that aim to produce its knowledge.

While Chapters 2 and 3 focus respectively on a valued and an excluded form of subjectivity in the West—the romantic subject and the addict—by showing how each is articulated within figurations of rhythm, space, and time, Chapter 4 comes closest to the present by arguing that recent formations of personhood in the West have been shaped by an investment in an idea of everydayness as the name for an aesthetic environment protected from the damaging, linear effects of history. In commercial Western films about terrorism since September 11, 2001, it is the right to the ordinariness of the everyday that is interrupted by the terrorist plot, which punctures the fantasy of national belonging as a temporal space in which nothing particular happens (as in "it was just another day, and then . . ."). The chapter argues that the fantasized referent of the ordinary American life is captured audiovisually in this repertory as a figuration of middle distance, where the specifics of plot, speech, and genre are blurred, leaving behind the hollow forms of clichés as the sensory texture by which national belonging is recognized.

Rather than proceeding chronologically, then, the chapters each look back from the present to take account of different ranges of history within which their respective concerns come into focus: sound cinema and video since 1940; the period, beginning in the middle of the nineteenth century, characterized by what Elissa Marder has called the addict's "quintessential malady of modernity, the inability to incorporate time into experience";[37] and the affective experience of nationality in the first twenty years of the twenty-first century. Across these asymmetrical engagements, the book develops, as it were laterally, a number of thematic concerns. One is that the epistemic accesses to feeling and interiority granted by the musical underscore are much more startling, more mysterious, and more historically revelatory of a broad formation of contemporary subjectivity than they are typically taken to be in the conventional procedures of film music and audiovisual media analysis. Another is an ongoing engagement with the theory of melodrama. Mobile across theater, literature, film, music, and more, melodrama has been said to extend a coherent mode of modern, liberal, and bourgeois representation from the eighteenth century to the present and future of mass culture as such—if, that is, Jameson is right that the end of melodrama would signal the end of popular culture as we know it.[38] But to imagine an end to something is also the expression of a desire to imagine that it existed, in a form concrete or stable enough for an end to be imaginable at all; endings are retroactive fantasies of coherence. The chapters thus track the unevenness of melodrama's appearances across their case studies, noting, in particular, the different stresses and emphases that different historical urgencies place on different parts of its formula. For example, if melodrama in one account classically hinges on a moment of revelation in which something hidden in the protagonist is expressed and recognized by the outside world, each of the chapters tracks what bearing this moment has within the articulation of its particular form of life. In doing so, they discover that melodrama's confessional, self-revelatory drive is not always directed toward receiving recognition in the world, either because recognition is less affirming than the expansiveness that the confessing voice itself articulates, or because the recognition is less of another than of a hidden register of signification within the ordinary recesses of one's own life, or because, in the stranger spaces of contemporary US publics, it is unclear whether melodrama can still figure the world as an audience, and so whether there even remains an other to whom one's revelations of virtue and interiority would count.

Finally, a note about this book's relation to the academic practice of music studies. At the moment, there seems to me to be no unifying metasystem of value, no common body of works or of writing that would determine the conditions from which new formations of knowledge could reliably be predicted to come. Perhaps there has never been such a consensus, only normative fantasies of it. In the heterogeneity of such eras, the friction between epistemic systems is likely to be felt most not in questions about the value of this or that object of study, but rather in, for instance, modes of evidence and argumentation, claims of tone and style, and the ways these mediate the affective recognition of what is called—as if it could be one—historical knowledge. With respect to method, some of this book's readers may wonder at stretches where it does not appear that I'm talking much about music or sound at all. I have tried to avoid engaging in the attentive elaboration of the musical example when it appeared to me that my reasons for doing so were primarily ones of disciplinary credentialization. As music scholars who have worked in interdisciplinary areas know, musical expertise can generate both an authorizing and a provincializing effect at the table of theory, granting them admission to film or media or cultural studies while at the same time cordoning off this expertise from the production of the field's general knowledge. If these modern effects are a result of the ongoing separation and credentialization of disciplines within the academy, another of its effects is that, within the closed borders of each discipline, it is rarely necessary to make the case for the relevance of music or visual art or philosophy *as such* when one begins one's inquiry. A consequence of taking the kind of knowledge generated from one's expertise to be self-evidently valuable is that one loses the occasion to ask the question of its relevance. In this book's question about the forms of historical, formal, and political knowledge that might be encoded in the audiovisual registers of opera, film, and video, the question of *whether* music or sound does something in relation to a specific question always begins as an open one. It is my sense that to begin, as a music scholar, by assuming that music or sound will have a predictable importance in an object or a scene, or that a certain method of description or analysis will yield discoveries that will be relevant to your question—even if this assumption turns out to be true—deprives you of the opportunity to observe what happens in the moments when music passes into importance. And to discover that one's analytic or descriptive or ethnographic or citational methods are not in fact relevant, or not tuned the right way, or that their production of an object of knowledge turns out itself to be the phenomenon that one wishes actually to be tracking, would equally be a discovery. As elsewhere, to lose the world-making norm of a practice and a convention allows one to become interested, as if for the first time, in where and how the music comes in, granting oneself the capacity for surprise.

※ 1 ※
Three Speeches Delivered by Colin Firth

Within a span of seven years, three movies, belonging by any ordinary use of the term to three different genres, end by placing the actor Colin Firth in scenarios whose similarities seem to call for an encompassing mode of reading. At the end of *Love Actually* (2003), Firth must propose to the Portuguese maid with whom, in private hours at his summer home, he's only communicated in pantomime and comic distortions of language. Now, having just cobbled together a little Portuguese from language-learning tapes, he stammers, crudely, the first words that she can understand. In *The King's Speech* (2010), Firth is now King George VI, who must find a way to overcome a vocal impediment that developed in childhood to deliver a radio address that would (the film strongly implies) unite the Allied resistance to the Nazi threat. And finally, in *A Single Man* (2009), Firth plays George Falconer, a gay English professor in 1960s Los Angeles who, in the midst of personal and historical upheavals, repeatedly states his desire to live in the "moment," a word that for him also names the ambition to "feel, rather than to think." Yet Falconer only achieves this dreamed-of state of sensuous presentness when he is at the point of death, when the loss of his physical ability to speak forces these final words into the mediated register of the voice-over.

On one hand, a romantic comedy aimed at mass pleasure, an Oscar-winning historical drama, and a smaller gay indie film would seem to index different formations and positions within an analysis of culture. And yet none of the three films can deliver their resolutions without proffering a nearly identical sonic scenario. A character played by Firth must deliver a speech, even though his capacity to speak has been hindered in some way by the plot; meanwhile, a lyrical orchestral cue blooms around his words, enacting the flow to which his voice aspires. Though these films engage different structures of social identity and coherence—the couple form, national sovereignty, and a metaphysics of the self that links feeling to presentness—it is in the outlines of this recurrent figure that these registers of social and political personhood converge, proposing a formal ground for their uneven meditations on privacy and publicity, voice and personhood, sexuality and normativity, time and history, intimacy and scale.

How does one make sense of this figure, which seems to belong to the repertory of conventional genre effects and yet fails to differentiate the genres of these three films from one another? The figure seems to resist the two most common paths that studies of genre typically follow. In the first, to write about genre is to write about difference. The genre analyst's task is to draw general features out of particular works, such that this general form can serve as a contract of expectation with its audience, distinguishing its offerings from those of other genres.[1] In this approach, the genre analyst aims to drive aesthetic material as much as possible toward an inside similarity and an outside dissimilarity, such that reading generically tends to favor a loss of richness in the object that is compensated for by the creation of belonging- and separation-effects, the simultaneously constituting recognitions of "that is me" and "that is not me." At the same time, the sonic figure that appears across these films also seems to resist genre studies' other primary use, which is the diachronic tracking of a single genre over time.[2] Instead of a synchronous snapshot of a marketplace of genre options, then, this approach instead tracks the persistence of a genre across a period of history, whether in service of an argument about its formal durability or to use it as a seismograph for historical perturbations.[3] Unlike the synchronic model, which tends to imagine culture or the market as an aesthetically neutral container that merely houses the genres available in its time, the diachronic model is more likely to offer an explanation for how genre's formal transformations relate to social and historical ones, though often at the temporary cost of narrowing its focus to a single genre at a time.

The two main tendencies of genre criticism, however, leave a third possibility uncovered at their juncture. Would it be possible, or even meaningful, to historicize the aesthetics of a mass-cultural public as a whole? This would be the view that popular culture in a given historical formation is not merely the sum of the works and genres that appear within it, but is also grounded in a syntax, a substratum of formal figuration, that enables the appearance of narrative, meaningfulness, and the differentiating activity of genre in the first place. Mode, for instance, is a word that theorists of melodrama have used to capture a structure of sense that spills across the containers of genre, animating the possibility of a general experience that *could be mine* in representations of the family, the romantic couple, the sports team, the military, and the achievement of self-definition in work and in leisure, among many more. Indeed, the scenes that open this chapter appear to be legible within melodrama's framework: in each film, the plot drives toward an affective and theatrical scene of disclosure in which the promise of resolution hinges on the epiphanic recognition of the protagonist's exposure. Scholars from literature, theatre, cinema, music, political theory, and many more fields of study have proposed that melodrama is a dominant cultural mode of the period from the bourgeois revolutions of late eighteenth-century Europe to contemporary popular culture, which some consider to be unthinkable without melodrama's structuring form.[4]

And yet, mode, which seems to solve the problem of naming a broad cultural figuration that extends beyond the formations of specific styles, identities, and localities of experience, ends up reproducing, rather than displacing, the very descriptive ambivalence at the heart of genre analysis. For to gather instances of cultural production across time and place under the term "melodrama" seems inevitably to flatten differences of tone and style, affect and situation, and crisis and solution, such that these begin to seem merely like local variations of a master code. At the same time, to reject the flattening view of a cultural mode would be to abandon one's insight that there is, in fact, something related about all of this cultural production—that there is not *nothing* in common between the spheres of domesticity and war, say, or between the dramas of symbolic restitution promised in the romantic couple and in sports. There are reasons, in other words, for the critical wish to read genre both for similarity and for difference, either of which is likely to lead the reader to emphasize different regions of a work's style, form, affect, and detail.

How does one honor the impulses both to particularize (into the specificity of experience, identity, historical situation) and to generalize (into form, affect, structure) within a reading of mass culture, especially when these impulses are immanent to the promise of mass culture itself? The audiovisual figure that repeats across these three films' endings offers a place to witness the formalism that resonates through fantasies of the self, the couple, and the national collective at the beginning of the twenty-first century. At the same time, the formal outline that repeats through these historically nonidentical scenes also ends up producing different engagements with the audiovisual apparatus. In the romantic comedy, for example, the plot drives toward the encounter of the couple in real space, where their locked eyes, as they face one another, facilitate the expressive event of a mutual confession. In the national scene, however, the importance of the king's speech is not that it is addressed to a single other (who is represented in the film's ending by the speech therapist), but that it can be picked up by the microphone between them and broadcast over the airwaves, as if the intimate couple's purpose within national fantasy were merely to facilitate the creation and transmission of a voice that could produce an empire as an audience. Finally, the facing context of romance's voice and the amplified and transmitted one of nationality become, in the third film, the voice of the self's achievement of presence and presentness, which is removed from the diegesis entirely. The similarities that bind the chapter's examples together thus also trace a process of increasing technical abstraction and intermediation, in which the love scene's theatrical schema becomes the technologically mediated one of national address, whose disembodiment of a real voice in the film's world becomes a disembodiment at the level of fictional structure in the final film's closing address.

Each of these films also contextualizes itself within a national crisis event. *Love Actually* opens with a monologue about the terrorist attacks on the Twin Towers in New York City; *The King's Speech* centers on the Second World War and its threat to the symbolic continuation of the British Empire; *A Single Man* opens with live news reports, playing in the background on the radio, of the Cuban Missile Crisis. Together, then, these films also constitute a loose archive of early twenty-first century attempts to reconstruct how the disturbances of national history in the twentieth century came to bear on the narrative coherence of the privately lived life. They do so by documenting the audiovisual figurations of self, couple, and nation that promised to restabilize the self in the face of historical threats to this stability, while also containing, within this ideological and generic variety, a common figure that occurs across these reassembled convictions of a livable life—a figure of the future becoming imaginable beyond the specific resolutions promised in any one genre.

> When the planes hit the Twin Towers, as far as I know, none of the phone calls from the people on board were messages of hate or revenge. They were all messages of love. If you look for it, I've got a sneaky feeling you'll find that love actually is all around.

Love Actually begins with an evocation of traumatic national history.[5] The account of this history comes in Hugh Grant's voice, though it is not yet identified by anything other than its celebrity grain. As he recalls the events of 9/11 for the viewer in voice-over, we see candid footage of people in the present reuniting, joyfully and tearfully, at the arrivals gate of Heathrow Airport. The reference to a real historical event by an actor in a romantic comedy over documentary footage of real people seems immediately to engage, as a question, the only word in the film's title beside the one that indicates its genre: actually. The actual refers to something other than the real, because "actually" is often used as a correction to some other proposed factuality: the "actual" is a reality that aims to dissipate some other proposed real as mere smoke and shadows. The historical reality of 9/11 does not overshadow but amplifies love's own reality, then, since it is only in contravening the national wound that the trumping insight of love's everywhereness achieves its particular force. Love promises fantasy and virtuality, but its fantasy and virtuality are not simply detachments from what is real. Instead, the opening of the film suggests that love becomes present to experience in the places where the hardness of life dissipates into intangibility, washed out by a kind of spreading hum that is both everywhere and yet hidden from overt sight ("If you look for it"; "I've got a sneaky feeling"). The formal figure for love's fantasy, then, is not escape but inversion, as love transposes its own dematerialization into the physical world and takes for itself the punctum of the real.

The arrivals gate spills out into a number of interrelated love plots that converge around one Christmas season in London. In one of them, Colin Firth plays Jamie, a recently heartbroken English writer who retreats to his holiday cottage. There he is introduced by the cottage's proprietor to his new maid, Aurélia. As it happens, Jamie and Aurélia both talk a lot, but apart from mimed gestures and the occasional cognate between Portuguese and English, the romance derives its comedy from the absence of language's relational utility. And its pathos: in one scene, Jamie and Aurélia, face to face, confess their romantic feelings for each other in a symmetry that can only be grasped by the film's audience, who are assisted by subtitles. That the achievement of a mutual confession of love does not produce a couple suggests what is still missing, and what the rest of this plot exists to supply: not the capacity to put one's confession into words, which they can already do, but the dimension of language that is social, that allows confession to have meaning for someone else.

The season ends, and the two leave the cottage. A montage shows glimpses of Jamie learning Portuguese. Then, a few weeks before Christmas, Jamie arrives at a family gathering bearing gifts, only to drop them suddenly and dash off to the airport. Running marks the point in romantic comedy when the last decision has been made, and all that remains is distance. Its purpose is ostensibly to bring Aurélia within hailing range of the voice, to bridge the distance within which feeling can be confessed and heard. *Love Actually*, in fact, includes three sequences in which a man, having decided to pursue his crush, hurtles through space, his headlong speed underscored by a triumphant orchestra.⁶ These balletic displays through streets and airports, supported by horns and crashing cymbals, tie the moment of romantic resolve to a delight in physical freedom, a joy in sheer motion that seems retroactively to frame everyday existence as inhibited. These triumphant runs are not only in service of producing a couple; they also suggest that the romantic comedy plot drives toward the event of the protagonist coming into knowledge of their own desire, and of the pleasure of being organized by its clarity after so much ambivalence, regardless of what the other's response turns out to be.

Alasdair MacIntyre has argued that desire becomes a material for subjectivity through the very terms of liberal political structure. While liberalism initially proposed only a political, legal, and economic framework in which people with "widely different and incompatible conceptions of the good life" could express and debate their preferences in a public arena, it followed that individuals would first have to know and express their preferences in order to become politically legible as persons.⁷ Under these conditions, desire becomes a fraught possession, for the individual must then be on constant alert for the emergence of new desires, which could then be voiced in public as both the raw material of democratic world-making and as badges of personhood. However, as MacIntyre suggests, the possibility of incoherent or contradictory desire hovers as a constant threat to the coherence of one's subjectivity. If saying "I want" in a liberal cultural order is also to announce "I am," the run in romantic comedy represents the clarity of desire as a freedom of the body. The run does not bridge a distance so much as it inaugurates a new spatiality: it marks the point where the drama of desire shifts from an internal to an external matter, as the subject's anxious interior monitoring comes to an end and the newly clear desire propels the body through the world. The business of noticing and expressing preferences is simplified into the mere crossing of a gap, traversable by taxis and planes—as if the universe's physical extension, its existence as a field of nonidentical locations, could itself be a diagram of desire.

Jamie's run takes him to the restaurant in the South of France where Aurélia works when she is not working at his cottage. When he storms in, the triumphant cue that underscored the run fades out, exposing the ordinary sounds of a restaurant: conversations, clinking silverware, and the sound of a house band. The camera cuts around the room, alighting on unfamiliar faces. Then Aurélia enters the frame. At this moment, the band stops playing, and a single, closely miked piano note over sustained strings saturates the sound mix. The entrance of this note replaces the restaurant's din with a warm aural focus that turns out to be the beginning of a melody: the love theme that had underscored the couple's previous scenes together. Then, as Jamie begins to speak, the restaurant goes quiet, and the camera pans around the room to reveal faces turned to him in rapt attention.

This moment marks the couple's first emergence from the privacy of the cottage, but it is also the storyline's first representation of a public. And the speech's effect is not just to communicate something to Aurélia. It also cuts through the dispersed temporalities of a dozen private dinner conversations and replaces them with a collective sense of a beginning, in the beginning of the speech. When Jamie first entered the restaurant, the band music that washed around its islands of conversation marked what Henri Bergson has called a spatial concept of time: metrical, a click track, free of contouring by specific human experience. When Jamie begins to speak, however, his voice cuts through the chatter and produces a collective apprehension of time in the time of his speech, in which each moment is not simply "one point alongside another" but is rather enmeshed in the movement of an "organic whole, as happens when we recall the notes of a tune, melting, so to speak, into one another."[8] It is fitting that musical melody was Bergson's chief example of the temporal experience he called "duration," since Jamie's voice is joined with a melody that extends across the length of the speech. Yet the underscore does not so much accompany an event in the narrative as it provides the condition for that event's possibility: its sound is tied to the voice that breaks through the restaurant's scattered pockets of time, forming its diners into a collective by shaping them as an audience.

That the feeling of togetherness can be taken as proof of actual togetherness is a basic feature of sentimentality. When politicians give speeches announcing a new day or a new beginning for the nation, this abstract claim feels credible in part because the speech itself enacts, for a dispersed audience, the experience of feeling a given moment in time as a collectively apprehended present. Yet this also suggests that a voice laden with feeling can produce an impression of the communal on its own, without needing the responses of others. To see the confession itself, rather than the other's acceptance and recognition of the confession, as the central formal event of romantic closure makes it possible to read for discrepancies in each person's role in producing its social form, as the English subtitles translating Jamie's mangled Portuguese seem to suggest: "I know I seems an insane person because I hardly knows you, but sometimes things are so transparency, they don't need evidential proof. And I will inhabit here, or you can inhabit with me in England." But the fact that Aurélia works in Marseille when she is not working at Jamie's cottage suggests that she may not be as free as he is to inhabit wherever she likes. Indeed, as Jamie delivers his plea to an audience of immigrants in the South of France, the insanity of what he knows without proof seems to reside in a vision of borderless freedom as an emblem of what desire could do.

To say that the romantic comedy's central event is the creation of this voice—rather than, say, the event of the voice's reception by another—departs from much work on sentimentality and the scene of recognition in liberal aesthetics, which tends to prioritize the contact of the gaze. James Chandler, for instance, describes sentiment as that which circulates through a relay of looks, while Elizabeth A. Povinelli, writing about the significance of the romantic couple in liberal cultures, summarizes its transformative promise with the motto, "In your gaze I become a new person, as do you in mine."[9] Implicit in these accounts is a certain way of imagining the relation between sight and feeling: the gaze marks an event of contact between people, and this contact is the scaffolding through which feeling flows. The connection of sight serves as the structural condition of feeling's possibility—witness, in figure 1.1, the portrait of the romantic couple as a closed visual loop.

The idea that feeling should accompany meaningful moments of interpersonal contact is also commonly found in political hope. Lauren Berlant, writing about the United States in particular, calls this national sentimentality, a "rhetoric of promise that a nation can be built across fields of social difference through channels of affective identification and empathy."[10] At the heart of this form of political belief is a link binding reciprocity and feeling, since affect is a sign that channels between people are open, that feeling is flowing *somewhere*. This somewhere, in turn, quickly becomes the *there* of narrative, since to feel moved by someone else's suffering can feel like *moving in* the right direction, evidence that something politically

FIGURE 1.1. The two-as-one visual loop of romantic love. Richard Curtis, dir., *Love Actually* (2003).

productive has already begun to happen. Feeling, reciprocity, narrative: the promise of national sentimentality is the algorithm that connects these terms into a seamless sequence.

Yet this promise leaves some details unaccounted for. Does the fact that Jamie has known Aurélia only in the capacity of an employee have any bearing on the liberal story of love's equally shared feeling? Or that Jamie, a British citizen, declares the feeling he cannot ignore to a roomful of Portuguese immigrants in the South of France, having abandoned everything to fly there under the aegis of love? These matters of plot only emphasize the way in which the conventional heterosexual love story is already founded on discrepancies of freedom and power, even while its ending promises the beautiful symmetry of one soul's recognition by another. The sentimental model of feeling can only account for the end of the story, since it understands all people's feeling to be equally suitable for eliciting the empathy and recognition of others. And this is an analytical weakness of the model that takes feeling to circulate through a relay of looks: its location of feeling in the *relay* presumes the points along its path to be essentially contentless and identical. When what matters is the feeling that flows between people, the generative details of the heterosexual or the immigrant story tend to blur out in the background of love's sharpness. Jamie's speech seems to promise that the individual voice of desire can lead directly to the representation of a social world, bypassing (we might say formally) the need for the other's response. The voice itself inaugurates the drama of communication, though not in the sense that the other absorbs and responds to it. It is rather that the social world is created with the creation of the voice, that the effort to produce a voice, to put into the world the thing he must say, *is* the culmination and ground of the social. In this sense, personhood's emblematic sensory figure is to be found not in his gaze but rather in his stammer, as it enacts the fledgling coming-into-being of the voice as the drama of love itself.

Several thematic continuities join *Love Actually* to *The King's Speech*. For one, *The King's Speech* centers on a couple, the titular monarch (played by Firth) and his speech therapist Lionel Logue (Geoffrey Rush), whose relationship has been compared by Firth to those found in romantic comedy (Firth: "boy meets therapist, boy loses therapist, boy gets therapist"). Note, too, that the director Tom Hooper's first choice to play the king was, reportedly, not Firth but Hugh Grant, who is famous for using his stammer in romantic comedies as an instrument of charm.[11] And yet stammering, in this historical drama, is not a quirk or a mere fact of the body that might take on any number of significances or narrativizations for its experiencing subject. It becomes, instead, an emblem of nationality.[12]

The film follows Bertie (as the king is known to intimates) as he ascends the throne and is faced with the task of delivering, over the radio, an address to the British Empire at the outbreak of the Second World War. But Bertie has had a speech impediment since childhood, a personal problem whose implications for public life are made visceral in the film's opening scene. The year is 1925, and Bertie, still a prince, must deliver his first live address over the radio at the closing ceremony of the British Royal Exhibition, staged at the cavernous Wembley Stadium. As Bertie ascends the stairs to a microphone placed squarely in the middle of the stands, the crowds all around him rise to face him (their wooden chairs scraping the ground noisily), their bodies and expectant faces pressed close. Alexandre Desplat's minimalist underscore—which here floats a high, isolated piano melody over a sustained string pedal, the musical equivalent of a held breath—evaporates just as the flashing red light next to the microphone goes solid, abandoning Bertie to the silence of dead air. We see Bertie's face up close as his mouth works silently. Then, a sound, but not a human one—a horse neighs from the field, and the camera cuts away from Bertie to the horse, as if grateful for a sound, any sound, to track. It is not just feedback from the human and animal bodies clustered around him that interrupt the voice's issuing in this opening scene, but also the way that the public-address system turns Bertie's voice against itself, picking up the surplus frictions in his stammer and sending them echoing around the arena until their mechanical repetitions overwhelm his faltering attempts to speak.

What seems to unravel Bertie's speech in this scene is its amplification in a social environment, the fact that it is transmitted into a real space filled with other bodies. His voice is broadcast widely, but it is also absorbed by the crowd gathered around him in the arena, which breathes and produces sound into the same air that carries the sound of his voice, and whose faces register in real time a growing embarrassment as the speech falters and grinds to a halt. The overpresence of other bodies in the stadium, their sounds and expectant stares, unnerve the voice and its efficient delivery. This is how the film introduces the problem whose remedy will occupy the remainder of the story, and which largely centers on the therapeutic relationship between Bertie and Lionel. The two meet only after Bertie is unsuccessfully matched with a series of other speech therapists, who all offer him prosthetic solutions that range from cigarettes to a mouthful of marbles. What distinguishes Lionel is that he does not, at first, treat the problem as a mechanical one, instead asking Bertie about his earliest memories and his relationships with his family.

The film's telling of the story of a stammer via the talk-therapy plot constitutes a metaphysical claim that it makes about the voice. Bertie initially resists Lionel's questions because he does not think of his speech problem as a personal matter. But, by the end, this romance will unite the voice's physical being with the imprint of personal history: the film's finale advances the argument that the voice generating national solidarity cannot just be a voice, something transmissible through radio waves, but must also have a backstory, specifically one whose narrative begins in a scene of childhood trauma. The moment in the film that most explicitly presents this idea takes place immediately after the death of Bertie's father, the current king, in the meeting between Lionel and Bertie that most resembles a session of psychotherapy. The mood on this occasion is more relaxed than usual: Bertie plays with a model airplane left behind by Lionel's sons while the therapist nudges him into recalling the various abuses to which he was subjected as a child. When he arrives at the story of the maid who deprived him of food for three years without his parents' knowledge, however, his voice falters in the telling and stops short of the essential detail. Lionel suggests that he try singing it, because, he says, "continuous sound will give you flow." What needs to flow is not just the voice but something in Bertie's relationship to his past, which is not so much a repressed memory as a lump of unredeemed pain that prevents the present from becoming expressive. There is a stalling-out in the narrative of his life, a knot that has never been smoothed over, and this knot, it seems, has been transfigured into the knot in the throat that afflicts him in the present. Because the narrative depends on the improbable notion that all hope of English resistance to the Nazis rests on Bertie's ability to deliver a speech, the stammer becomes the hinge where personal and national history meet—or, as Rush glosses the plot on the DVD commentary, "it's the journey toward becoming a king and becoming a human being."[13]

To complete the narrative line from the failed speech that opens the movie to the successful one that ends it, the plot must first introduce another narrative line via the psychoanalysis plot: that of autobiography. Bertie is compelled to narrate his life from his earliest memories, but the story stalls, and this stall turns out to be what keeps the other story, the film's plot, from reaching its end. In the notion that the people will not be ready for war unless the king acknowledges his voice's history and confronts its origin in traumatic experience, we find an exceptionally literal instance of the nationally sentimental notion that significant political change will come about when those who do not have a particular experience of being socially subordinated are exposed to poignant and moving evocations of the pain experienced by people who do. Under this model, an individual's pain is linked to a vision of a healed or whole social order through an act of testimony, a genre of speech that represents private experience in narrative form in order to circulate it as social material.[14]

Stammering, therefore, is never represented as something that Bertie may learn to live with, in an ongoing and ordinary way.[15] Instead, the film conceives of life as something strung out on a narrative trellis between trauma and transformation and imagines the eventual release of the voice to be the sign that the self is no longer stuck in past trauma but has "moved on," fulfilling its life trajectory. *The King's Speech*, then, is structured like a superhero film: an initial trauma wracks the body with both pain and promise, since the pain is not just itself but also the beginning of something, an incipient moment that already contains the kernel of some future redemption. The same is true of pain in sentimental politics. If testimonies of pain are supposed to lead to healed and whole social orders, then it is as if the initial experience of pain retroactively becomes the birth of the social itself, which the suffering subject incubates painfully until it can be spoken into existence. It is significant for this point that the film's protagonist is the king, who, as Bertie himself admits, has no purpose outside of the people's belief that "when I speak, I speak for them." If sentimental politics holds that it is through testimonies of pain that a nation is able, through the identification and empathy those testimonies elicit, to renew and heal itself, the film selects as its protagonist the one person for whom an inability to speak presents a national dilemma. Thus the king, who is by definition not a subject, becomes in his very exceptionality the general model of a liberal political subjectivity.

How does the film represent the conversion of pain into a socially cohering affective force? In the film's climactic scene, Bertie and Lionel are huddled in a small, soundproofed recording booth, the receiver of a microphone bisecting their eyeline. When the speech is about to begin, Lionel delivers a sweeping conductor's gesture, and the Allegretto from Beethoven's Seventh Symphony cues on the soundtrack. The movement begins with a single chord in the orchestra, but in the film, the chord is intoned twice, a kind of instrumental stammer that delays the beginning at the beginning. As Bertie begins to speak, however, the strings' dactylic rhythm chops up the mostly static string textures heard so far in Desplat's score, driving the texture forward as the cue expands in pitch range and instrumental thickness. The scene seems to recall Lionel's earlier advice to Bertie that the continuous sound of singing would give his voice flow. And flow is invoked here again, though in the metadiegetic register of the director's commentary: until this point, Hooper says, the film's visual style had been dominated by static shots and the slight shakiness of a handheld camera. But, in the speech scene, "the camera really starts to move for the first time," the earlier style giving way to the lyricism of the Steadicam.[16] When the stammer in Bertie's throat releases into flow, the camera also begins to roam, cutting away from the little recording booth to reveal shots of ordinary people gathered in tableaus of absorbed listening, the radio becoming the organizing center of citizens' bodies in pubs, factories, and battlefields across the land.[17] When the speech ends and the music stops, the camera ceases its roaming across the vast expanses of the British Empire and returns to the confinement of the little recording booth.

What are the differences between this scene of successful speech and the failed one at the beginning? Their settings seem related in their extreme contrast: where Bertie was earlier flummoxed by the crowding of bodies around him and the sounds that ricocheted back to him in Wembley's cavernous arena, he now disappears into a tiny room draped with fabric meant to absorb all extraneous sound, including his own voice as it returns to him. The king can only speak when he removes himself from an environment populated by others, and when his voice is no longer pitched to and absorbed by bodies who use the same air and who can affect him in turn. That is, it is only when he recuses himself from *the scene of the social itself* that his voice, paradoxically, can generate an image of the national in the film's visual field. It is true that the speech is spoken to an intimate other, Lionel, who tells Bertie before he begins to "say it to me as a friend." And yet Lionel is not the speech's addressee. The ears it is meant for are out there, somewhere through the medium's relay. The fact that Lionel's conducting gestures seem to invoke the presence of music (even though the Beethoven is nondiegetic) seems to indicate what is essential in the speech: less the sense of its words than, say, its musicality, the simple fact that it is expressive. Lionel's role in the booth is not to receive a message, though his presence there makes the message possible.

Taking these two films together allows us to understand Jamie's speech in *Love Actually* differently. *The King's Speech* allows us to consider the possibility that the speech's addressee in the Portuguese restaurant was not Aurélia but the crowd, and that the intimate relay with Aurélia served only to generate the kind of voice through which the crowd could sense itself as a collective, held together by a shared affective contour, a rhythm of being-together opened by the voice of feeling. In this model's theory, the social is not what emerges after the other absorbs the voice's claims and, in responding, opens a second realm of desire that might force Jamie to compromise or abandon the shining futures he has imagined. Rather, Aurélia's assent is like the necessary cadence that rounds off a melody whose impression has already been made. The scene ends, it is true, with

Aurélia and Jamie mirroring each other as they step into frame, their eyes locked in the classic two-shot of romantic closure. Yet it is instructive to note that *The King's Speech* frames Lionel and Bertie in the same way, but bisects the gaze with a microphone that picks up the voice made possible by their intimacy (see fig. 1.2). The couple's intimate contact is not the end, but rather the means, by which Bertie comes to generate the voice of a king.

The shift in the voice's address from an intimate to a public context also attends the music selected for the scene. Hooper justifies his use of Beethoven to underscore the speech (instead of music by Desplat) because of its recognizability, which, he says, "elevates the scene to the status of a public event." This is in contrast to scores written for a film, which Hooper considers "internal" to the movie that they are scored for. Thus the shift from Desplat to Beethoven in the speech scene amounts to a shift in how the audience is interpellated: no longer as the "private" audience of this film's score, but, in their recognition and prior knowledge of the Beethoven cue, as part of a larger publicity. Yet Hooper's attempts to describe exactly who is included in this larger public reveal the structural limitations of a climactic scene that is, in principle and by Hollywood convention, supposed to generate recognition for anyone who can relate to the king's specific and universal story. Hooper explains his choice of the symphony by saying that "we all have some memory, or most of us have some memory, of this music. Some of us know it very well." Who is this "we" that becomes "most of us" and then a "some of us" that he does

FIGURE 1.2. Lionel and Bertie, a microphone bisecting their eyeline. Tom Hooper, dir., *The King's Speech* (2010).

not specify? It is a claim that might be less plausible, for instance, if made by an American director on the DVD commentary of a film peopled with an American cast. Note too that Hooper emphasizes not "our" collective familiarity with the music in the present, but rather the fact that we have "some memory" of it, projecting a shared past of collective listening. Is Hooper, speaking in the first-person plural, thinking about growing up with the BBC's broadcasts of classical music, a cultural signifier that the BBC has long associated with itself and thereby with national identity as such? Such a connection would be corroborated by the narrative's framing as a history of English broadcasting and by the delicately cultured voice of the BBC presenter that opens the film.

We might notice the circularity of romanticizing a major event of English broadcasting by using music that, in its location within what Hooper calls "public consciousness," presupposes an audience already formed by that history of broadcasting. On this point, Sara Ahmed has described the circularity by which a sense of national coherence arises through "loyalty to what has already been established as a national ideal."[18] The Beethoven cue, therefore, does not do quite what the film's form seems to suggest, which is to open channels of affect between national subjects who are otherwise fractured and dispersed. Hooper's comments suggest instead that those he means to bind with the cue have, in a sense, already been bound, which complicates the scene's depiction of a structural event of coming together. Feeling's flow is not proof that a wall has collapsed, nor that some new structural configuration has viscerally come into being. In the film's climactic scene, it is more like a leftover charge that flushes through old wires.

If the movie asks whether a monarch can produce the coherence of an empire, and the answer takes the form of the king producing the empire as an audience, then we learn something about what audience means for this film. Unlike the audience in the Portuguese restaurant, whose collectivity, we might say, is guaranteed by the fact that they exist physically together in a room, the audience of the king's speech can only be counted as a collective through their mutual absorption in the speech. It is as if there is no room or hall that could guarantee a priori the togetherness of a group of people, but instead this togetherness can exist only so long as the expressive utterance persists in producing them as an audience. Here, the film introduces a variation or further development of the melodramatic trope of the protagonist's exposure of a moral or emotional truth, a trope that presumes the existence of an audience, often a metonym for society, that is present to witness and recognize this truth. This would be the fantasy, as in *Love Actually*, that there is an audience for a character's declarations, for whom their proofs of goodness or innocence will count, and this would be the comedy in romantic comedy, where the ending figures not just individual or even coupled happiness, but the happiness of the individual's or the couple's reintegration into, and transformation of, society. But the question animating *The King's Speech* is not only whether someone can assert or expose their essential goodness (this is the Manichean concern of the nationalist war plot), but also whether there exists an audience at all to whom one's confessions could be presented, an audience that could either affirm or deny one's place in the world. When it takes the mediated and distributed amplification of the utterance itself to produce the very audience it needs for its own recognition, then collectives and publics in this world will likely be ad hoc, occasional, and the effects of speech acts rather than their presumptive condition.

Both *Love Actually* and *The King's Speech* end with the ratification of social worlds. But what purchase does the social have when both films show their protagonists in the process of learning to speak (which suggests that they cannot yet fully speak), and when the climax of each film centers not just on an act of speech, but with the impression that the protagonist has finally achieved speech—that he is, in a sense, speaking for the first time? To end a film with the birth of speech indicates the primary interest that a film takes in speech. It is not primarily an instrument used to provoke, cajole, persuade, soothe, or otherwise affect another, a model in which the life of speech takes place after the birth of speech. Instead, the films locate most of their plots before the moment of its birth, an event that ends each film and thereby compresses the time of a shared life in language to a momentary gasp. It would seem that the power carried by speech in these endings is possible only in the face of a denial that recognition and identity may come belatedly, after the interval of the other's response. It might be useful, here, to conceive of the other's difference not as a spatial displacement (implied in the returned gaze) but in the temporal lag of response. It is a lag that these films deny to sustain their closing scenes' power, bringing up the credits almost as soon as the protagonist's speech is done.

The lag is suppressed, and the time of plot takes its place. Could we not now conceptualize the commercial narrative that culminates in feeling in a different way? Conventionally, a movie unfolds a narrative in which actions take place. The flow of feeling, recognition's reward, will come at some point along the narrative, tied to some event within its sequence of action. Alternatively, we might begin, rather than end, with feeling, with sheer sensation in the present. But at some point, fantasies of personhood are loaded onto affectivity, so that a suffused and sonorous being-in-the-body is imagined to be the proof and experience of subjectivity. It is when the visceral becomes imprinted with this intangible promise that feeling no longer operates only in the present, but projects backward the horizontal dimension of a narrative that culminates in the achievement of presence. Narrative itself is a vital component of the fantasy that the true self *emerges* at an incandescent point when what I say is also who I am, merging the voice's inner and outer halves to produce the sense that I exist in the fact that I speak. It is the story that I will become myself when I become completely communicative, an event always to come that turns the interest of the life before into simply its becoming.

In *Love Actually* and *The King's Speech*, the voice is ordinary and sonorous and at the same time the name of an intangible property that is nearly synonymous with personhood itself. Thus, "having a voice" and "finding one's voice" are phrases not about your voice, but about you; when used in a creative context, they mean that traces of you are recognizable in your utterances, as if they each bore the imprimatur of who you are. A voice is something that defines you by virtue of your ownership of it (something you "have"); at the same time, it is not something you generate or fashion, but rather something you stumble upon, as if it were concealed somewhere (something you "find"). These idioms imagine the achievement of expressive personhood as an archaeology, and the task of the voice's possessor to be one simply of uncovering or unearthing that which was always waiting to be discovered. They also imply the narrative goal of reaching a point at which your expressions begin to communicate something like an identity, some core of consistency whose value is measured by the extent to which its signature spreads outward while remaining, at its foundation, a thing that cannot be copied.

In its political connotation, "voicelessness" is the term used to indicate an absence of power, a condition that requires others who do have voices to speak "for" you. Under such a conception, an equal society is figured as one in which the power of voice is equally distributed, as if the voice itself contained the premise or promise of equality. But the use of "voice" as a metaphor for (valuable) personhood contains contradictions that are inseparable from its power. "Voice" speaks at once to the irreducible core of your personhood and to the degree and form of others' response to your personhood (in the political sense, it is not you who may determine, at least initially, how much of a voice you have). If the proof of a voice's singularity lies in the fact that it is often imitated but never duplicated, it would mean that a voice's singularity could not be determined without first looking elsewhere. Imagine the singular voice on a spray graph: a shining dot around which imitations cluster, drawn by its gravity, yet where no other point has quite the identical color—as if the value of the singular voice were simply its possession, within a field of economy, of a property that cannot be repeated. Yet if it makes sense to say that one can only measure the singularity of a voice socially, that is, after the voice has spoken, how can the concept also claim to represent an innate property that existed in you before it was "found"? The fantasy of having a voice seems to express an ambivalence toward the social as such: it is the fantasy of having an existence that is both determined and undeterminable by the social.

In these films, this ambivalence is tracked first in the immediately social scene of love and then the abstractly social one of nation. A further recession takes place in a third film that ends with an extended passage of Colin Firth's voice: Tom Ford's 2009 film *A Single Man*.[19] This speech, however, is not delivered to anyone except for the film's audience: the scene is empty, and the voice exists only in voice-over. The romantic other is gone, or, as we shall see, asleep; so is the audience addressed by the intimate voice that Firth used to speak a nation into existence. The film distills this chapter's earlier cases: there is no final recognition in the world by those around the speaker, and no suggestion that the speech is heard by anyone other than the audience of the film.

Firth plays George Falconer, an English professor in Los Angeles in the 1960s who is living in the wake of two events, one public and one private, that have both eroded the reliable expectation of narrative's continuation: it is a month after the Cuban Missile Crisis, news of which still comes over the radio, and it is an unspecified amount of time after the death of Jim, George's partner, in a car crash. In the midst of these derailments to the assured continuations of history and autobiography, the film does not so much begin as merely open, detailing the mundanity of dressing, eating, and driving to work that George forces himself through just to "get through the goddamn day." The problem of the voice's flow in the earlier films is transposed into the scene of living itself, which threatens to end before its stuck repetitions can resolve into something else: the film opens on this particular day only because George has resolved to commit suicide at the end of it.

Over the course of the film, George flirts with one of his students, who then meets him for a drink and at the end of the day returns to George's house. They drink, and George falls asleep. When he wakes up, he discovers the young man asleep on his couch, cradling the gun that George had planned to use on himself. He puts it away in a drawer and then opens a door that leads outside: as he does this, an owl startles up from a branch, shot at a stuttered frame rate that registers his sudden sensory acuity while also slowing the scene down. The shot brings the film audience's perception in line with shutter speed, with the suddenly apprehensible rate of film perception. The implication seems to be that the audience's visual acuity in this moment becomes mechanical, divested of subjectivity: it sees all that there is to see. George gives the slightest of nods, the tiniest trace of a smile. Then, his voice, intimately miked, sounds in a voice-over as the film's main string theme plays: "A few times in my life, I've had moments of absolute clarity. When, for a few brief seconds, the silence drowns out the noise, and I can feel rather than think. Things seem so sharp. The world seems so fresh. It's as though it'd all just come into existence. [Deep exhalation] I can never make these moments last. I cling to them, but like everything they fade. I've lived my life on these moments. They pull me back to the present. And I realize that everything is exactly the way it's meant to be." As in the king's speech, there is an intimate other in this scene, though this apotheosis doesn't center on the formation of a couple through the gaze: indeed, the student's eyes are closed, and the fact that he is asleep seems to be part of what allows George to experience what he calls a moment in which "the silence drowns out the noise." In fact, this figurative phrase also literally describes the drowning out of the quiet night scene by the saturation of the string cue: unheard music that washes out the night's crickets. The sleeping student is proximate but not present—he cannot speak or interject—and this promises that the voice-over will not be interrupted and will go on as long as George remains in this most precious of states.

George's speech seems to end affirmatively: everything is "exactly the way it's meant to be." Yet this final line can't quite conceal that the speech in its entirety is in the genre of lament, whose language iterates a certain set of familiar idioms about the temporality of the present. Consider the following lament in Hans Ulrich Gumbrecht's *Production of Presence*, which comes in the course of his description of an experience he calls "the perfect day": "I suspect that what lies behind my fixation on the form and the substance of the 'perfect day' is a longing—disappointment of which is ultimately, needless to say, for the better—for those moments of intensity to last, which, of course, they never will. Short of ever letting myself be convinced that a day was a homogenously perfect day indeed, I have come to accept that an alternation between intensity and perfect quietness would probably be good enough."[20] The same terms recur: clinging to that which "of course" cannot last, and a heavy sigh of grandiloquent resignation that almost conceals all the riches that must go unremarked for the "perfect day" to be the focus of someone's most desperate pursuit. The lament of presence is a lament about narrative, and specifically of one's helplessness to make sense of or predict the appearance of moments of future intensity. And its almost inevitable wish must be for death to come in the midst of one of those moments of presence, since no other option would be acceptable for someone for whom life consists of an "alternation" between intensity and its other.

This is precisely what happens in *A Single Man*: earlier in the film, we see George attempt to commit suicide. This sequence begins when the end of the day so carefully planned by George—all his papers in order, his funeral clothes laid out—is disturbed by sounds of merriment coming through the window from the next-door neighbor's party. George goes to put on a record in order to drown out the noise with music, but picking up the record stimulates a flight of memory, rendered in the film as a flashback. But what the film flashes back to is not just a memory of listening to records with Jim: it is, more specifically, of a moment when, as George and Jim are sitting together on the couch, a record has just come to an end, and the silence it opens as the disc's empty spinning fails to produce more sound transitions into a period of recitative, of talking before the next number begins. In this suspended moment between records, in the reawakening to the present and to the ordinary sounds of the day produced by returning from the music's transport to another time and rhythm, it strikes Jim to say about animals, wistfully, that "they really just live in the moment. It's like now—what could be better than being tucked up here with you. I mean if I died right now, it would be O.K."[21] It is the return to ordinary time from music's transport, rather than music's transport itself, that produces what the film's metaphysics cherish as that rarest of experiences: a narratorial access to the significance of the moment while at the same time living it, as if one could be both a character in the story and the agent of the fiction's omniscient enunciation.

When the flashback ends and the memory stops rolling, the sounds of the party return. George puts the record on: it is a soprano aria, "Ebben? Ne andrò lontana," from Alfredo Catalani's 1892 opera *La Wally*. The sentiment of the aria's title, "Well, then? I'll go far away," had also been expressed by George to a stranger he had met earlier in a parking lot. And yet it seems that George cannot simply decide the moment—or the soundtrack—of his departure. As he props himself up in bed with the gun, no posture or position he occupies seems like the right one in which to die. It is as if *any* bodily configuration he tries is inadequate, because each of them seems too specific and too banal for a life's final frame. At this moment, he is like Jamie in the restaurant before the underscore comes in and the speech begins: time and space are external, measured by the clock's objectivity; human actions can only take place within them and do not encompass them. Try as he might, George cannot reproduce the feeling of presentness that listening to records had led to with Jim.

The first two films demonstrated that sentimental fantasies of unison in love and in collectivity model themselves on the theoretical model of the facing gaze, a model whose imagelike instantaneousness underemphasizes the temporal dimension that opens between speech and its response. It is this temporal dimension that the endings of these films, which take place nearly as soon as the voice comes into being, aim to foreclose. As a result, their enactments of the protagonists' coming-into-presence via the movement of speech itself cuts off their entry into the social region of responsiveness that Stanley Cavell describes as "an invitation to improvisation in the disorders of desire."[22] The performativity of speech, Cavell writes, requires that one must wait to discover what effect one's speech has, and so what new status one bears in relation to the world, after which one might speak again, in a process that never arrives but is "endless." Presence is not settled by the fact of speech; rather, it comes only after the interval of the other's response, which exposes the extent and nature of the effects that the speech produced. The desire to experience one's presence in the present, to feel one's subjectivity viscerally, is also the desire to protect oneself from the temporality of the other's response, from admitting that presence in the social can only be negotiated within the social.

George's discovery that he cannot simply decide to drown out what he calls silence with music whenever he wants to suggests that the soundtrack's arrival in the film's final scene must index more than its ordinarily transportive effects. In the end, George is finally able to experience—and to narrate, in a voice that postdates his last words—the presentness he craves only when a heart attack dutifully and punctually takes him out (see fig. 1.3), an end not intended or prepared by him.[23] The suppression of the response of the other, which these films must enact in order to produce the mirage that personhood emanates from its own expressive authorization, is further abstracted in this ending from the other of love or the recognitions of one's people into the impassive externality of world and of history itself.

If these three films are not arbitrary cases but instances of a pattern, we could see how the voice that is catalyzed by the presence of another in *Love Actually* is picked up by a microphone and transmitted as the abstract yet intimate voice of nation in *The King's Speech*, and that the voice that is separated from the body by the microphone in *The King's Speech* is removed by yet another order of mediation in *A Single Man*, stashed into the nondiegetic register of the voice-over. The three images in this chapter locate *The King's Speech* in a kind of middle stage between the fusion of the

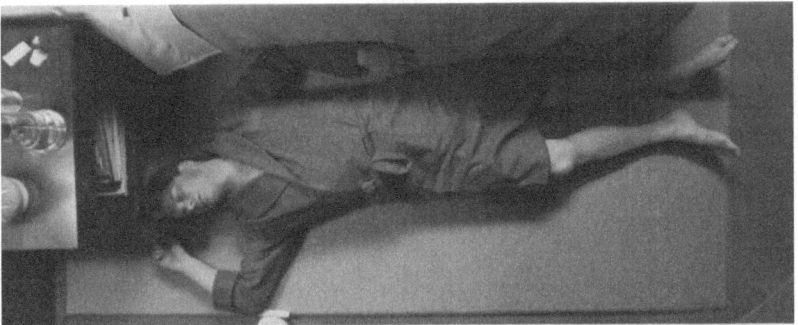

FIGURE 1.3. The film's last shot, with speech pushed into voice-over at the moment of death. Tom Ford, dir., *A Single Man* (2009).

intimate couple and the speech delivered only to the film's mass audience, completing a process of abstraction in which the position occupied by Aurélia in the first film is sequentially displaced onto Lionel/the nation and then finally onto the film audience itself. The lyrical promise that one's personhood is best accessed through the self-authorizing force of one's own feeling, then, is delivered not only in the overt lyricism of the soundtrack or in the mellifluousness of the voice, but also in a modular architecture of speech and address that operates not within genre's details but across or below them, uniting these films' collective ambitions to deliver a sense of what it would finally feel like to achieve the atmospheric promises of love, self, or nation. At the same time, the roaming referent of the intimate recipient of the voice, which appears in these films in differently mediated forms and across different positions within the fiction's enunciation, suggests that these genres of personhood might appropriate specific audiovisual affordances in order to deliver their implicit and diffuse promises to locate the self *somewhere* in the reflection of mass-cultural representation. In other words, it is in attending to audiovisual form, to the structure of fictional enunciation within which narrative and representation become possible, that one can trace the lines of similarity and of difference that run through personhood's formal legacies.

✷ 2 ✷
White Love

ROMANTIC COMEDY, THE '90S, AND
GENRE IN THE BACKGROUND

To write about romantic love is not just to contend with a field already saturated with language—that is, advice (often unsolicited), theory, cautionary tales, clichés—but also one in which a commonly encountered claim is that the thing you are after cannot be described. Perfectly standard responses to the question of what romantic love feels like, or how one identifies it, might include statements like "I don't know," "I can't describe it," "you just know it when you feel it," or simply the silence of thinking or trailing off. One might even imagine the avoidance of description to be followed with a smile, and the person who asked the question then nodding, the two interlocutors sharing a moment of speechlessness before a great and unifying mystery. In other words, in the scene of the transmission of certain kinds of intimate or heightened knowledge, to fail or refuse to answer a question does not always result in the questioner's disappointment, but sometimes in their satisfaction. Romantic love participates in a form of cultural reproduction in which the speech act "I can't describe it" can serve as a successful description, fulfilling a contract in which the one who supposedly holds knowledge conspires with the one who does not to keep certain parts of a shared culture implicit.

A study of romantic love cannot, then, simply promise to deliver knowledge. It must also track the effects of knowledge—its veiling, its tantalizing promises, its exposure events—as components of the experience of love itself. For example, as with many things that feel too close to describe, a concept's clarity can be a factor of distance. Hemangini Gupta writes about what her ethnographic subjects in India call modern love, "a companionate model of marriage increasingly witnessed the world over that emphasizes courtship, intimacy, support, and mutual respect as integral aspects of love."¹ From the view of a place in which Westernness can be felt and paced as an encroaching phenomenon, love is not so easily deracinated from its historical specificity. "Modern love" makes it plain that the concept's attractiveness is related to its status as a marker of civilizational progress and national contemporaneity, a framework unavailable in the term "true love," which obscures its historical desire. We can see, in the differences between "modern love" and "true love," or between "love marriage" and "marriage," the way in which qualifiers get stripped away the closer one gets to an ideological epicenter. For Gupta's subjects, to imagine this form of love is simultaneously to imagine a place—the "West"—whereas in the time and place from which I write, nation and history tend to disappear as love claims for itself a transcendent universality.[2]

How, then, should we define the proper geographic scope of a study of romantic love? A location can strip an abstraction of its abstraction—"Western love"—but it also seems to elide the very phenomenon one meant to capture, which is how love's sharpening of its subjects against blurred out backgrounds of time and space constitutes a central formal promise. In the essay "On Being White . . . and Other Lies," James Baldwin tackles the problem of defining the geographical scope of his object in this way: "My frame of reference is, of course, America, or that portion of the North American continent that calls itself America. And this means I am speaking essentially of the European vision of the world—or more precisely, perhaps the European vision of the universe."[3] In giving the essay's frame of reference, Baldwin simultaneously suggests that it does not need to be given—that it is, "of course," America. "Of course" can mark that something does not need elaboration, that it is obvious. And yet, when Baldwin continues, it is precisely to elaborate it ("or that portion of the North American continent that calls itself America," etc.), an elaboration that increasingly undermines the original frame of reference as it expands. If to say what "America" means is to show, in a series of surfacings, all that has disappeared from the word, then there is nothing actually obvious about the frame of reference at all. What, then, should Baldwin's "of course" be taken to mean? If not that it is obvious what "America" refers to, then perhaps that America is a concept whose meaning resides in its nonelaboration—for instance, when the word is used as a complete sentence. Like love, it circulates socially not just as knowledge but as *obvious* knowledge, a rhetorical mode in which elaboration's recession signals the positive existence of a collective culture so natural that it is shared before the intercession of language.

We might think of ways in which the performance of obviousness is key to the reproduction of norms, and in particular norms of sensation and feeling. Consider how sexual and romantic knowledge are often transmitted generationally (from parents and other adults) or microgenerationally (from siblings and older kids), or via the decontextualized research offered by the internet: the child is confronted with information, images, that they have no way of evaluating, but which they must assume coheres on some plane into a full knowledge that they will one day possess. What becomes erotic in the process is not only the putatively sexual or romantic content of the information, but also the structure of unveiling a mystery. And yet, the promised arrival of future knowledge in formulations like "you'll know when it happens" or "you'll know when you feel it" produces an affective paradox: how am I supposed to recognize a feeling when it comes if I've never felt it before? "You'll know when you feel it" thus performs a lexical antecedent that the child might themselves one day close with the sentence, "*This* must be what it feels like." In declining description, the initial speaker presumes that there is an affective plane of consistency whose existence the second speaker will one day corroborate. Though "you'll know when you feel it" appears to withhold definition, it nevertheless projects a metaregister of feeling that presumes romantic experience and sensation to be self-evident and identical, an affective common sense to which anyone naturalized in that culture will have an instinctive and unteachable access.

It is in the intervals of this culturally reproductive inexplicitness that popular cinema, and in particular the genre of the romantic comedy, stages in audiovisual form what it might feel like for love's promised happening to deliver a world worth living in. And yet love's representation takes place not only in the space of a film's content, that is, in the arenas of character, situation, plot, and setting. Rather, as this chapter will show, if to become love's subject is to take up a position within a field of knowledge relations and effects, then the attempt to render love on-screen will almost inevitably engage with, and become thematized within, the epistemic conventions of the audiovisual medium itself. These include, familiarly, the sense that characters cannot hear the soundtrack that glosses their world, including those feelings and thoughts that remain unexpressed and internal, or that the audience or consumer of the work sits in a position across this line of knowledge, able to take in both. If these audiovisual conventions have been naturalized in the narrative practices of mass cinema and video for the last century, it is also my sense that part of this naturalization involves the widespread belief that these conventions exist primarily to standardize efficient storytelling and to modulate an audience's moods, interpretations, and investments—and not as themselves encoding or revealing the formal conditions that frame the appearance of a historically particular kind of personhood. What is more, in the case of love in particular, to recover the historical relation between the form of mass audiovisual storytelling and its content would be, necessarily, to become engaged with the promise of love itself, insofar as this promise involves dissipating the peculiarities of its own historical formation, and, by proxy, those of its subjects as well.

This chapter thus extends scholarship in sociology, anthropology, sexuality studies, and other domains that have tried to show how romantic love not only belongs to one's intimate or personal registers of experience, but is inseparable from the historical formation of the liberal state and of capitalist structurings of time, labor, and aesthetics. Eva Illouz's work, for example, shows how the "meanings" of love and sex are constantly being tuned and reconfigured by institutions and markets, all while producing the impression that "desire" is something that belongs to you.[4] In the tradition after Foucault, sex is made an object of (self-)knowledge for the same reason that you might plant drugs on someone's body: to expand the discursive and practical reach of the law.[5] Here, as in Lauren Berlant and Michael Warner's work, heterosexuality, along with love as its morally impeccable relational form, functions as the one blind spot and exemption to the law's reach, thus structuring all other kinds of sex as marked, public, and within the narrative frame of history rather than floating amorphously outside of it.[6] For Elizabeth Povinelli, romantic love can be related historically to Western liberal subjectivity because it is the switch that turns on one's access to the register of common liberal humanity, functioning, as it does, as the name for a kind of relation that exfoliates the incidentalities of embodiment: love acts as a decontaminating shower that scrubs the subject clean of race, class, and other sedimentations of history, preparing its pink body for entry into neutral and universal subject forms, like "citizen," like "person."[7]

Formal theorists of love tend to locate its appeal in the offer of a place of repetition and stability through the future's unpredictable variation. This structure might be seen optimistically, as bell hooks does, as something that affords a better anchor than default options such as capitalist ambition, or neutrally, as Eugenie Brinkema does, as simply the form of a recurrence of a dyad in time, which only then becomes a canvas for cathexis and interpretation.[8] Writers interested in normativity as well as love, such as those extending queer theory and psychoanalysis, think of love's promise of a stable place of return over time as also a fantasy, one that trades an openness to the difference of the future for a mummified anchor that at least promises more of the same.[9] This chapter shares with these accounts an interest in thinking of love as a form, a structure in time and space that is repeatable enough to want (and want again). And yet, engaging with mainstream and amateur productions that attempt to capture or induce love's feeling in audiovisual form leads elsewhere, too. If, as Berlant argues, love provides a setting or scene in which desire can stabilize into something solid enough to imagine, love is desire's entry into representation, with the psychoanalytic scene functioning as a kind of mise-en-scène. While the romantic comedy, like all mass and unprestigious genres, is typically seen merely as a vehicle for the transmission of ideology, this chapter argues that romantic comedies encode not only normative ideas or arguments about love but also audiovisual forms, patterns of sound and image, and configurations of foreground and background that convey in love's transmission a tacit and felt secret of Western cultural belonging.

This chapter unfolds in three sections. The first traces the general audiovisual features of the scene of love as it is described and imagined in a range of romantic comedies, most of which appeared between the 1990s and 2010s. It also asks about the function of comedy in romantic comedy, focusing on what shifts when the punch line lands. The second section asks what these formal features have to do with the historical period in which they appear. Attending to love's audiovisual form, it turns out, reveals broader transformations and anxieties in public culture, the notion of the "political," and the need for genre in the mediation of ordinary existence. Finally, the third section traces some of the transformations that lead up to the 1990s by attending to a line of film remakes that span twentieth-century sound film and culminate in Nora Ephron's *You've Got Mail*. As I will argue, the audiovisual formulation of love frames it not merely as a desire for a legible kind of feeling, relation, object, or subjectivity: it also becomes a wish for a sensory and formal structure within which historical contradictions in the present might achieve an at least symbolic resolution, at least temporarily, as long as the feeling lasts.

Three Punch Lines (What's Comedy Doing in Romantic Comedy?)

In 2014 *Saturday Night Live* ran a sketch on its news segment, "Weekend Update," in which Michael Che, as the anchor, interviews a "romantic comedy expert" played by Vanessa Bayer. Bayer is there ostensibly to deliver a report on new television programming, but the joke turns out to be that she belongs to the genre on which she reports: an adorable klutz, Bayer claims to have accidentally stumbled onto the program (even though Che has just introduced her) and blushes furiously at every question she is asked. Meanwhile, Che's deadpan replies bring out the absurdity of Bayer's clichés:

CHE: So as a romantic comedy expert, what do you think of these new shows?
BAYER: What do I think? What do I think honestly? [Gentle acoustic guitar strumming begins] I think that um, that maybe I was meant to be here tonight. Because I was meant to meet you.
CHE: That is not actually why we brought you here.
BAYER: It's just that—and I think—well, you go first.
CHE: You're the only one going! So maybe get back to talking about romantic comedies.
BAYER: [Electric guitar enters as music gets louder] Look, I guess what I'm saying is, it's New York City! And it's six days before Halloween! So do you want to just go somewhere, and talk, or . . .
CHE: Daisy, I can't go anywhere now, I'm in the middle of "Update."
BAYER: You're always in the middle of "Update." Well, why not be at the beginning of something? Stop reading the cue cards out there and start reading the ones in here [touches her heart].[10]

When the strummed guitar comes in, Bayer's megawatt smile never flickers, but Che's eyes flit suspiciously up and around the hall, as if seeking the source of the music or the studio laughter that follows it. Alongside the parody of romantic comedy's stock phrases, then, the scene also lampoons the genre's musical praxis: the guitar's entrance, and Che's befuddled look, are enough of a punch line to get a laugh from the audience.

This musical punch line depends on the aesthetic convention that the nondiegetic cue should be imperceptible within the world whose events are, motivationally, its source. That Che seems to be startled by the cue is a sign that, for him, the cue is not a trope. It is as natural to her genre as it is alien to his; the difference in their hearing registers their gendered and racialized difference within the show as a difference in musical convention. The entrance of the guitar functions as a punch line because it exposes an expectation that has been implicit but underarticulated in the material that precedes it, a detail in the background of the world's coasting that the punch line wrests suddenly into the open.

If part of the skit's comedy turns on a difference of hearing as a difference in genre, it reminds us that genres can contain phenomenologies, ways of experiencing the world. For example, Bayer continually invests the moment with significances that Che can hardly register as such. These include familiar romantic tropes of predestination ("I think that um, that maybe I was meant to be here tonight") and sudden marvel at the specificity of the present ("It's New York City! And it's six days before Halloween!"), but also the sudden feeling of access to stretches of utopian, suspended time somewhere else ("So do you want to just go somewhere, and talk, or . . .") and the proliferation of hypothetical worlds that pressure the present's contingency ("If I don't leave now, I'll miss my flight and you'll lose me forever!"; "If we're not both married in, I don't know, fifteen, twenty minutes, do you wanna, um, meet at our special place?"). The contingency of expression itself becomes palpable when there is more to say than time needed to say it ("Well, you go first"). To be in the space of love means to feel confidence not just in feeling's continuation ("Why not be at the beginning of something?") but also in narrativity itself, in the hidden linkages that make it possible to speak of beginnings and endings at all.

In other words, love is imagined to be transformative and magical, but that does not mean that it is abstract or unspecific. In fact, Bayer's exemplary genre protagonist offers a clear vision of how love would vector time and space around the chronometry of the present. Wanting love seems to be as much about wanting this particular kind of aesthetic experience as it is about wanting another person; Che's flat refusal to get involved in Bayer's fantasy seems to have no impact whatsoever on her sense of romantic achievement (when Bayer asks Che if he wants to take a chance on "us," he says, "Absolutely not," to which she responds, "You had me at 'absolutely'!"). The skit, in other words, removes one half of the romantic couple and reveals that this has *absolutely no effect* on the production of romance's promised ending. Bayer's triumph shows us that the participation of a second person is not, in the end, the most essential component of romantic fantasy. What romance refers to in this context is not the same as what Stanley Cavell saw as the goal of remarriage comedies from the 1930s and '40s, which was the achievement of conversation, of finding a way of talking together.[11] Instead, in the romantic aesthetics that the skit both parodies and represents, the essential transformation happens not with another person but in the dawning of a new mode of feeling oneself in relation to the world.

Here is how the eponymous protagonist in *Frances Ha* (2012) describes the mode of relation to the world that love is supposed to induce:

> I want this one moment. It's what I want in a relationship, which might explain why I'm single now, ha ha . . . It's that thing when you're with someone and you love them and they know it, and they love you and you know it, but it's a party, and you're both talking to other people and you're laughing and shining. And you look across the room and catch each other's eyes—but not because you're possessive, or it's precisely sexual—but because that is your person in this life. And it's funny and sad but only because this life will end, and it's this secret world that exists right there,

in public, unnoticed, that no one else knows about. It's sort of like how they say that other dimensions exist all around us but we don't have the ability to perceive them. That's what I want out of a relationship, or just life, I guess. Love.[12]

Frances wants so much from so many things that disappoint her, chief among them an uncomplicated and eternal intimacy with her best friend, Sophie, and a successful career as a dancer in New York City. And yet she—like Vanessa Bayer's expert at the "Update" desk—turns out to be a romantic comedy protagonist who isn't in a romantic comedy. The film processes millennial economic uncertainty and the disappointments of friend and lover intimacy in a comic tone of disavowal (the "ha" in "Frances Ha"). Within these disappointments, Frances's insight that her romantic fantasy is "not precisely sexual" indicates that what's more important than the differences between whatever a lover, a friend, or a calling might provide is that they all become potential settings for a more general fantasy: an aesthetic experience in which the sound of a party and its conversation dims around a secret world that "exists right there, in public, unnoticed." Giorgio Biancorosso writes that love on film is rendered as an anesthetic effect, in which "the senses are temporarily numbed and the physical world recedes into the background of one's consciousness."[13] In Frances's monologue, this phenomenological reduction and intensification also grants love's subject a kind of narrative power: within the secret world, her ordinarily first-person living opens into an omniscient perspective that is able to take in, as from a floating eye above, the whole of things ("this life will end"). And yet this funny-but-sad realization is counterbalanced by a certainty—"that is your person in this life"—that forestalls the future's threatening difference, as if in the place of tomorrows is the promise of an intensified and continuous today.

A version of the moment that Frances describes ends up taking place at the end of the film. At a party after a dance show that Frances directs, she and Sophie see each other across a crowded room while talking to other people. At first there's the sound of Frances's conversation with her former boss, mixed with the hubbub of party chatter and a light underscore in which a wind motif is passed around but doesn't really begin to coalesce into melody. The camera frames the intimate conversation not intimately but from across the room, improbably picking up the closeness of their voices across the movement of bodies in the frame's blurred foreground. Then, just as Frances breaks the conversation's intimate contract to look across the room at Sophie, the idling motifs in the underscore finally catch the gust of meter and start spinning out a melody, propelled along by pulsed hurdy-gurdy strings. Now, finally, the camera pulls in to frame Frances's and Sophie's faces in alternating close-ups, and as the underscore is turned up, the sound of the party and the conversational other both disappear from the mix.

Both "Romantic Comedy Expert" and *Frances Ha* process a postmillennial distance from romantic saturation and immediacy, a desire for which animates their protagonists but no longer seems to be guaranteed in their worlds. Yet though this genre disappointment produces satire in the first and awkward comedy in the second, both audiovisual texts model the longed-for experience in a surprisingly consistent way. In the *SNL* skit, the romantic protagonist is marked in part by her inability to hear, or to note, sounds in the room that others are perfectly able to hear; in *Frances Ha*, the sounds of the party and of conversation are shut out of the membrane that envelops love's relay. In other words, the purpose of the music cue that enters in the background of both scenes is not, or not only, to introduce its mimetic or emotional properties to the scene, nor to produce an intensely focalized sensory experience, one belonging either to the character or to the audience. It is also to provide an aural figure of the world *dimming*.

Love as a fantasy of the recession of the world's sound occurs twice in Alice Wu's *Saving Face* (2004).[14] The film revolves socially around the East Buffet & Restaurant, a ballroom rented out for weekly gatherings by a set of interlinked Chinese immigrant families in Queens, New York. Its younger attendees call it Planet China, which better captures its ecosystem of interdependence and the pull it exerts on those drifting around its orbit. The blueprint of the hall itself is important for the analysis to come. It features buffet and private tables that ring a central dance floor, and it is there that men and women pair up for a song to fulfill a variety of social needs: romance, sure, but also simple catching up, gossip, and cover for queer pals to produce counterscopic commentary about the watchers on the sidelines. To go out to Planet China is to go out in public, but to step on the dance floor is to enter a surveilled space in which every gesture offers itself up to the crowd's interpretive pleasure.

It's on this dance floor that Wilhelmina, the film's lead, first sees Vivian, who's also part of the Chinese pod. It is key to this meet-cute that it happens while Wil's grandfather, who is also Planet China's de facto patriarch, is giving a speech to the assembled crowd. The grandfather begins by saying, "Let me say a few words," ushering in not so much the beginning of words as the beginning of words marked as words. When speech assumes the condition of performance, all other speech that is not explicitly invited becomes an interruption; as a result, people around the room start to settle in for the long haul, their eyes showing that they've gone internal. Wil is no exception, and when the camera cuts to her, the grandfather's voice now sounds fuzzed out, the way a voice might sound if you weren't paying attention to it. In the space of focus and attention that comes from inattention to something else, Wil sees a girl in the hall's upper balcony.

Accounts of meet-cutes—fictional or otherwise—often focus on matters of plot: she did this, then this happened. The meet-cute appears as an improbable and sometimes comic event sequence that follows a narrative arc from the ordinary day to the unordinary contact ("I was just minding my business at Planet China when, out of nowhere . . ."). But the meet-cute in *Saving Face* also takes place under notable sonic conditions. As the grandfather's voice fades to a faint murmur, we see Wil look at Vivian, then look away; Wil look at Vivian again and, when her look is returned, turn away in embarrassment; Wil look at Vivian a third time, this time meeting her gaze in acknowledgment of the exposure of interest that had caught her by surprise. Then the grandfather's voice is turned back up to its ordinary volume and fidelity.

This scene realizes in practice what *Frances Ha* set forth as a sonic theory: namely, that when your attention drifts in the middle of a conversation to alight on the object of love, it is as if the voice you were listening to suddenly becomes muddled. How do we account, technically or conceptually, for this change in sound? The voice itself hasn't gotten quieter or moved farther away; nor is there a sense that the voice has been superseded by another sound (in fact, Frances seems to describe a situation that is acoustically paradoxical, that of noise drowned out by quietness). It feels more accurate to say that the sounds of the room, or of the world, are no longer immediately present to the person in the ambit of love. Ordinary sound and speech now have the quality of being submerged, as if the hearer had crossed into some other substance—say, from air to water.

That the grandfather's voice can nevertheless still be heard as an indistinct murmur is evidence of some intervening surface as well as of this surface's porousness. The world's sounds become something like the scene's background, a register that is sonically delineated from the foreground event of love's incitement, in which Viv's scraping of a chair and the magical appearance of wind chimes come through with perfect clarity. If, in a now classical line of film music analysis, we identify the chimes as a nondiegetic addition to the scene's diegesis, figuring some line that separates the inside and the outside of this romantic comedy's sound world, this is both an accurate and an incomplete description of the ways in which a sense of world-line emerges from the scene's sound.[15] To mobilize the reading of an inside and an outside world of sound only via the convention of the soundtrack's use in narrative cinema is to pass over the fact that the film has already produced an audiovisual image of romance as a partition of inside and outside sound *within* the diegesis, as the soft aural focus of the grandfather's voice sharpens the sounds that are most present to Wil. It is as if the representation of love depends, at least partly, on the possibility of splitting hearing into backgrounds and foregrounds, and the world into sheets or layers of sense.

The final coming-together of Wil and Viv turns on a punch line about this very difference. Here is the plot that has transpired: Wil and Viv get together, but Viv leaves for a ballet gig in France when Wil, among other avoidances, refuses to kiss her at the airport, "right here, in front of all these people." At the end of the movie Wil and Viv run into each other again at Planet China. As Wil starts to walk across the floor toward Viv, the dance hall's diegetic music fades out and the movie's soundtrack, all soft winds and strings, takes its place. The camera assumes Wil's point of view as she floats toward Viv, parting a sea of couples as Viv grows nearer in the frame. Then, as she pulls up to Viv, the soundtrack fades out again as the noise of the hall returns just as a song is ending. Then this:

WIL: Dance with me.
VIV: Wil...
WIL: Vivian Shing, I am asking you to dance with me.
VIV: I can't. [long pause] There's no music.

Nothing more is needed after that; the film's question about love closes on these words.

What does this exchange overcome that could not be overcome before? Wil opens with a veiled, or doubled, meaning: "dance with me" is a question not just about dancing, of course, but also about Viv being with her. Viv's response, however, is to feign ignorance of the fact that language has been doubled and to answer only *one* of the possible hearings, the literal or explicit question about the dance. By collapsing the split that Wil introduced into a single, explicit hearing, Viv in essence denies that there *is* a veiled question that needs an answer. It is as if she is saying, when there is no question about whether I would be with you, you could only be asking me to (literally) dance with you.

This play of gesture and metalanguage ends with this section's second punch line—"there's no music"—which recalls the underscore joke in *SNL*, in which the possibility of a shared world of escape also turned on the question of whether two people could hear the same cue. In fact, it is possible to read Viv's punch line about music as a double entendre of its own, one that registers the parallel existence of inside and outside music, or of the figurative and literal senses of the dance. After all, to give "there's no music" as a reason for not wanting to date someone is perfectly comprehensible, if a little purple. Music might just be a word for a metaphysics—like "connection," "spark," "vibes"—that marks something felt, there, and invisible. Viv's "there's no music" could refer to the kind of music that swells up in romantic comedies, legitimating a romance as real, as when Wil walked across the dance floor toward her and the DJ's music dialed down to make space for the film underscore. The two hearings of "there's no music" seem to correspond to the two kinds of music that give way to each other in this scene, the diegetic and nondiegetic registers making and taking space from each other in an aural pas de deux.

But it is also that the difference between inside and outside music, or love's secretly lived and publicly expressible forms, is the very issue that has separated them to this point. In these final lines, then, they are engaging, continuing to engage, the still-unsettled question of their future possibility. As in *SNL* and *Frances Ha*, to think about love depends on the capacity to imagine that language, and the world's sound, have both an inside and an outside: an objective, formal, recorded register that establishes public mutuality and copresence, and a secret, removed, temporally alien space from which the world's sound recedes even when one is in it with others. Romance is as much a fantasy that the world is split between this outside and this inside, that anywhere in what we call the public could be found secret pockets of a different time and place, as it is of the relation between one and two.

That love might name an aesthetic configuration of the world—one in which sound's public face is doubled in a realm of private hearing—could be one way to account for the notable presences, in the endings of *Brown Sugar* (2002) and *Notting Hill* (1999), of specific technologies and occasions of audiovisual mediation. In *Brown Sugar*, the couple's final exchange takes place on the air when Dre (Taye Diggs) calls in to a radio show where Syd (Sanaa Lathan) is being interviewed as the author of a new book on hip hop.[16] In *Notting Hill*, the film's final revelations happen only because Will (Hugh Grant), masquerading as a reporter, has sneaked into a press conference that Anna (Julia Roberts) is giving on the occasion of the release of a movie in which she stars.[17] Neither movie, in other words, stages the revelation of romance in the context of ordinary speech; instead, both place these crucial lines within the professionally and technologically mediated language game of the Q&A.

That these two films would marshal these peculiar, and peculiarly similar, performative settings for their finales would seem to suggest that there is something about what an interview does to language that the films' endings require. In *Brown Sugar*, when Dre's call goes live on-air, he begins by asking a question that might plausibly be asked by an anonymous radio caller: "Sydney Shaw, when did you fall in love with hip hop?" When she starts to answer, however, he cuts her off, claiming that she misunderstood the question. He now asks, again: "Syd, when did you fall in love with hip hop?" We have learned that for Dre and Syd, "hip hop" means hip hop before the genre's mainstream and commercial successes, and also that it is their metonym for original and unspoiled love. Hip hop, therefore, also means them, since they met in the prelapsarian space of childhood while watching local MCs battle in the park, before these figures became the names they would become.

When Dre switches from her public name to her nickname, Sydney realizes who the anonymous caller is and also now hears the question embedded in the question. Two changes then occur. The first is that the unobtrusive beat holding time in the background—the kind that might play as a radio DJ talks between tracks—is now drowned out by soft, synthy strings that start to creep into the sonic texture. The second is that Syd now addresses Dre directly or intimately, no longer as the anonymous caller and no longer from her professional capacity as an author being interviewed on the radio: "Dre, I've been in love with you from the first day I saw you." The nickname, like Viv's line about music, finally collapses the doubled public and private meanings of Dre's opening question into a single possible hearing.

And yet, the collapse of the double entendre does not simply remove the couple from the scene's public setting. Even as the strings draw a sonic curtain around words uttered in the intimate mode, dimming the presence of the interviewer and the sounds of the studio, Dre and Syd are still speaking on the air, their private moment broadcast to places such as the taxi from which Dre calls as he speeds to the studio. The question of why the film contrives a situation in which the final revelation happens during a publicly broadcast radio program is related to the question of why, to imagine love, Frances had to first imagine a party. The film itself gives some clues: as Dre enters the radio station, still speaking to Syd on his phone, we also hear his voice coming through the building's speakers, which are broadcasting the interview live through the station's halls. As the film approaches its romantic culmination, then, the voice of its disclosure is not just the soft and near one of the lover, but one that is in the process of becoming public. It is Dre's voice, but relayed through a cell phone and filtered back through the radio, such that the voice that issues from his body is layered on top of another: its recorded, mediated, and disseminated form, an echoed and delayed double.

Brown Sugar's ending is calibrated not only to produce a couple, then, but also to create something like the public form of Dre's voice, which emerges as he gets close to romance's closing event. Similarly, the formation of a couple at the end of *Notting Hill* produces, almost as its effect, the public version or existence of Will Thacker, the ordinary man who falls in love with an American film star. In the film's closing sequences, Will crashes Anna's final press conference before the end of her stay in England. Like Dre, Will begins by speaking within the language game of the interview. Following another reporter's question about photos of him and Anna that had circulated in the tabloids, Will is then called upon by the moderator as another reporter on the floor. "Ms. Scott," he asks, "are there any circumstances in which the two of you might be more than just good friends?" Anna, recognizing him, responds that she had hoped that there might be, but has been assured that there aren't. They continue to speak like this, the private context embedded in the public one, until Anna finally admits that she would consider taking "Thacker" back. To which Will responds, "That's very good news."

News is what people are sometimes inclined to call personal developments in the love plot—a new cutie, an engagement, a pregnancy. News is also what the press conference is structured to produce, as reporters transform interviewed speech into publishable material. This double hearing of the word "news" in Will's line—the news of Anna's reciprocated desire, which will also become the news printed in tomorrow's tabloid—is facilitated by the architecture of the press conference, in which a room is staged to make it appear as if the central communicative act takes place between two people, the questioner and the answerer. But this apparent exchange only facilitates the primary function and form of address that the press conference exists to stage, which is the dissemination of that exchange to a wider audience. The purpose of the "direct" address between reporter and subject is primarily for it to be overheard, say, by a third party—the public—which may or may not be present in the room. This is especially obvious with interviews in professional contexts such as sports, in which reporters sometimes ask leading questions, which is to say questions whose answers they already know (for example, "How much grit and resolve did it take to get the win tonight?"). But to see this kind of question as a failure of the reporter's task is to misunderstand the function of questions in the interview context. The fact that the space of an interview is, by default, on the record—a fact assured by professional conventions as well as the presence of microphones and cameras as technologies of transmission—means that it is a space between quotation marks. We might then see the reporter's job differently: it is not only to discover facts about the respondent that they and the public do not yet know, but also to *shift language into the space of quotation*. We might think of the press conference as a mechanism that converts language into news, which is why it is important for the respondent to say it in their own words, even if what they say is already essentially known.

The endings of *Brown Sugar* and *Notting Hill* both produce and stage the transformation of words into their official and public form, into material that might enter the public record. As Bayer's *SNL* performance suggested, you might confess your romantic secret in order to get nearer to the object of love, but then again, you might not. You might do it instead because the occasion of love allows you to stage the entrance of thoughts and words deemed secret into the hearing and memory of the world. If disclosure, and not desire, were the central erotic operation of romantic comedy, its theoretical model would center less on relationality and the couple and more on the operation of becoming a public thing, on the difference between private information and the public status of the news.

This difference becomes the subject of a punch line from the film *Happiest Season* (2020), a holiday rom-com about a woman who brings her girlfriend home to her conservative family for Christmas.[18] For most of the movie, various kinds of sexual information are kept secret as the children attempt to become the frozen portrait that the parents desire. Then there is a scene where everything shifts. It begins when the closeted daughter comes out to her parents in the middle of their living room; then, unprompted, her sister adds that she is getting a divorce and had been hiding this news for fear of her parents' disappointment; then the third sister steps up and announces, "I don't have any secrets, but I am an ally."

To what or to whom is the third sister declaring her allyship? To the lesbian sister, or to the straight sister whose divorce nevertheless makes her sexually perverse in her family context, or to both? Or is she an ally to anyone with a secret, whatever the secret happens to be? This scene invokes Foucault's genealogy of a tradition in the West in which the socially integrated individual must periodically confess their innermost urges and secrets to an "impartial" institutional figure, which in different eras and contexts might take the form of the priest, the judge, or the therapist.[19] But as D. A. Miller has pointed out, the secret that you are most ashamed of and find most difficult to confess is often the *least* surprising and individuating thing about you (for example, in a conservative religious world, the fact that you have sexual desire). Why, then, is it so hard to confess the sexual secret, the addictive secret, or the secret of one's shame? Miller suggests that there are reasons to want to keep *and* to tell your most secret secret, which is both utterly common and yet feels like it pins you down so particularly: "I can't quite tell my secret, because then it would be known that there was nothing really special to hide, and *no one really special* to hide it. But I can't quite keep it either, because then it would not be believed that there *was* something to hide and *someone to hide it.*"[20] In other words, the secret is precious not because of what it contains (because its content was never an individual material to begin with), but because the form of the secret allows the self to imagine itself as a private and hidden space, separate from others and the public. In Miller's description, personhood emerges as an effect of secrecy, since simply revealing my secret would be an admission that there was nothing particularly special about it in the first place—or about me. Thus, while social personhood is threatened by the secret, it is also that the concept of personhood needs the secret to produce the difference of inside and outside, of private and public, as a difference of what is kept and released.

What is revealing about the punch line of the third sister's addition to the other confessions is that she declares herself an ally not to a specific identity formation, but to the *structure of disclosure* itself. Or, as the movie's tagline puts it, "This holiday, everyone's secrets are coming out." Repeating the progression enacted by the three sisters, what begins as the particularizing queer phrase and speech act of "coming out" is eventually generalized until it refers to "everyone's secrets," an operation that draws on an essential ambivalence that Eve Sedgwick noted about the theorization of minoritarian forms of life: that is, is queerness primarily "about" individuals and forms of life marked as queer, or does its pertinence in fact encompass the scope of "virtually any aspect of modern Western culture"? As the film bridges the shift from the particularity of a queer rom-com to the end of secrets as such, its operative theme shifts from the realm of sexuality and desire to the eradication of privacy (and of one's ambivalence about privacy). Romance's question is then no longer "Is there someone out there for me?" but rather "What if there were nothing left for me to hide?" We might then see the romantic comedy as a genre driven energetically toward pushing everything out into the open, toward converting, like the press conference, "private" facts into a fully disseminable register of publicity. Then the appearance of Will's face on television screens as cameras turn to him after his confession of love, or the way that Dre's voice starts to ring out over the radio station's public-address system as he gets closer to Syd, might not be contrivances specific to these two plots so much as depictions of the general procedure and fantasy of romantic comedy. If this is so, then the genre's emblematic figure would not be the couple but rather the celebrity—the figure of the fully public individual.

Notting Hill, of course, centers on the fantasy of a romance between an ordinary person and a celebrity, although knowing this does not yet mean that we know whose fantasy it is or what the fantasy consists of. It is also difficult to determine, at certain moments in the movie, whether the fact of Anna Scott's celebrity is there as the content of a specific fantasy (i.e., dating a famous movie star), or whether her celebrity is there to illustrate, via its exaggeration of the ordinary, certain common and generic features of romantic experience. For example, when Will and Anna break up halfway into the film's running time, there follows a standard montage in which we observe Will's despondency as he wanders the city, alone. The film's twist, however, is that Anna is a celebrity, and so Anna is everywhere. Will attempts to fill the empty hours by going to the movies, but Anna is in the movies, watched by him and countless other people who also imagine themselves privileged with an intimate and possessive relation to the star. When he takes the bus home, Anna's face is on the side of the bus. It is formulaic for the despondent lover to see their lost love everywhere, but in this case the Romantic trope of the lover's disembodiment and dispersal into the world's natural forms becomes literal in the structure of the celebrity's technological dissemination.

The celebrity's function in the film as both the content of a specific romantic fantasy and a concrete embodiment of the general form of romance ends up producing an unstable lexical field in which the general and the particular constantly undermine each other. For example, a phrase like "Haven't I seen you somewhere before?" is no longer just a cliché when it is spoken to a celebrity. When Anna first walks into Will's bookstore, his look of surprise registers both the fact that he is seeing someone for the first time and also that he has seen her before. The sense of meeting a new person with whom you already feel a mysterious sense of intimacy, as if you already know them, or toward whom you feel a sense of entitlement, as if you deserve access to them because you have always had it, is a psychic aspect of romantic projection that becomes material in the modern celebrity's mediated form. If it is a cliché in love to feel an unusually deep familiarity within someone new, a sense of belonging incommensurate with experience, it is also because the cliché, like the commodity, hovers between the promise of its force and the open secret of its indifferent fabrication. The usually disparaged asymmetry between time and affect invoked in judgments of the cliché and of the commodity is thus valenced differently in romantic love: there, it is a lovely mystery that the absence of strangeness in the stranger seems out of proportion to the time of your acquaintance, as if there were a duration unaccounted for in the ledger of intimacy.[21]

The casting of Julia Roberts in the role of a major Hollywood actor itself contends with one of romantic comedy's constitutive ironies, namely the casting of a film star to play someone whose only purpose, at the beginning of the romance plot, is often to index someone who is socially unremarkable and invisible. In *Notting Hill*, however, the fact that Roberts plays the role of a movie star, albeit a fictitious one, complicates what it would mean for an audience to separate from the plot their knowledge that Roberts, or indeed Hugh Grant, is already a star. This separation of plot and metatext is further complicated, for example, in scenes that seem to refer to the actors hidden within the performances of their characters, as when Will opens his front door to a horde of reporters flashing their cameras in his face or when, at the end of the closing press conference, Will's and Anna's faces begin to appear on screens assembled in the press room (fig. 2.1), as if the revelation of love also revealed the true natures of the stars that had been, until now, concealed beneath character.

The stripping away of the fiction of character continues in the film's epilogue, where narrative time also begins to speed up. The press conference cuts forward in time to Anna and Will's wedding, and then to Will and Anna on a red carpet, presumably at a film premiere. It is at this point that a viewer might be forgiven for experiencing an *unsuspension of disbelief*, following the generically contractual suspension of disbelief that allowed them, for the majority of the film, to see Grant as a romantically hopeless nobody who lives in Notting Hill. That is, one would be forgiven for seeing, in the shot of Will Thacker and Anna Scott on the red carpet,

FIGURE 2.1. Will and Anna appearing on screens as their romance is ratified. Roger Michell, dir., *Notting Hill* (1999).

not the characters in the film, but rather Hugh Grant and Julia Roberts in their natural habitat. For *Notting Hill*, in other words, there is no difference between becoming a subject of love and a subject of the public. Its claim is that to be ushered into the halls of romance and its personhood-granting effects *is* to achieve a form of legibility and publicity of which the celebrity is not a social exception but an affectively metonymic form. We might think of the romantic comedy plot that ends with its protagonists in a public place, cheered on by the public around them, as a plot that follows the peeling back of character to reveal the star underneath, returning the celebrity who plays them to their proper place at the center of things. In this reading, the fantasy promised in romantic comedies is not only that any nobody could achieve, via love, a kind of public visibility and existence normally accorded to a figure like the celebrity; it is also that our drabness is a fiction that covers our actual stardom, and that the purpose of plot is to reveal what was always our essential form. It is to become the bearer, and the subject, of news.

Though *Notting Hill*, *Brown Sugar*, and *Saving Face* all end with the emergence of some private or secret version of the self into a publicly articulable or disseminable form, the codas of these films also frame the significance of these emergences differently. In *Notting Hill*, as soon as the couple is clinched and the plot is effectively over, the most notable aspect of the coda that follows is its tremendous and nearly incoherent acceleration. Elvis Costello's "She" takes over the sound mix as the press conference cuts through Anna and Will's wedding and then to their appearance at a film premiere, and then finally to a nondescript park in the city. We arrive to find the camera already in motion as it follows a child going down a slide, after which it picks up (or is picked up by) the motion of two other children running and follows them past a scene of mothers picnicking with their children before finally alighting on a park bench, where it circles around a pregnant Anna with her head laid in Will's lap. The film fades out to this final image, the two children still running circles around the bench as the camera circles in the opposite direction, centering the complex of mommy-daddy-baby as a still image in the midst of all this concentric rotation. This visual distillation to the final image is accompanied by a final lyrical distillation of the Costello song to a simple repetition of the word "she," which projects femininity as an atmosphere of underexplanation, taking as self-evident its purest representation in the nuclear efficiency of the white family.[22]

In *Saving Face*, the visual event of Wil and Viv starting to dance on Planet China's central stage produces not the universal recognition of melodrama's standing ovation, but something more uneven. Some people are delighted; some couples return to their ordinary squabbling; others flee the scene, while their companions are more concerned about getting their dinner's worth than about what might have just shifted in Planet China's normative scene. In a post-credits sequence, queerness is shown not to explode but rather to be integrable into various normativities that allow the people in a scene not to be completely indecipherable to each other. One man says of the couple's revelation, "I didn't get it—but at least she's marrying a doctor." Later, Vivian promises Wil's mother that she'll inherit the parental project of getting Wil to dress less butch (the two then clink glasses). As if clinching that the film's ultimate genre is not just comedy but slapstick comedy, the last shot we see is a spit take, delivered by Wil when her mother says, "So, Wil, there's only one thing left. When are you going to have a baby?" This is no queer tragedy, but it isn't utopian either. It does what comedy does in the classic literary sense: it offers a vision of the integration of the couple into a social order.[23] Slapstick, unlike sentimentality, doesn't need things to line up perfectly for a whole world to be there.

Brown Sugar presents yet another formal model for the end of the story. After Dre and Syd get together on-air, the film follows not the couple, as in *Notting Hill*, but the song. As Dre and Syd kiss in the booth, the DJ puts on the track that caps Dre's search as a music executive for what the film has called real—by which it means pre-mainstream—hip hop, located fantasmatically by the film in the New York City public park where Syd and Dre witnessed their first rap battle as children. The film's opening sequence—and subsequently, its romantic metaphysics—unfolds from this tension. Its first line of dialogue is a voice-over from Syd: "I've started every interview I've ever given in the same way for over ten years: so, when did you fall in love with hip hop?" Then the film intercuts talking head–style documentary clips of real MCs, from De La Soul to Black Thought to Common, who, in answering, unfold a collective memory of the time before they became the names that identify them at the bottom of the screen.

The film's opening, in other words, takes pleasure in a particular kind of frisson available in the phenomenon of fame: that of recalling the ordinary origins of someone who would turn out to be a star. Then Syd says, "I remember the exact *day* I fell in love with hip hop. It was July 18, 1984." At this moment, the present tense of the voice-over cuts to the memory it describes: we are now watching Syd and Dre discover each other as kids discovering hip hop. When the present tense of the voice-over returns, pushing the memory once again into the past, this is what Syd says: "The day I saw Slick Rick, who went by Ricky D back then, Dana Dane, and Doug E. Fresh battle in the Bronx was the day I truly met hip hop. Little did I know a year later Ricky D would join the Get Fresh Crew and record the hip hop classic 'The Show,' and of course the B side, 'La Di Da Di.' Dana Dane would drop a couple years later with his classic 'Cinderfella.' But little did I know how much hip hop would be a part of my life." "Little did I know" is the secret wish buried inside the wish for romance. It is a phrase that marks one of the few occasions where one's ignorance is a source of pleasure, as the present self enjoys how little the past self knew about how things would turn out. The pleasure of "little did I know" is, in part, the pleasure that there are narrative forces and genre protections at work of which you might be completely unaware. The phrase thus demonstrates the willingness to sacrifice a total self-knowledge in favor of the existence of a narrative position somewhere, perhaps in the distant future, from which the present's stuckness could be seen to have been merely a failure of knowledge.

Brown Sugar locates knowledge as an erotics of difference in both the romance plot and the film's romance about hip hop, where Ricky D would eventually come to be known as Slick Rick, and no one knew on that day in 1984 of the things that the men in that park would go on to do. The film's final image, instead of accelerating into *Notting Hill*'s reproductive future, thus circles back to the past: the track that Dre gave up the profits of commercialized hip hop to produce plays over the airwaves as the camera cuts to a park not unlike the park in which he and Syd had first discovered hip hop. Now it is *his* track that plays as the soundtrack of the park, and the camera alights on a bench on which a little girl and boy sit listening. The film's form is circular: the end point of the plot feeds back to its beginning as another scene in which love, or hip hop, might catch.

In other words, though all three films propose that the coming-together of the couple coincides with the point at which they become maximally public and on display, *Notting Hill*'s innocence of racial and sexual specification ends up with a very different idealization of what happens after this moment in the film's coda. Perhaps because, unlike the first two films, there is no racial or sexual public in *Notting Hill* to which the characters belong within the implicitly white and homogenizing public of US or UK "diversity," white love comes to be figured in the film as pure publicity, as pure escape and release from the stagnating and isolating effects of privacy. At the same time, the camera's motion also cuts the white family off from the public as such, driving them centripetally to the center of things until the world appears only as a background blur. Romantic love's magic is that it is paradoxically both publicizing and isolating; its recognition effects, which affirm at last that you are normal in the world, are also a compensation for your separation from it, for your removal from the public world at last.

All three films also end with the image of a child, although the aesthetic import of these figures varies. In *Brown Sugar*, the children we see listening to the final track on a park bench might be unrelated to Syd and Dre, but they could also be their children, or even their own past or future incarnations. It doesn't much matter; what matters is that the official and professional public that hip hop has come to occupy, and which Syd and Dre mostly lament, has not precluded hip hop's other and original space. The film's romantic essentialism about hip hop's former purity is thus also a way of recognizing the existence of a Black public before and apart from the public of the American mainstream, a space for language and social form between the individual and the commercial whole, a kind of semi-private public of which the opening documentary shots of storied Black figures in hip hop serves as an emblem. In *Saving Face*, the baby in the closing line is a channel for others' normative demands and desires; like other normativities, it produces for the aberrant subject a slapstick rhythm in which a tense anticipation inevitably gives way to the dreaded comment you knew was coming: *splat!* In *Notting Hill*, however, reproduction is a paradoxically anti-generational act. The child is a gesture of beginning that is also strangely frozen and final, as if true love meant staying on that bench forever. Unlike the figure of the baby in *Saving Face*, which reveals the couple's entrenchment in the social, the finality of the baby in *Notting Hill* more closely resembles the eternally frozen space child at the close of *2001: A Space Odyssey* (1968).

And, as with that film, *Notting Hill* frames the cadential baby in the aesthetic envelope of a nearly incoherent narrative acceleration. It is here that romantic fantasy's impatience to know the end, to fast forward to love's established and establishing events, to reveal in the future what one already knows it must hold, approaches a different kind of aesthetic form: the musical montage. Once the dilation of time around the confessional scene closes, the film leaves the present behind to draw a straightening and narrowing line as the time of the Costello song stitches together snapshots from love's future. It is here that the filmic close-up of love's union gives way to the filmic cut as the coda's central technical device, capturing the shift as the narrative time of romantic fantasy accelerates into the time of the montage.

Musical Montage, or Heterosexual Aesthetics

Romantic love doesn't just name a kind of relation, like friendship or the family. It also names a longing for the shared tempo of public life to recede into the blurred background, as the focus of love enables a dilation of time and space that untethers you from merely being anchored in the present. The crush or the lover—whose presence seems to frame love as a problem of relation, of the two—is also there just to facilitate one's flight into this other place, into the secretly possible world to which the technical device of the double entendre hints. In the modernity of the era subtended by the examples so far—but whose outer bounds, historical beginnings and ends, have not yet been traced—the wish for this other kind of place does not occur primarily as an image of a utopian elsewhere, but rather in the sonic fantasy of the world's sound dimming, which is often achieved technically by the entrance, or increase, of music in the soundtrack. As the underscore draws a boundary around the silence that falls around you and your person, masking out the world's hubbub, romantic fantasy furnishes stock images for a slideshow of the future that the mind can't help generating, perhaps, of the life that could now come. Romance culminates in the shedding of the time of plot, of causally connected action, of the ordinary time of living, as if its fantasy were centrally one of phasing out of narrative time and into the time of montage.

This chapter's contention has been that the formal or aesthetic properties subtending the experience of romance are not only to be found in analysis of commercial films themselves, but are also part of a formal and aesthetic pedagogy in personhood. The transmission of romantic love as cultural ideology depends not only, say, on the affective persistence of certain normative values and concepts, but also on one's lifelong absorption of shadings of space and time, on sense memories of density and porousness, on contours of speed and slowness that precipitate from encounters with love's mediation. But where to look, not for the aesthetic forms of romance's mainstream representation, but for evidence of the formal lessons that the ordinary consumers of romance's cultures might have learned? Where could we trace the forms that have become internal resources, instinctive modes of parsing and realizing the world, upon which the ordinary consumer of love might draw when attempting to imagine or represent the event of romantic love within their own life?

We might look to a video like "The 365 Day Proposal," uploaded to YouTube in 2015 by Dean Smith.[24] The video documents the event of Dean's marriage proposal to Jennifer on the occasion of her birthday at a resort in Aruba. The proposal itself involves Jennifer being shown a video that Dean has been making in secret for the past year; the video uploaded to YouTube includes the proposal video that Jennifer watches as well as additional documentary of the events leading up to this event of spectatorship, plus some narrative framing for the YouTube audience.

As an amateur production, "The 365 Day Proposal" emerges from the aperture of a few historical windows. It is, first, a proposal video from the mid-2010s, and its tone and atmosphere owe much to an enculturation in pop-cultural romance, say, from the 1990s to the 2000s. But it is also an only recently possible kind of aesthetic text, historically demarcated by the mass commercial availability of digital camcorders and consumer-facing video editing software, which had only been widely in use for a nonspecialist audience for about a decade. These conjunctures made it possible that someone with conceivably no training in audiovisual post-production could be faced with a nonspecialist interface with which to clip, reorder, reanimate, annotate, and score images collected from the everyday, evincing, perhaps, the instinctive audiovisual habits that might have sedimented in a consumer of pop culture of the era.

Specifically, the form that Dean elects to use for his proposal video is a musical montage. As he explains at the beginning of the video, he will take a brief video clip of himself every day for a year and then splice these clips together into a montage that he will present to Jennifer on her birthday. In most of the montage's shots, we see Dean engaging in activities that belong to the genre of the everyday: waking up, getting dressed, eating cereal, showering, shaving, being at work. The montage lasts around ten minutes and is set to three consecutive pop songs—Bruno Mars's "Marry You," Pharrell's "Happy," and Anthem Lights' "Best Thing."

Why does he choose the montage as the proposal video's form? In the lead-up to the montage, Dean describes the video's form as an attempt to solve a "problem": the problem of planning a "perfect proposal," one that would demonstrate to Jennifer that she is in his thoughts "literally every moment of every day." This problem is, in a sense, an aesthetic one: how does one represent in audiovisual form a magnitude of love that encodes, specifically, the sense or conviction of a thought that permeates all of the moments that make up all days? To solve it would mean to reconcile the challenge of affect and scale posed by the two forms of time that Dean juxtaposes in his articulation of the proposal's formal conundrum: on one hand, the literal constancy of thought in "every moment of every day," and on the other, the climactic wish of the perfect proposal, which invokes the wedding's broader association with the temporal idiom of the best day of your life. This idiom, however, betrays the problem of a perspective that is technically impossible in the present tense: the best day of your life, after all, is a day that stands out not only from all the days that have come before, but also all the days that remain. This is, from the standpoint of ordinary perception, impossible to ascertain. In thinking "the best day of your life," one also must think a position of futurity and omniscience from which such a judgment would be possible. The wish for a day of your life to be the best, then, is in part the expression of a wish for the ordering clarity of retrospection while still in the present—to be both the person to whom the event is happening and the one reading the book of what has happened, who still has a mind and a memory after the book is closed.

As it happens, a future-omniscient narratorial position can be discerned in the peculiar composition of the YouTube video itself. The first image in "The 365 Day Proposal" is a black text screen with white lettering (fig. 2.2), which then cuts to handheld video footage. Jennifer's sister Jaclyn is knocking on a hotel door, which opens to reveal Jennifer. Jaclyn holds up a small whiteboard for Jennifer to read—she does, and responds with "aww!" But the whiteboard is not shown to the camera. Instead, we learn of the whiteboard's comments from a second black text screen, which informs the video's viewer that the whiteboard had contained instructions for Jennifer to go down to the lobby.

"The 365 Day Proposal" thus begins with two deferrals. The "birthday surprise" with which Jaclyn is supposed to arrive turns out to be a message on a whiteboard that defers the actual moment of surprise. Furthermore, this message, which arrives on a rectangular surface of text, is kept hidden from the video's viewer, thus requiring the insertion of a second or doubled rectangular text screen in the video's shot sequence, the black screen that interprets and relays the white board's contents to the video audience. This opening play around knowledge and its concealment has the effect of establishing a formal symmetry between Jennifer (the object of the

FIGURE 2.2. The opening text screen. Dean Smith, "The 365 Day Proposal."

proposal's address) and the spectator (the object of the video's address). That is, they (or we) are both participants, let's say, whose knowledge of the unfolding situation is mediated by a frame containing text; they (or we) are the recipients, or perhaps the targets, of the surprise promised in the video's first screen. Both the spectator and Jennifer are placed into a relation of dependence to an invisible writer, who controls what and how much they will know about what's coming. This is the gift of the "surprise": that someone else will titrate the emergence of the scene for you, allowing you to remain in the openness and abeyance of the first screen's ellipsis ("...").

But then something changes in the implied voice behind the text screens. At the beginning, it was possible to believe that the text screens were simply a helpful and neutral textual presence, like the title cards used in silent cinema. But the purely formal justification of the text screens' existence is disturbed by a new message: "Happy Birthday, Jennifer!" In a reverse prosopopoeia, the absent impersonality of narration starts to speak for "itself," as if there were suddenly someone *there*. The conventions of the narratorial function are stripped of their purely technical justifications: the convention of the narrator's access to knowledge of the world now feels more like a privileged access carried by *somebody* in the video's world, while the narrator's conventional disembodiment now becomes a curious absence of embodiment. But it is also that the birthday wish, which is addressed to Jennifer *but only readable by the viewer*, complicates the prior identification of the viewer with Jennifer alone. The aside suggests that there is a narratorial vantage that the spectator can occupy alongside the narrator (or, to be more precise, that the narrator shares this vantage with the spectator) even as the spectator continues to be aligned with Jennifer as a recipient of surprise—that is, as a bearer of the ignorance of what's to come that is formally required for the possibility of surprise. The spectator of the video finds themselves doubled, sharing the positions both of the surpriser and the surprisee.

To complicate this already dense network of positions, the sudden subjective presence implied in "Happy Birthday, Jennifer!" suggests that Dean is not only one of the two protagonists within a love narrative, but also occupies a triangulating or third position above or outside the video, in a space we might think of as belonging to the editor or the narrator. In fact, when Jennifer arrives on the beach and is handed the phone on which Dean's prepared video begins to play, the preamble to the musical montage reflects this very split of Deans. The video begins with Dean explaining that "I've actually been planning this birthday surprise for over a year now." This shot then cuts to another Dean, Dean from precisely one year before, who begins to talk to Dean from the present, a conversation facilitated (presumably) by a third Dean, Dean-as-editor:

DEAN FROM A YEAR AGO: I just want to make this video to tell you that today is the day that I decided that I want to spend the rest of my life with you.

DEAN IN THE PRESENT: That's right, Dean from a year ago! Exactly one year ago, I realized that you were the person I wanted to spend the rest of my life with. The only problem was, how do I plan the perfect proposal, one that shows you how much I love you and how you're in my thoughts literally every moment of every day? And then I came up with a brilliant idea.

The idea he comes up with, as we know, is the musical montage. But how is the montage supposed to solve the aesthetic problem of romance's representational impossibility, which must capture both the ordinary of "every moment of every day" as well as the possibility of sensing one event, say, the event of proposal or marriage, as ultimately unsurpassable, even as life continues?

Let us examine some of its details. To begin, we might notice that the montage features a notational redundancy: each day's shot notates its chronology twice, first in a date, scribbled American-style on a whiteboard in the shot's frame, and also in a number, added to the top left corner in post-production, that counts down the days from 365 (fig. 2.3). The video thus commingles the sentimental effects of Dean's mugging and the pop soundtrack with traces of an administrative fastidiousness, as if answers to the constant question *what day is it?* were both so crucial and so liable to slip away that they required not one but two forms of textual anchoring in every shot. The notational zealousness with which the calendrical difference of days is recorded seems to stand in contrast with, and in fact be compelled as a response to, the daily sameness of the footage itself. It seems, in other words, to admit via overinsistence that the content of each shot could have been filmed on almost any of the year's days. And this is crucial: for what unites the types of activity performed by Dean is their complete inability to refer to a *particular* day. As such, the video plays with what Hayden White characterizes as the difference between chronicle and the narrative impulse of history:

> Chronicles are, strictly speaking, open-ended. In principle they have no *inaugurations*; they simply "begin" when the chronicler starts recording events. And they have no culminations or resolutions; they can go on

indefinitely. Stories, however, have a discernible form (even when that form is an image of a state of chaos) which marks off the events contained in them from the other events that might appear in a comprehensive chronicle of the years covered in their unfoldings.

It is sometimes said that the aim of the historian is to explain the past by "finding," "identifying," or "uncovering" the "stories" that lie buried in chronicles.[25]

But the aim of the normative romantic is different. Whereas the historian's process eventually discards chronicle, separating the wheat of difference from the chaff of daily inconsequentiality, it is the romantic's task to turn events into history while also preserving the affects of chronicle—hence the video's commitment to showing essentially only those parts of the day that are in effect useless for the differentiation of days. They record precisely what is normally sieved out to create the consequentiality of history.

"Every moment of every day," as the expression of a temporal wish of attentiveness, requires that the chronicle's meticulous and purposeless accounting not disappear in the making of history, but instead that the noncumulative persist alongside the cumulative within the ordering structure of a story. It is precisely to the problem of witnessing the little parts of life that don't make it into grand narrative that one can understand the effect of Dean beginning to lip-synch along to the pop songs, somewhere around the montage's fiftieth day. The lip-synching is, first of all, an arduous editorial task that announces its arduousness, since Dean must each day film

FIGURE 2.3. Notational redundancy in an archive of the everyday. Dean Smith, "The 365 Day Proposal."

himself singing along to a different two-to-three-second excerpt of a song and then edit these clips together to form a seamless performance. The lip-synching act thus references the concealment and revelation of hidden labor that is normative to the proposal gesture, the work that happened while you weren't looking. But it is also that the lip-synch disturbs the ordinary logic of the cinematic montage sequence. Typically, a montage juxtaposes shots of time and space that are discontinuous, such that the persons in each scene are not aware of one another or of the fact of being assembled in this way. The coherence of the montage is only available from the position of the editor, who is the only one who "sees" the montage and who lends to the viewer this omniscient perspective. In montages underscored with music, like the paradigmatic training sequence in *Rocky* (1976), it is the song that marks the presence of this omniscient position by marking how time passes from its perspective. In his montage, Dean appears first as a character or a constellation of characters, each anchored to a separate day of the year via the video's rigorous numerical accounting. But in lip-synching to songs that play not in the temporality of the segments of the montage but in the temporal register of the edit, Dean demonstrates that he can access both temporalities and both narrative positions simultaneously.

In "The 365 Day Proposal," heterosexuality is a musical structure in which the man lives both in the everyday and in the soundtrack of the montage, both within and across editing. He thereby keeps one foot in the ordinary mundanity of work, driving, eating breakfast, and shaving, while his lip-synching also gives him purchase in a transcendent register in which the year—which is too long for anyone to experience in any coherent sense—is spanned within the rhythm and momentum of three pop songs. And he does this so that he can return to the woman from this adventure at the end of the year—the woman who lives only in the ordinary temporality, within editing and not across it—and deliver to her the gift of this perspective, of how a day could be more than a day, of how the ordinary accumulation of a year might be felt all at once, and of how omniscience could be accessed from within the mundane. Heterosexuality's gender difference is figured here not only as a difference between performer and spectator, or motion and stillness, or actant and actee, say, but also as an asymmetrical distribution of narratorial access to time. As Jennifer finishes the video, montage speed ends, and she returns to the ordinary temporality of the present, to the dailiness of the day. And that is when the real Dean appears before her on the beach, as if stepping out of the video and back into their shared world, bearing the trace of his travels.

Though love appears to be a binary form—that is, a form about the relation of two elements—the proposal video reveals that its form is, in fact, triangular. It is only from the vantage of a third position "above" the daily and first-person experiences of the couple—a position figured in the technical positions of the editor or the narrator of the montage—that romantic fantasy can formally organize a felt relation between the little behaviors that fill an ordinary day and some broader structure of significance. The soundtrack under the montage holds out the promise that the long *durée* of a life should be sensible as a rhythm or tone that threads through that which threatens to be lost: the promise of romance is also a promise that love's form will scoop up all of this detritus and breathe plot into it.

When this video from the early twenty-first century attempts to capture or produce the experience of romantic love, it turns to capturing or producing an experience of the everyday, a register of the ordinary whose banality and recursiveness seem to resist this very attempt at accounting or inscription, since there is nothing outside of the notation itself to distinguish one day's footage from another's. Why is *this* what an audiovisual representation of romantic love looks like in this period?

For example: can we relate what the proposal video works through formally to Lisa Duggan's broader description of the 1990s as a decade that formed from the privatization of political energies that had formerly textured the US experience of political publics from the '60s through the '80s?[26] Duggan argues that while the postwar decades saw marginalized groups organize politically around the precise insistence that the "intimate" arenas of, say, gender, sexuality, and race were properly descriptions of the social distribution of resources and of power, the '90s marked a shift inward in the symbolic content of the "political." Where the focus of the political had once targeted the structures that produced the uneven experiences registered in identity formations, corporations and other political actors now began to adopt languages and styles of "equality" or "diversity" that were consistent with, and even dependent upon, the maintenance of existing consolidations of power. For Lauren Berlant, these jarring epistemic shifts toward the end of the twentieth century produced a new historical sensorium characterized by "class unconsciousness that looks like consciousness."[27] Central to this new articulation of the public political sphere is a private figure that Berlant calls "the subject of true feeling," which names a theory of justice and aesthetics centered not on the structures that organize living but on individual empathy and the eradication of pain. The aesthetic configuration of this public is a marginalized theater that compels expression of the "personal" content of intimate political experience before a public now construed primarily as an audience.

It was into this disorienting zone of unconsciousness and contradiction that the romantic comedy film entered the decade in which it produced its most canonically exemplary works, and in which it achieved unprecedented status as a tentpole mass entertainment genre.[28] The retraction of the public political energies of the preceding decades into the privacy of individual recognition and self-expression can be felt in, among other places, the odd absence of sexuality in the best-remembered examples of this era. Unlike the teen sex comedies that populated the genre in the 1960s and '70s, the typical '90s protagonist is an adult whose world acknowledges the literal existence of sex and yet whose fantasies are textured by a kind of presexual innocence and sweetness.[29] An emblem of this imagination of sex can be found in an early scene in *Sleepless in Seattle* in which Meg Ryan tries on her mother's traditional, white wedding dress. At this point she is engaged to a man who will turn out not to be the film's romantic hero. While wearing the dress, she intimates to her mother that she and Walter have already had sex, something her mother both acknowledges and dismisses. And yet the effect of the exchange is less to introduce the concerns of sex into the romantic comedy than to acknowledge that sex can be placed beside the point, removing its question from the film's concerns. It is as if, for the straight, white, middle-class adults who populate the mainstream films of this era, sex itself had become too associated with the political events of public life, too tainted by the emergence of sex as a public problem, to retain its once undisturbed implicitness—in a way affirming the successes of the previous era in relocating the content of the political from the private to the public sphere. An effect of these shifts is that the '90s romantic comedy is generally textured by a sense of disappointment with the world of adulthood and its too-complicated modernity, such that romance appears as the promise of a retreat to a simpler and prior childlike coziness and innocence.

Berlant and other theorists of liberalism relate this promise to the juridical concept of privacy: *Griswold v. Connecticut*, the US Supreme Court decision that accorded to married heterosexual couples the right to use contraceptives, did so by imagining heterosexual love as occupying a sacred space exempt from the law's eyes and reach. As Berlant writes, "Privacy is the Oz of America. Based on a notion of safe space, a hybrid space of home and law in which people will act legally and lovingly toward one another, free from the determinations of history or the coercions of pain, the constitutional theorization of sexual privacy is drawn from a lexicon of romantic sentiment, a longing for a space where there is no trouble, a place whose constitution in law would be so powerful that desire would meet moral discipline there, making real the dreamy rule."[30] Heterosexual love is figured as always anachronistic in the present of political public life, since its reference is always to an elsewhere untouched by the impingements of history. This reference to an amorphous zone beyond history or plot, in fact, seems resonant with the archival efforts of "The 365 Day Proposal," in which the attempt to capture the everyday as a register of reality seems also to occur under the hazy recognition that a historical representation of the self and its story might be wanted—that is, missing. What the form of the video suggests, in other words, is that the amorphous and ahistorical zone of romantic love might also pose a problem of self-representation for its unmarked and ordinary subject, whose sense of the passage of historical time "out there" seems oddly out of touch with their most immediate and intimate experience of the everyday. In a moment like this, and under these historical conditions, a function of romantic love might be to offer a formal structure in which these disparate scales or sheets of time are reconciled.

Revelations of Form: A Reading of You've Got Mail

In the amateur aesthetics of "The 365 Day Proposal," the musical montage is an audiovisual device that attempts to solve—and, in doing so, exposes—an anxiety that ordinary existence for the ordinary citizen has lost touch with something that might be called history. By history, I refer to the public world of news and event that makes sexuality, among other things, appear to be a "contemporary" issue, but it also refers to a more diffuse sense of adding up to something that the subject who enjoys sexuality as a mostly private phenomenon might sense as existing out there, that is, outside the temporal zone of the everyday. This is essentially what Dean articulates as intimacy's representational problem, a problem he resolves in part by reaching for the device of the musical montage.

I've focused on this scene of aesthetic problem-solving in the space of everyday life because it offers what seems to me a substantially different way of thinking about music's presence in audiovisual works—that is, different from seeing the soundtrack as bearing a function in relation to the image or film world (i.e., mimetic, disruptive, representational), or in relation to an audience (i.e., pedagogical, affective, ideological). Certainly the presence of soundtracks in this chapter's commercial and populist archive can be explained by these functions. But I am also trying to demonstrate via these examples that the soundtrack as a technical convention is in some sense immanent to the formal structure of romantic love itself.

To feel the presence of love in this chapter's contemporary contexts would be isomorphic to sensing the nearness of an aesthetic form.

If the marriage plot in the novel, in Ann Ducille's description, is traditionally a convention of the white middle class in which marriage as a legal and fantasied event anchors various symbolic infrastructures—like citizenship, like narrative as such—the juridical frame with which this chapter contends might be imagined to extend from *Loving v. Virginia* in 1967 to 2015, when the US Supreme Court struck down state bans on same-sex marriage, a period in which marriage law intersects with romantic love's promise to exfoliate the particularities of politically marked personhood in the name of the universally promised subject of love.[31] Juridically as well as in the popular vernacular, the last half century has seen in the United States shifts to deracinate love from the heterosexual, white, middle-class property that it traditionally existed to index and to protect, and to construct in discourse a sense that this deracinated form had always been love's referent, and not the result, as Chandan Reddy writes, of a liberal redefinition of personhood after the fact.[32] And yet, popular aesthetics constitutes one place in which the translation of love's metaphysics into audiovisual form remains archived in spite of later revisionist histories.

This section's examples, spanning the period 1940–98, trace a trajectory in which romantic love acquires its universality by shedding its localization in the body, becoming instead a ubiquitous, atmospheric thing untethered to historical or political form. The aim, then, is not to isolate and identify white love as a culturally dominant form that is different from other kinds of love. This is the counternormative approach taken, for example, in David M. Halperin's work on queer love, which attempts to recover "other forms of pleasures, of relationships, coexistences, attachments, loves, intensities" that fail to become legible within the hegemonic scripts of love's dominant and legitimating form.[33] My approach, however, is not to contrast or oppose the hegemonic form of romantic love that issues from the West with minoritarian, unexampled, or promissory practices of radical love, in part because contrasting or opposing are operations that presume an at least categorical equivalence between the terms being opposed. I am interested, rather, in the impossibility of opposition that appears in a passage like this one: "When I think romcom, I think white.... So does *The Undefeated* culture critic Soraya Nadia McDonald, who attended a predominantly black high school and remembers kids 'losing their minds' over *Love & Basketball*. Yet the first thing that enters her mind when she thinks of romcoms is her favorite, *Bridget Jones's Diary*."[34] Notice the difference between what one remembers and "the first thing that enters [one's] mind": the white rom-com becomes an emblem of genre knowledge as such ("when I think romcom") and avoids becoming recontained as an ethnic "content," while the Black film is unable to shake its particularity and is thus disqualified from becoming genre knowledge as such. This sketch of popular culture as an always fissured memory for its minoritarian inhabitant has tended to suggest a certain kind of path for public political strategy. The most optimistic version of one such strategy, under mottoes such as "representation matters," contends that minoritarian material will eventually be sufficient to produce not just a statistical but an epistemic shift at the level of genre knowledge, such that a distribution of pop-cultural representation more in line with demographic reality would undo the hierarchical relations of value, pleasure, and disgust that also animate these materials internally. And yet, it's been this book's formal claim that the deprovincializing of racial and other particularizing knowledges cannot happen merely through a statistical redress of the field of representation, since such redresses are already preceded and contained by the placement of minoritarian knowledges under the sign of "content." What is needed, then, is modes of reading audiovisual works that bring out the formal lineaments of whiteness as a deracializing form, which negates its own appearance as a particular racial content in order to become formally isomorphic with love and genre itself.

This last section returns to the soundtrack and to Hollywood film to show what an analysis that follows from this thought might produce. I focus on a line of three films across different eras of sound film that each remake the same story: *The Shop Around the Corner* (1940), *In the Good Old Summertime* (1949), and *You've Got Mail* (1998). The base plot shared by all three films involves a man and a woman who are enemies in the public world of business but have also, unbeknownst to them, struck up a romantic correspondence via letters or e-mail. In all three films, it is the man who first discovers the woman's doubled identity and also chooses to conceal this knowledge from her, which frames the ending of the plot as a matter of the woman's discovery. As we shall see, of particular interest to our analysis will be moments when a later film encounters a plot event that has become anachronistic within its updated present. The film must then find a way of retaining the essential structure of the adapted story while infusing it with a new causality, such that the film's form becomes a record of the transformations needed to refurbish an old convention in a changed cultural context.[35]

One transformation that takes place across this series of films concerns the status of the photographic image. Perhaps the most glaring plot difference along this line of remakes is Ephron's change to the ending, in the version from the 1990s. In the earlier versions, the last scene takes place in the store where the protagonists work as the woman is about to leave to rendezvous with her pen pal (she thinks) for the first time. It is at this moment that the man tells her that he met her "dear friend" the other day, and that he is, for instance, ugly, dull, and unemployed. These revelations cause the woman to crumple in despair as the fantasy of the romantic partner bursts, and it is at this moment that the man, who has just been promoted to manager, reveals his doubled identity to her. The possibility of romance, in other words, is confirmed or disconfirmed along lines of sight: in the man's "sighting" of the other, which disqualifies him, and in the camera's subsequent witnessing of the viability of his own body. The fact that the camera becomes the instrument of romantic confirmation is made clear at the end of *The Shop Around the Corner*. After the man's revelation, the woman still hesitates: she has heard a rumor that he might be bowlegged. The camera then cuts down as he hikes up his trouser legs, revealing pasty flesh and the intimate sight of sock garters (fig. 2.4).[36]

In *You've Got Mail*, however, Joe (Tom Hanks) attempts and fails to execute the very strategy that was sufficient to bring the earlier narratives to an end.[37] Near the end of the film, Joe and Kathleen (Meg Ryan) have overcome, or at least suspended, the animosities of their business rivalry and become friends. When Kathleen confides in him about her e-mail

FIGURE 2.4. The shot of legs at the end of *The Shop Around the Corner*. Ernst Lubitsch, dir., *The Shop Around the Corner* (1940).

exchange with a man whose screenname is NY152, Joe, like his former incarnations, tries to suggest the man's undesirability through guesses of what the number might represent: 152 could refer to his age, or the number of pockmarks on his face, or the number of souvenir shot glasses he owns, or the stitches from his nose job. Yet Kathleen, unlike her earlier incarnations, seems unmoved by these visions of hideousness, and retorts: "152 insights into my soul!" Where the former men in the role could marshal a disgust for class, taste, and embodiment that was sufficient to override the intimate connection forged through the exchange of letters, the concept of love in *You've Got Mail* has become the socially negating one of liberal love. As Elizabeth Povinelli writes, "in matters of love, the issue is the humanity of the person, not the accident of birth or forced enclosure within a social skin. . . . Love is a political event. It expands humanity, creating the human by exfoliating its social skin, and this expansion is critical to the liberal Enlightenment project, including the languages of many of its most progressive legacies."[38] For this kind of love, the skin's historical memory demonstrates negatively love's expansive and humanizing possibilities; only when its "forced enclosure" is exfoliated does love become sensible and conceivable. The 1990s film, in other words, posits a different relation between the possibility of love and its photographic evidence, a difference that stands in explicit contrast to the shot of legs that closes its earlier version.

In fact, an early sequence in *You've Got Mail* stages a musical montage whose function is seemingly only to demonstrate the camera's incapacity to produce love's photographic evidence. The montage consists of shots of Joe and Kathleen repeatedly crossing paths on the Upper West Side, oblivious to each other, as they walk their separate ways to work. Set to the song "Dreams" by the Cranberries, we see Kathleen walking just behind Joe on the sidewalk, then Kathleen leaving a Starbucks just as Joe enters, then Kathleen and Joe passing each other at a flower stand, and so on. What is the effect that this montage is meant to produce? It seems to find something significant in the fact that there could be an intangible but real bond that remains hidden in the everyday, in the public world of streets and markets and strangers. This is a montage of the city coming to life, and in it Joe and Kathleen are just two more strangers, no different from any others they might pass by. The camera's agnosticism or neutrality in simply recording people wherever it is pointed reveals nothing about the specialness of one stranger over another. The point seems to be that the visible ordinary, that which photography is equipped to record and represent—the positivity of photographic presence—is also the concealment of something, which it is the task of the romantic comedy plot to bring out. When true love is required to disavow its exclusive reliance on the legible attributes of looks, wealth, and class and becomes instead a form directed to the attributeless "anyone," the "anyone" in turn conceals the content of romance from the province of the photographable. And this way of positing the relation of genre to medium—of the way in which romance becomes a subject of film—seems to suggest that the medium's achievement of a representation of love will need to take the form of an unconcealment.

As this line of remakes records an emergent liberal love as an attendant loss in the capacity of the image to secure the kind of knowledge that it once could, certain transformations also occur in the symbolic freighting of diegetic and nondiegetic appearances of musical sound. It is particularly instructive to compare *In the Good Old Summertime*, a film with musical and performance numbers starring Judy Garland, with *You've Got Mail* as an emblem of '90s commercial narrative underscoring. Consider a song that Veronica (Garland) sings near the end of her film. She has just heard that Andrew (Van Johnson), the coworker for whom she has recently begun to develop feelings, is already engaged to a girl with whom he keeps up a correspondence. Andrew knows that Veronica is the person to whom he has been writing, but he continues to withhold this information from her; when she exposes her feelings to him and he continues not to reciprocate, she turns on him angrily and declares that she will quit her job at the end of the day. As she returns to the sales floor, however, a customer asks to hear "Merry Christmas," a melancholy version of a Christmas ode written for the film by Fred Spielman and Janice Torre. With Buster Keaton (who plays another sales clerk) accompanying on the organ, the film's setting in an early twentieth-century sheet-music store allows Garland, via Veronica, to deliver a performance whose ironically hopeful lyrics are made wistful by their narrative context and the song's slow tempo:

> Merry Christmas, have a very very merry Christmas
> Dream about your heart's desire
> Christmas Eve when you retire
> Santa Claus will stop and I know he'll drop
> Exactly what you wanted from your chimney top[39]

As she sings, the organ's reedy consistency fades into the warmer tone of a body of strings garlanded by chimes, even though no other musicians are playing in the store. Instead, a crowd of customers has gathered around her and Keaton. Not surprisingly, the format of the musical demands and delivers a situation for Veronica to express her feelings at the precise moment that such a scene is needed. But the performance also conceals them: though the moment gathers listeners for her expression of sadness, they are also, in the world of the film, holiday shoppers who believe her merely to be at work. Garland's performance is connected to her feelings as a subject of love, but it is also demanded of her by her employment in a sheet-music store before the age of commercial recording. Only Andrew, who stands to the side and somewhat behind her, as if listening in rather than addressed by the performance, understands more fully the irony of the song's delivery against the lyrics' cheerful platitudes.

Unable to tell Andrew the truth about why she is upset, the film's genre provides Veronica with a stage and an audience. By the time we arrive at *You've Got Mail*, however, Kathleen Kelly has neither access to a music shop nor the film musical's generic affordance of narrative intercessions reserved for the expression of feeling in song. In an early scene of despair—prompted by the threat Joe Fox's chain bookstore poses to her small independent shop and by a self-absorbed boyfriend who claims to speak for her anguish, thus leaving her anguish unexpressed—we see Kathleen retreat to the privacy of her laptop, the camera outside her window peering from the dark of evening into the circle of lamplight that illuminates her (fig. 2.5). As she begins to type, we hear her voice speak the typed words in voice-over as a soft string cue suffuses the scene's uninterrupted shot: "Sometimes I wonder about my life. I lead a small life—well, valuable but small. And sometimes I wonder, do I do it because I like it? Or because I haven't been brave? So much of what I see reminds me of something I read in a book, when—shouldn't it be the other way around? I don't really want an answer, I just want to send this cosmic question out into the void. So. Good night, dear void." The cue, in the idiom of a gently tinkling piano line warmed up by strings, begins with a series of closed antecedent-consequent phrases but then swells lushly into a prolonged high note when Kathleen speaks of sending her "cosmic question out into the void." Like Garland's performance of "Merry Christmas," the cue fills out a duration in which a character is given time to express what the world of the narrative does not permit her to express. The scene is part of the story, of course, but it is also a kind of aside, a suspension of the narrative time of action for a lyrical time free from the risk of interruption.

Insofar as Kathleen's monologue is given a formal wholeness by the scene's single shot and the cue of music that expands around it, and in its expansion of a privately held feeling that contrasts with the recitative-like patter of the scenes of action and dialogue before and after, we may think of it as her aria. Though *You've Got Mail* features almost no diegetic music, we can nevertheless see how the film musical's number structure,

FIGURE 2.5. Kathleen types an e-mail in her apartment. Nora Ephron, dir., *You've Got Mail* (1998).

inherited from operetta and opera, survives into nonmusical narrative film as a rhythm of action and expression, or of linear time and lyrical time. Yet the difference between Garland's singing and the unheard nondiegetic cue has important implications for how each of these film worlds imagines agency, privacy, and the relation between characters and the medium in which they exist. In the musical, the film's musical register is sustained by characters through their performative charisma and skill; it is only after Garland begins singing that her and Keaton's diegetic performance is able to call up the nondiegetic string underscore, which then continues on into the next scene after the performance ends, echoing the song's melody into the next stretch of action. In *You've Got Mail*'s aesthetic universe, however, music disappears from the world of representation and takes up residence entirely in the underscore. Music's expressivity no longer issues directly from the activity of characters who suffer and feel; rather, the camera's placement outside the apartment and the soft underscore suggest the location of these sounds at the periphery of Kathleen's world, kept at bay by the circle of lamplight. In this version of the aria, music's expressivity does not issue from her body but hovers at the unheard edges of her world.

If *In the Good Old Summertime* produces an audience of holiday shoppers to receive, and therefore authorize, the performance of a song that both reveals and conceals Veronica's inner life under the guise of the sale of a commodity, what is the audience for Kathleen's expression? Though it is implied that Kathleen is typing the words to Joe, since he is the only person she types to in the film, it is worth noting that this is also the film's only e-mailing scene to not explicitly indicate the addressee: she writes not to Joe but to "the void." What does she, or the film, mean by this word? It is dark outside; the lit frame of the window takes up only a small portion of the film's frame and is further obscured by a tree's branches, out of focus in the shot's foreground. It looks, in fact, as though the camera is peeking through the branches, as if using them for visual cover, even though it is too dark for Kathleen to see out. The out-of-focus tree against the apartment interior's visual sharpness seems to suggest that the branches and its gently shivering leaves are *very close* to the camera, as if the lens were right up against them. The implication of the scene's visual composition seems to be not that the camera's position is merely efficient, a neutral choice in service of optimal film narration, but that it occupies this specific point in the film's world, tucked behind the tree outside Kathleen's apartment. It is the kind of shot that would be used in a horror film to suggest the presence of someone outside of whom the protagonist is not yet aware, and to project a future moment in which whatever occupies the camera's POV and the person in the house will come face-to-face.

Both horror and romantic comedy are genres in which the protagonist might sense, affectively, that *something is out there*, a something they might shiveringly sense has to do with them and yet whose confirmation is held in abeyance, such that their inhabitation of genre is, at the beginning, mostly atmospheric and not yet consolidated in knowledge. The purely formal arc of both genres consists of the staging of an encounter between character and atmosphere, as the thing that was initially sensed only as slight perturbations to the outside edges of the perceptible now collides with the trajectory of plot. Perhaps the romantic hero is romantic comedy's monster, the fleshly form that (sometimes disappointingly) ends up displacing atmosphere at the plot's close. Yet there are some indications that this simple translation is not the end of the story. For one, "The 365 Day Proposal" proposed romantic comedy not as a dyad but as a triangular form, requiring the positions of editor, protagonist, and audience to produce its symbolic closure. It is also that, unlike horror, where the shot hovering outside the window would belong to the point of view of the monster who later appears, the shot outside Kathleen's window does not belong to anybody (if it did, this would be a stalker film), even though it is somewhat meticulously staged *as* a perspective. If romance in this historical period requires the unconcealment of that which is concealed by photographic presence, what would count as an unconcealment of *this* perspective?

A demonstration of how the ordinarily visible and perceptible—framed as the concealment of something—might then be unconcealed takes place in a sequence near the end of the film. It is a sequence in which something is thrust forward as an object to be read, and yet for which the interpretive frame necessary to crystallize a reading is withheld or tampered with. At this point in the film, Joe knows that Kathleen is his secret pen pal, and he arrives at her apartment with a bouquet of flowers. Is it obvious what it means when someone shows up at your door with flowers? It does not seem so for Kathleen, at first, since she asks Joe several times why he is there, first on the intercom before she buzzes him up to her apartment, and then again when he is at her apartment door. He evades the question the first time; the second time he offers a string of statements that don't quite add up to an answer: "I heard you were sick. And I was worried. And I wanted to make sure . . . is there somebody here?" Joe leans past the doorframe, peering around: he has heard the Home Shopping Network that Kathleen has left on, and as she goes to shut it off, he enters the apartment without being invited and shuts the door behind him.

It is only after Kathleen asks the question a third time that he offers an answer that sounds like a truth, or perhaps a half-truth: he says, "I wanted to be your friend." How might Kathleen receive this answer? It might sound like any number of things to her—"I wanted to see if you would forgive me," for instance. Or perhaps he really is looking for friendship, for a relation with her that is, we might say, personal and not business. Or perhaps she suspects that "friend" euphemistically indicates romance. Yet "friend" also has a fourth hearing, one she doesn't likely register: "friend" is the salutation and signature they use in their e-mails, the chosen noun that allows them to omit their names and thereby remain anonymous. When Joe tells her that he wants to be her friend, he is (also) meaning the word in the particular, and not only in the categorical, sense.

Like the bouquet, the answer he gives to her question about motives is both thrust plainly forward (willingly given to be read) and presented in a context that has been tampered with or left deliberately incomplete. She doesn't pick up the valence of the word that is available to him because he has not yet chosen to bring her into his fold of knowledge. In that sense, the hearing she needs to decode his sign lies ahead, in a future moment when the withholding stops. It may be that then she will think back to this conversation and the correct reading of the line will dawn on her (no less than the correct reading of the bouquet). We might understand Joe's privacy or hiddenness not only as a position that opposes unconcealment or the open, then. It is also a kind of writing or marking of the present that is not meant to be read now, but in some future moment that unfurls the coiled doubleness of the signs of the past.

Joe, in other words, instrumentalizes the hiddenness he has created by deciding to keep the secret. The temporal form that connects a prior "text" with a later hermeneutic dawning becomes something like a medium that Joe now uses to deliver messages. This is a kind of gain in power, of his rising, we might say, a little above the level of character, not only acting in the present but also controlling to some extent the narrative's structure of enunciation. And this power is granted to him because he has withheld his knowledge of Kathleen's and his other identity from her, knowledge that he cannot come out with lest he lose this power and be reduced again to speaking only in the literal present.

His encoded signs are a challenge not only for Kathleen but also for the film's audience. For example, can we know for sure if there is a second hearing in the following lines?

JOE: Tea?
KATHLEEN: Yes. I was upset and horrible—
JOE: Honey?
KATHLEEN: Yes.
JOE: I was the horrible one.

Joe delivers these lines in such a way that the last two statements could be heard as a continuous thought: "Honey, I was the horrible one." On the last statement, Ephron cuts to a single shot of Joe, generating a slight directorial underline. What the word "honey" means depends on whether it is tied to the statement before it ("Tea?") or the statement after it ("I was the horrible one"). Its ambiguity, in other words, is possible only in talking, not in writing, which could show in punctuation how and what the phrase means. The sense that Joe has just emerged from the world of writing into that of speech is also present when he asks her for a vase, but tests out both pronunciations—"a vah-se? a vai-se?"—as if exhibiting a self-consciousness in the migration to sound.

It is, I would say, not difficult to hear the word "honey" in this way, but it does require an active hearing-for. But to hear for it means to unearth a pattern of emergent meaning in Joe and Kathleen's dialogue, from the line about the friend to the exchange, right before Joe decides to reveal his identity to Kathleen, in which she tells him that she thinks his mango is ripe and he responds, "I think it is." These are all statements with second hearings that are available only to those who know the full story. "I think it is" is a line delivered half to an audience, though there is no audience in the world on the screen as Joe walks with Kathleen. If it is half delivered to us, the movie audience on the other side of the screen, it means that he is half speaking in a voice intended for this form of hearing, that he is speaking in a voice that corresponds to the form of overhearing characteristic of the watching of movies.

But what is the point of hiding this sentence, of concealing its hearing, in his address to Kathleen? "Honey, I was the horrible one" sounds like a rote phrase in a long domestic union, something repeated ritualistically in a couple's bedroom in the debrief after a night out. The quality of domesticity it supplies in Kathleen's apartment is mirrored by Joe's increasing fluency in her kitchen. Though he could not locate the vase, he is soon pulling things together effortlessly for tea, putting the kettle on and finding mugs and teabags without missing a beat. This happens at the back of a shot that centers on Kathleen in front, and it is very easy to miss Joe's sudden mastery of her kitchen. But that is, we might say, exactly the quality of domesticity that he wishes to impress upon her. Not to make her notice it, but precisely to accommodate her within a sphere of domesticity that feels so natural it passes beneath her notice. He wants to show her—but not exactly show her—that it is something the two of them can do.

It turns out that Joe's relation to Kathleen in this sequence is formally related to a way in which the film frames its own relation to the audience. In the movie's closing scene, Harry Nilsson's rendition of "Over the Rainbow" begins in the soundtrack just as Kathleen sees Joe Fox round the corner to greet her at the park, where she has been waiting for the pen pal whose identity she still does not know. And yet, while the song only appears here, at the movie's end, this appearance is preceded, or foreshadowed, by a series of not-quite appearances and half-hidden fragments threaded throughout the movie from the very beginning. The song first appears as a motivic thread in the DNA of the movie's opening sounds: as we hear the dial-up tones that accompany the opening zoom through pixelated space, an oscillating interval drifts by, just a minor third followed by a major second. It is almost certainly not enough to identify as a motif from the bridge of "Over the Rainbow," unless it's already something you're looking for—which is to say, unless you already know that the song appears at the end. If this reference is meant to be part of the experience of the film, it would imply a mode of attention in which the viewer is either recalled to this moment at the end (the fragment flaring in the memory at the moment of the final song's appearance), or the film is watched more than once. Either way, the first appearance of music projects the film as something not only to be watched linearly, but to be remembered and grasped retrospectively in a moment of realization; the opening motivic fragment is like a puzzle piece awaiting the completion of the frame that will pick it up and imbue it with significance.

Elements of the song appear again before the first date that Kathleen arranges with her pen pal, but only as a kind of background piano filigree that evades the most identifiable part of the tune. Similarly, the timbral signature of Harry Nilsson's voice appears twice before the ending, on "Remember" and "The Puppy Song," the latter of which plays over the opening credits. These preparations before the final number are joined by a visual reference so slight that it would almost certainly remain uninterpreted during an ordinary viewing: an ornament in the form of a pair of ruby slippers that Kathleen hangs on her Christmas tree (fig. 2.6). As she hangs them on the tree, Kathleen is reciting the lyrics to a Joni Mitchell song in voice-over while Harry Nilsson's "Remember" plays in the soundtrack. The slippers are the brightest point in the shot and the focus of Kathleen's action. Yet they too are not overtly emphasized—the camera does not cut to them in close-up, for instance. The visual composition of the reference is like the aural composition of the fragments of "Over the Rainbow" that omit the most recognizable leap in the melody: they are references that are both plainly present, available to be grasped, and yet composed in such a way as to minimize the possibility that someone might grasp them. They seem to be elements placed in the audiovisual composition in order to pass beneath notice.

There is, therefore, a structural rhyme between the way fragments of "Over the Rainbow" are flashed before the film audience and the way Joe offers the bouquet and the line about the friend to Kathleen. Just as Kathleen encounters signs that gain significance only when Joe

FIGURE 2.6. Ruby slippers, thrust forward to be seen, but without an invitation to perceive them. Nora Ephron, dir., *You've Got Mail* (1998).

reveals himself later at the park, the film's audience encounters signs that gain significance only when Ephron reveals "Over the Rainbow," also at the park. In both cases, the saturated feeling-moment promised in romantic genre is preceded or prepared by a long and deliberate textual hiddenness.

What happens when the film eventually stages the unconcealment of this hiddenness? As *You've Got Mail*'s inheritance of the aria or number form suggests, this is also a question about who would now count as a witness in the film's contemporary world. The line of remakes seems to indicate that the role of the witness can no longer be fulfilled by someone in the world, in the way that Andrew could by hearing through Veronica's performance, standing a little to the side of and apart from the holiday crowd. The kind of witness demanded in liberal love's metaphysics, the one who can narratively rescue the arbitrariness of living, has to come from outside the world—for instance, in the abstraction of the camera shot outside Kathleen's apartment. In "The 365 Day Proposal," Dean resolves the problem of the witness by doubling himself as both the protagonist and the editor of the montage, and in that way creates a position from which the duration of a year might be grasped lyrically rather than from the incoherent and wandering experience of living it. This is, then, what Joe must do before this movie can end and why he, unlike the earlier characters in his position, could not simply assume the fantasmatic position of the male lead by dismissing the other on the basis of his attributes. The promise of romance is no longer only the promise of a suitable partner, which is emphasized, perhaps, by the fact that Nora Ephron's characters are often already partnered and nearly engaged at the beginning of their stories, as if to say that the social achievement of marriage is no longer what the fantasy of romance would be answered by.

What would answer it now? Near the end of *You've Got Mail*, Joe, like Dean, begins to double himself as both the participant and the orchestrator of surprise. First, appearing not from his apartment but rather from what looks like the dark cabin of a ship's bridge, Joe, as NY152, sends Kathleen a deliberately cryptic message: "I'm in the middle of a project," he types, "that needs tweaking." Later Joe happens upon Kathleen in a Starbucks and helps her to decrypt the message—or so Kathleen thinks. What Joe actually does is to feed her interpretations of the text that send her back to NY152 with questions, questions to which Joe has already formulated yet more cryptic responses. During this sequence, the camera cuts back and forth *from* Joe (in the ship's cabin) *to* Joe (with Kathleen), visually emphasizing his bifurcated self.

The sense that Joe is directing or scripting the conversation—suggesting action, feeding lines—joins with his increasing control over the movie's final scenes, during which he physically points to locations that the film then cuts to. Consider the scene where he asks Kathleen to meet him on Saturday around lunchtime as he points offscreen. There is then a cut back to Joe on his ship's bridge and a voice-over that narrates his typing: "How about meeting Saturday. Four o'clock. There's a place in Riverside Park at 91st street where the path curves and there's a garden. Brinkley and I will be waiting." This e-mail amounts essentially to a location description, the kind written into screenplays at the beginning of the scene; the shot then cuts to Joe and Kathleen standing in the restaurant to which Joe had just pointed. As we come to the end of the story, Joe begins to assume more and more the roles of the writer, producer, and director of a film—the very roles that Kathleen had earlier accused him of occupying after their initial encounter in her bookshop. We might say that one of Joe's responses to the loss of the power to disqualify the other man on the basis of his looks and social standing is to assert control not over the content of the fantasy but its mise-en-scène—determining pace, setting, the quality of light at a particular time of day—such that Kathleen's discovery of her lover's identity will take place within his elaborate orchestration. It is as if these aspects of the mode of production of Hollywood movies, whose concealment is necessary for the production of the effect of an independent and autonomous world of action, now begin to intrude into the fabric of the diegesis.

As a result, when Kathleen finally discovers the identity of her pen pal in the film's final scene, she also discovers the presence of an elaborate and artificial production which had until now been operating in the background of her life. When Joe rounds the corner at the park, she is seeing not only Joe, but also a whole retroactive chain of events whose narrative linkages now spring into her awareness. It dawns on her, for example, that Joe had set up this meeting in the park, that he had known it would end this way when he confessed his love on the street in front of her apartment. It dawns on her why he had become her friend, and also what it had meant for her to go to Joe for advice about NY152. The meaning of the bouquet must eventually dawn on her as well, as does the reason she had been stood up at the café, and what was still invisible to both of them when they first met in the bookshop. What dawns on her, in other words, is something like the entire plot of the film *You've Got Mail*, and the knowledge that she has been a protagonist in a story that looks very much like a romantic comedy. The moment of revelation at the end, though it looks like the revelation merely of the romantic partner's identity, is also and more crucially the revelation that genre has been operating in the background of the ordinary, in a historical period in which one could not be certain whether genre still operated in the world as it did in the old romantic novels and films in which Ephron's protagonists are deeply literate.

When Joe rounds the corner and "Over the Rainbow" begins to play, then, Kathleen also approaches more closely than at any other point in the film the presence of the star who plays her. The climax of the romantic comedy offers a kind of resolution to the problem of the star-actor, whose recognizability on-screen always exists in tension with the requirement, imposed by genre, that she be believed initially to be just an ordinary person. Kathleen's discovery of herself as the lead in a story that has been scripted and prepared is also the discovery that Joe has been a director of sorts, one whose emergence out of hiddenness at the end is a sign that this ending was not arbitrary but designed, that she has been secure in the structure of genre. Here the soundtrack's glossiness is doubly indicative: gloss refers to the saturating sheen that an underscore imparts on a scene, brightening it, as Adorno says of music that plays in cafés, as if someone had turned on a spotlight,[40] but the addition of the soundtrack's metatextual presence also constitutes an editorial gloss on the existing text that exposes the presence of an eye over the world, a sense that the present moment is also one remembered and ordered by an editor or reader above and after the story is done. The creepiness of romantic comedies cannot just be excised without substantially changing the genre's psychic form; creepiness is an affective coin flip away from romance's promise of a witness, of an eye over the senselessness of past living that redeems its senselessness. The camera that hovers outside Kathleen's window, structurally identical to the perspective of a stalker or of horror's monster, is also the promise of a form, if not yet an affect, of a narrative line that will someday intersect with the plot in a moment of future convergence.

What Kathleen discovers in the park, or what Jennifer discovers on the beach, thus offers in its modernity a further development or variation of the classical trope of recognition in literary romance, which, as Jameson writes, operates in periods of history in which the foreign other must be reconciled with an emergent and enlightened recognition that the other is, at the same time, a person *just like me*: "The hostile knight, in armor, his identity unknown, exudes that insolence which marks a fundamental refusal of recognition and stamps him as the bearer of the category of evil, up to the moment when, defeated and unmasked, he asks for mercy by telling his name: 'Sire, Yidiers, li filz Nut, ai non' (*Erec et Enide*, 1042), at which point, reinserted into the unity of the social class, he becomes one more knight among others and loses all his sinister unfamiliarity."[41] For Jameson, historical dissonances between the polarizing code of melodrama and the universalizing one of personhood are resolved in an affective gesture of unconcealment, as the evil knight removes his armor to reveal his essential sameness. At a glance, this description seems to map more or less well onto the endings of romantic comedy and seems nearly a mythic formula for *You've Got Mail*'s interest in the enemy of the public world who can, and perhaps even must be, one's soulmate, since the extremity of this coincidence would best enable love's argument of the concealment of surfaces.

And yet, though the classical plots of romance and of comedy often culminate in the dramatic revelation of someone's formerly hidden identity, the modern endings of romantic comedy suggest that what their protagonists must recognize—in order to produce the formally necessary conciliations between self and society that these genres promise—now extends beyond the simple recognition of the identity of the one under the mask. This is especially clear in "The 365 Day Proposal," in which it cannot be said that Jennifer discovers anything particularly new or revelatory about Dean. Instead, like Kathleen in the park, Jennifer must now reconcile her memory of the past year with the scenes that now flash before her, which reveal the optical contents of what had been going on, in secret, in the backgrounds of her ordinary life, when she was turned away, or in the other room, or out of frame. Her discovery is less about the identity of the other, in other words, than it is of an aspect of her own existence, and specifically that there has been a veil separating what she is able to perceive from backgrounds that now turn out to have concealed a vast and orchestrated secret. She learns, say, that what ordinarily lies outside of the frame of her experience is not merely an extension of the world within it, governed by the same arbitrariness and callous indifference. Instead, this space outside of the frame is *busy*—busy with secretive preparations and plans, all of them designed to produce an experience for her. This is what Kathleen discovers about genre, and what the film's audience discovers via the soundtrack: not that the modern world is sheltering and protective rather than indifferent and callous, but rather that one's accurate sense of the modern world's indifference and unsheltered callousness is, paradoxically, the conscious effect of a meticulous and interested care, of a force that must convince you, every day, of the world's indifference to your plans and wishes, if only to prepare a future moment when the preciously held secret of your protagonicity, kept in abeyance in the background, will someday flood the foreground of your experience and erase the line between them.

Modern romantic comedies have for some time now taken care to demonstrate that their protagonists are often experts and fans of the genre in which they appear, which suggests that to be interested in romance is also to be interested in genre's formal effects of categorization and difference. After all, what the normative romantic wonders is not whether romance's promises are real or a lie, but whether they will turn out to be real or a lie *for me*—whether they will turn out to be the form of my life, or whether the form of my life will be something alien to them and to the predictability of the conventional more generally. If nearly every scholarly study of the romantic comedy film points out the particular trouble that this genre poses for class membership—such that nearly every writer on the genre raises, at some point, the problem of how to determine whether a film constitutes a romantic comedy—it is also that a film cannot be a romantic comedy unless the protagonist feels or asks this question. And it is as important that they ask the question as it is that they cannot know the answer.

✵ 3 ✵
Metarhythms of the Addict

TANNHÄUSER IN THE COMPULSION ARCHIVE

Get Better

Jonathan M. Metzl and Anna Kirkland's wonderful volume *Against Health* articulates, among other things, a familiar crux in political pedagogy.[1] On one hand, the book performs political critique in a predictable way: it exposes what is damaging and normative in a concept, debunking its moralizing essentialisms in favor of a systemic account of conditions under which individuals are forced to make a life. We should be against health, we learn, because it is under its name that health and wellness industries continue to massively expand their profits—having discovered, as any form of capital must, a far broader field of extraction in health's ongoing concern than in illness's perhaps occasional and temporary episodes. We should be against health because health so often becomes a vector for the old story of self-discipline and will, trading a properly biopolitical account of state power for neoliberal melodramas of virtue and failure. We should be against health because, as Mimi Khúc also reminds us, the World Health Organization equates health with the capacity to work.[2] Also, what one thinks of as healthy is often just a retroactive justification for the kinds of bodies and practices that one happens to like, sanitizing class and other disgusts by giving them a compassionate and progressive-sounding name. Yet health endures—for who, Metzl and Kirkland ask rhetorically, could possibly be against it?

At the same time, the book acknowledges that this kind of political pedagogy—the debunking of bad ideology in favor of a more properly political reading—is by now a practiced and even fluent operation. "This part," Metzl writes, "the theoretical part, comes relatively easily."[3] Metzl seems to be naming an unease not with what the theory teaches, exactly, but with theory's sensory-affective experience. To debunk ideological thinking, for example, may produce a hit of epiphany, an *aha!* feeling of suddenly seeing through power and grasping something that feels like the truth. This feeling may have salutary effects for a concept of the self predicated on its own autonomy and rational self-possession—*I am not merely indoctrinated*, one may think, *for by seeing through power's operation I have salvaged a sense of my individual coherence and separateness from the systems in which I also live*. In this image of political learning, one may desire the advent of the theoretical frame because it comes with an image of autonomous and rational individuality and allows one to feel narratively more advanced than those who still "believe" in the ideological norms (including, of course, the self of the past that one now sacrifices).

In other words, attending to theory's affects exposes that the move from health to its radical critique quietly retains a formal feature that is central to health's normativity: the idea of a moral line that separates a passively symptomatic population from those who are strong or smart enough to distinguish themselves within their damaging circumstances. If, as Metzl seems to worry, the satisfaction of the debunking perspective comes too easily, it may be because the arrival of this knowledge nevertheless allows one to keep something that one is not yet willing to let go—in this case, to remain staked to the question of whether one is subject or object, of whether one's acts of thinking and intention are powerful enough to make one self-determining rather than merely determined. This remnant—a crystallization of an impulse for a certain kind of legible selfhood—is where a historical particularity echoes through the terms of the contest around health and its moral centrality, supplying the grounds and the language for the struggle.

Metzl writes that though it is easy to understand abstractly what is damaging about the concept of health, the "much more difficult task is to ask what we should do about it."[4] Yet, might moving to the question of solutions also offer a comfort to the questioner, as difficult as solutions undeniably are? For if the difficult task ahead is simply one of action, then it means that there is nothing decisive left to uncover in one's understanding of a problem. It may be less unbearable not to know what to do than to allow that one has not fully understood the problem, that mysteries remain that are not yet modeled by the formulations we have. For example, the model of the bad (individual) reading that is replaced with the better (systemic) one, with its affective promise of triumphant arrival and resolution, of the relief of sharp categorical edges, fails to capture how utterly confusing it can be for someone to live under the aegis of health today, even if they have all the right kinds of knowledge. If imagining damage as indoctrination (i.e., into the self-evidences of neoliberalism and capitalism) perhaps necessarily leads to images of purification and escape, of eventual arrival at a liberating freedom, the neat narrativity of these imagined codas seems also to flatten and mischaracterize the conceptual haziness and narrative uncertainties of the subject who must, at the end of the day, make a life within the conditions and languages that are available to them.

How might we stay descriptively closer to this subject's muddled motion, and thereby to the lived textures of compulsive repetition that might accrete into the medicalized and identitarian significations of illness and addiction? We might look to what is recorded in compulsion's aesthetic archives—for instance, in a song like "Maybe This Time," sung by Liza Minelli's Sally Bowles in the 1972 film *Cabaret*.[5] The title's "this time" seems first to suggest the linearity of a sequence of other times that the present moment follows in order. But "maybe" also destabilizes any possibility of reading the sequence's sense or even its promise of continuity, since it splits into one future in which this time will end up like the other ones, and another in which the painful past will turn out to have been merely the setup for a transformative event:

> Maybe this time, I'll be lucky
> Maybe this time, he'll stay
> Maybe this time, for the first time
> Love won't hurry away

In this intermediary space, caught in a repetition whose end cannot yet be seen—when one perhaps has time and space to overthink things—the atmosphere becomes hypermetaphorized, as if everything the singer encounters becomes an omen; hence what "he" does this time will reveal the intention of love itself as the master name for the series' abstract pattern. But it's not enough to say that this consciousness moves along the points of a sequence, continuing to repeat the same old thing, even if it looks precisely like this to an outsider. The thought of "maybe this time," in the attempt to load the potential for difference into *this* instance, also destabilizes itself in the stark reality that this instance, this song, has been sung before:

> He will hold me fast
> I'll be home at last
> Not a loser anymore
> Like the last time and the time before . . .

That is, the song must allow—even though it cannot fully admit—the fact that every earlier point along the sequence was once a possible *this* time, an occasion, say, for the incursion of a number, in the parlance of the musical. The consciousness in the hovering space expresses awareness that there is a pattern, while also needing to disavow this knowledge in order to generate belief in the difference-making potential that each fresh instance brings. If the formal trail of disavowed knowledges is recorded anywhere, it may be in the contour of the opening melody itself, which, even while voicing the hopeful "maybe," begins the song by ascending eight times to the third of the chord before falling back each time to the place where it began.

We might imagine that if this time does turn out to be different, it will mean the end of the song—not just the singing of this particular moment, but of the metasong that spans the sequence and in which any particular instance (including "this" one) occurs as just one manifestation. And so, while there is a clear pattern that looks like repetition to the outsider, the consciousness who is living it experiences the points of the sequence not as a repetition of the same but as fresh explosions of possibility into an elsewhere—a sequence that becomes a sequence only after the fact, as it settles into the constellation of a biography. While the subject is determined to wrest a truth about the self from the sequence's unfolding—will I succeed or fail? will I change or remain the same?—the song's repetition is quietly generating, as if in the background, the outline of a life that is strung across these moments of speculation, which become something like the overarching structure of a life lived in pursuit of freedom.

This chapter focuses on an aesthetic object at the emergence of the modern West's compulsion archive: Richard Wagner's opera *Tannhäuser*, which premiered in 1845. If "Maybe This Time" projects the line of a sequence within which the song occurs in medias res, the opera extends this pattern across (and beyond) the entire narrative frame of an audiovisual work. Tannhäuser is a protagonist who feels constantly unfulfilled in the present yet persists in fantasizing that some solution or scene around the corner, some new person or way of life, will finally deliver the satisfaction that his questing has as yet failed to produce. The ordinariness of compulsion and the dream of what might be called salvation, health, or recovery in different historical situations and contexts intersect in these moments of fantasy, in which clarity and conviction about *what to do* hits Tannhäuser as a flooding feeling that propels him from one scene to the next, generating in its optimistic force the shape of the plot. As I will argue, such moments of being struck by thought are a key formal feature of life within the affective experience of contemporary health. When the everyday, default person is thought of not as implicitly healthy but as implicitly ill—a sign of which can be found in the growth of talk and other forms of psychotherapy as treatments that, in theory, anyone could benefit from—it is in the hopeful subjunctive of "maybe" that the dream of health touches down on the body as the sudden thought of how you could otherwise, or someday, be.

To invest attachment in an object (such as a diet, a practice, or a theory) as a way of imagining your continuance in the world is what Berlant describes formally as optimism.[6] Yet optimism can be "cruel" if the thing that sustains your attachment to life is also the source of your enduring misery. What is striking about the epiphanic moments in *Tannhäuser* is that they are not always events in which a hit of knowledge, felt as a sensory and bodily shock, means that a character has finally grasped a truth that has eluded them until now—a standard way of thinking about the dramatic function of epiphanies since Aristotelian poetics.[7] Rather, we may detect in *Tannhäuser* and in the dread that hovers around the performance of "Maybe This Time"—where the audience is liable increasingly to feel, the more hopeful and insistent the song becomes, that repetition of the past is all but certain—the outline of an aesthetic tradition that conceptualizes the epiphany differently. In this alternate tradition, the force of a realization comes not because a formerly concealed truth has been revealed (as in the convergence of knowledge and feeling found in the classical theatrical functions of anagnorisis and catharsis) but rather because a truth, and a transformation, have been averted. In this aesthetic archive, the epiphanic sensation of fullness is not an indication of truth revealed but rather an effect of a change that has not taken place, thus allowing the satisfying experience of fullness to continue.

This aesthetic archive converges with a critical one, ranging from the published texts of Alcoholics Anonymous to antimoralizing accounts of addiction from writers such as Helen Keane and Gabor Maté, in which the addict subject is historicized within the ongoing frame of the Enlightenment as a period broadly permeated with dreams of self-determination and the promotion of thinking as the determining agent that overcomes the impulsive repetitions of the animal.[8] This alternate critical genealogy offers a different view of agency and self-determination from that found in the much more pervasive aesthetic theory of "if you want it/believe it/dream it enough, it will happen," a theory of interiority, affect, action, and politics in which an inner felt force comes ex nihilo to transform the external world. If this is the aesthetic theory that implicitly undergirds meritocratic and neoliberal imaginations of social and political worlds, the alternate tradition offers a different theory. It sees in compulsion texts such as "Maybe This Time" that moments of thinking, which are also moments of song, are not the places in which the subject's willpower breaks the cycles of the past, but are rather the very nodes of the compulsive repetition itself—that thinking forms the infrastructure of, rather than providing escape from, addictive repetition. The proper compulsion is not to love or to the sequential occupants of the pronoun "he," but rather to an idea of the self that is free, self-determining, nonrepetitive, and the subject rather than the object of the forces that shape it—in other words, to the achievement rather than the failure of the kind of personhood recognized as true and real within an Enlightenment frame. It is the inability to let go of this wish that brings the person to the song's hope again and again.

Two Concepts of Tragedy

It may be too generous to describe the ideology of health as simply damaging, for key to its particular forms of damage is its conceptual and grammatical incoherence. Currently, health operates simultaneously within two discursive frames. In the first, it refers to an unmarked, default state, while "illness" names the disturbance and interruption of that state. At the same time, there are other uses—for example, in language surrounding the concept of mental health—in which it is illness instead that names the ongoing and ordinary texture of a person's life, while health speaks to a dreamy future in which one is finally free of the sabotaging tendencies. Just as the latter paradigm relocates the sense of ordinariness from health to illness, so too does it relocate the term associated with consciousness. In the first understanding, health is the state that you are not conscious of until illness arrives, which imposes among its debilitating effects the added effect of awareness of illness: to be healthy is to be doubly lucky, since it also means that you don't have to think about health. But in the reframing that has taken place in mental health's therapeutic discourses, it is the state of toxicity that is thought of as the unconscious one, into which the process of recovery may enter as a process of becoming conscious. To be "healthy" in the paradigm of mental health means to cultivate an intimate and moral practice of awareness, a practice that points toward health without ever getting there, since to drop the constant vigilance that marks the subject-oriented-toward-health is to risk relapsing into the subject-not-aware-of-unconscious-impulses.

This shift in the grammatical location and tense of health is reflected in public pedagogies of addiction science. In an article published in *The New York Times* in 2012, "The D.S.M. Gets Addiction Right," Howard Markel writes that the old sinful nouns—drugs, alcohol—are being replaced with a story of attachment drama that can take any object: gambling, sex, work, gender, and love, to name a few.[9] The site of addiction migrates from something traditionally rooted in the concept of the object—for instance, the properties of alcohol or the "alcoholic personality"[10]—toward a person's psychic affordances for comfort, need, and getting by, which are instead rooted in their history of relationships with other persons and objects. If there is a new materialism of addiction, it is centered not on bad objects but on chemicals of attraction and pleasure, such as dopamine, that live in the addicted subjects themselves and tell the story as a generalized one of need and relief. To locate addiction in the brain means that, within this model, removal of the addictive object and "its" effects cannot be a complete cure, for the addictive infrastructure will remain, theoretically open to finding new objects. When the location of addiction migrates from the exogenous substance that is ingested to the disease process played out by the brain, the reference of health also shifts from the achievement of a state to recovery as a constant practice.

The medical and diagnostic reading of addiction—which depends, like any discourse of disease, on the possibility of separating a normatively healthy population from an ill (but potentially treatable) minority—is thus in constant formal interference with the contemporary model of mental health, in which it is increasingly impossible, and discursively nonsensical, to identify *any* normal person as definitively and conclusively occupying a state of health.[11] Although the linear way in which Markel tells the story of addiction medicine offers a reassuring progression from bad old knowledge to the ever truer science of the future, then, it fails to describe the discursively incoherent conditions under which persons who aspire to health must actually live. For these subjects occupy both discourse worlds, both historical and linguistic frames, simultaneously. As Eve Sedgwick remarks, if you say (granting yourself agency, but also speaking in a mood of chastisement), "Well, I could have chosen differently," then you are blatantly disregarding the fact that you are subject to biochemical and other factors beyond your control; at the same time, "one's assertion that one was, after all, compelled, shrivels in the equally stark light of the open secret that one might indeed at any moment have chosen differently."[12] The status of the addict's agency becomes the site of an unanswerable question—unanswerable because neither answer, "I was compelled" or "I was free to choose," seems completely to describe how a given sequence of living occurred the way that it did.

In the interference zone of overlapping discourse worlds, something has happened to the language of freedom and compulsion. Specifically, claims about one or the other do not function in the way that claims typically do. The claims "I am free" and "I am compelled" each attach a descriptive quality to the self, but unlike other claims that follow this construction ("I am Canadian," "I am hungry")—which narrow and specify the self's qualities to the exclusion of other possibilities ("I am not Canadian," "I am full")—claims of freedom or compulsion seem to double back on themselves and dismantle their own assertive clarity. We might say that claims of freedom and compulsion are inoperative; they slip off the experiences they are meant to be attached to; they may not be the right words—or claiming might not be the right kind of speech act—to offer the clarity that they seem to promise in the opaque reaches of compulsive thought and action.

Sedgwick writes that in the particularly obsessive and intense determination to answer questions of freedom, coercion, and self-reliance in the political and popular registers of US culture, "acts of refusal and rebellion in this wasting landscape need to muster real rhetorical and political cunning to remain secret, partial, tangible, true."[13] As wise as this advice is in practice, it also marks a return, in the essay's solution section, to an idea of individual inventiveness and virtuosity, to the heroic effort to remain incompletely captured within systems of signifying use. The vision of a subject slippery, courageous and brilliant enough to evade the entangling mess of language and culture retains once more the historical frame in which the truest and most desirable subjective form is the one that gains coherence apart from the normative overdeterminations of culture, by dint of its grit and mettle.

This solution, then, is not a way out of health and addiction's incoherences, but is rather internal to their terms, constituting one of the poles—along with the specter of nonagency—of a historical blueprint for subjectivity. If claims of freedom and of compulsion seem to be strangely defective, such that one can never seem to establish the absolute truth of one or the other, then the continued attempt to determine such a truth would simply play into the abyssal question's hands. Instead, we might suspend the question and proceed in a descriptive and formal mode. What effects, for instance, does the quest to become self-determined, to resist compulsive damage, leave in the shape of a life over time? How and when does the feeling-thought of agency and autonomy show up in the discourse worlds of contemporary health, and what happens when it does? And does the subject of compulsion and freedom leave a temporal wake from which we might discern shapes that amount to a cultural and historical form?

Tannhäuser's usefulness in tracing the emergence of a modern discourse of health comes from its location at the overlapping juncture of two different modes of reading its tragedy. The story follows Tannhäuser, a minnesinger who had left his home to take up residence in the grotto where Venus, the goddess of love, resides, drawn by its promise of sexual pleasures. When the opera opens, however, he has already grown tired of the Venusberg and expresses a wish for salvation. Over the course of the opera, he will shuttle between renunciations of and expressions of fealty toward both Venusberg and Rome as the opera's metonyms for sensuous pleasure and religious redemption.

In one conception of the opera's ending, descended from classical European literature and its critical traditions, its tragic sense emerges at the point where human agency ends and helplessness begins. Its literary tropes include coincidences and bad timing, epiphanies and revelations that come too late, and the inevitable catching up of fate to those who thought that it could be outrun.[14] Some versions of the *Tannhäuser* legend are legible within this framework: for instance, in one telling, when Tannhäuser visits the pope to seek salvation for his sins, he is told that his chance of being redeemed is as good as that of a dead branch flowering. Days later, the pope's staff produces flowers. He sends a messenger to intercept Tannhäuser with the news, but the knight has already returned to the Venusberg and is never heard from again. In this ending pattern, the transubstantiation of the ordinary (dead wood) into the magical (a flowering staff) indicates a shift in the story's mood from the indicative to the subjunctive, to *if only* and *what could have been*. The key figure who makes the ending generically tragic and not simply unfortunate is the messenger, who converts the moral and emotional stakes of the tale into a flat matter of $\frac{\text{distance}}{\text{time}}$: there is a physical limit to how fast the messenger can go, and this speed, which nobody can accelerate, temporarily takes the question of human control out of the story's universe and aligns the other characters with the audience's passively spectatorial position. There is nothing more they can do now but wait. The sense that the ending is inevitable and out of human control, that one is helpless before the logic of its inexorable unfolding, requires something like the messenger's run for its dramatization.

Tannhäuser allows itself to be read within this older formula. But there is also a more contemporary diagnosis of its misfortune in Carolyn Abbate's "Metempsychotic Wagner." Abbate notes that when Tannhäuser, sick of sex in the Venusberg at the start of the plot, cries out for Maria as symbol of spiritual purity, and when Wolfram, in act 1, scene 4, enjoins him to "bleib bei Elisabeth" (stay by Elisabeth), and again when Tannhäuser, in act 2 scene 4, declares his will to return to the Venusberg on the words "zieht in den Berg der Venus ein" (go to Venus's mountain)—that in each of these cases of a man calling out a woman's name at a critical point of personal and narrative renewal, the name is sung to a recognizably identical interval, a high tenor D–A.[15] Reinhold Brinkmann refers to this precise instance of a repeated interval as an example of proto-leitmotif—an early development of the musical fragment that transcends the single number.[16] The fact that women who represent polar opposites for Tannhäuser might all have their names sung to the same music presents what Abbate calls "the puzzle of two women seen as essentially the same," as if "the male characters mysteriously sense an essence that is one Woman."[17]

A puzzle names an atmosphere of withheld knowledge, jittery with faint perturbations, in which the answer hovers as a clouded yet proximate event of arrival. To describe something as a puzzle is to suggest that an answer does exist, however inaccessible it may be. In using the language of puzzles and mysteries to describe what is hidden to these men, then, Abbate raises the possibility that their ignorance need not be a permanent state. We might note here a conceptual shift from the earlier model of tragedy. In the classical version, tragedy comes from the fact that, in spite of a character's most desperate efforts, there was nothing they could do to change their fate—fate, that is, circumscribes human awareness and agency. But in the more modern telling, the emphasis is instead on what a character fails to see and to solve, on the patterns hiding in plain sight that would release them from a compulsion to repetition, *if only* they would notice them—a failure symbolized in the repetition of a musical interval that they themselves sing and yet cannot recognize.

The repetition of the D–A figure enters both the symbolic nets of an emergent discourse of leitmotivic analysis and an emergent discourse of contemporary health, both of which emphasize the necessity of interpretation as an activity that draws meaningful continuities out of a continuous dramatic fabric. If the emergence of the leitmotif also implies the invention of a particular kind of musical reader—the analyst who looks beyond individual scenes to draw out instances of similarity across the entire span of a work, finding in them a larger symbolic significance that floats across the moment-to-moment concerns of the plot—the same phenomenon also foreshadows the appearance of the therapeutic subject as a kind of reader, who is similarly trained to scan the past and pull out significances from the ongoing texture of living. That this mode of reading now requires something like interpretation, rather than simply identification, is one of the distinctions that has separated an understanding of Wagner's leitmotivic practice from simpler structures of thematic recollection and repetition.[18] While the latter tend to evoke, in critical reading, the image of the listener much more than of the analyst, and usually an unsophisticated, passive one who needs aural flashcards to follow the story, the Wagnerian leitmotif is typically differentiated by noting that its units of musical sense are lexically stable enough to be placed within patterns, and yet also complex, transformed, buried, or abstracted enough within processes of formal and musical emergence to require reading *for* as an interpretive activity.[19]

This temporal and structural figuration of the position of a reader who comes "after" and "outside" the text comes also to inflect the convention of the diegesis, which holds that an operatic character is not typically "aware" of the fact of their own and others' singing (unless such singing is marked as actually taking place within the world, such as during the song contest). In *Tannhäuser*, the fact that the men can't "hear" that they are repeating the D–A interval in their invocations of different women could now be taken not just as an aesthetic convention, but also as a clinical observation. Tannhäuser's downfall, then, might be said to stem from his inability to harness a technique of reading that the emergent technique of the leitmotif requires to be understood. In the place of a classical pathos that comes from a helpless witnessing of the unavoidable end, there is now the pathos of that which *could be otherwise*, the subjunctive dream of health that plagues the state of compulsion. In the modern version's reformulation, the tragic protagonist becomes the addict protagonist. There is no news that a messenger could deliver that would make a difference; rather, it is when tragedy resides in the fact that there is something that Tannhäuser himself must do, but continues not to do, that the story joins the contemporary genres and discourse realms of health, self-help, illness, and recovery.

In the course of the opera, whenever Tannhäuser seems to access the thought of a future world that contains a different version of himself—one who wants the things that he currently only wants to want—this thought comes in the affective genre of an epiphany, a knowledge event whose sudden clarity can manifest a sharp intake of breath, as if an idea were literally keeping you alive. An example of this comes at the end of act 2. He has just sung an ode to Venus and to sexual desire in a singing contest devoted to spiritual love, which prompts Elisabeth and the assembled knights to call for him to admit his sins and seek salvation. It is not that Tannhäuser disagrees with them. He knows his desire to return to the Venusberg is socially unacceptable, and he knows (in the same way—abstractly but not yet as desire) that he should go to Rome and perform penitence before the pope. He is acknowledging the rightness of these facts as the assembled knights and Elisabeth are shouting over him and each other. But then, seconds before the end of the act, all of this noise suddenly cuts out—the orchestra, the characters, the chorus. They have heard something "in the background, deep, as if sounding out of the valley":[20] a group of young pilgrims headed to Rome who are singing a chorale that they have been singing, from the wings and the deep background of the stage, since the first act:

> At the sublime festival of clemency and grace. / I will atone for my sin in humility.
> Blessed is he who truly believes! / He shall be saved through penitence and repentance.

The orchestra then returns, *allegro* and *fortissimo*. In a sudden reversal, Tannhäuser now cries out, "Nach Rom!" (To Rome!), which is immediately echoed by everyone else. The act ends eleven bars later.

When Wagner revised the score for the opera's Paris premiere in 1861, he changed the stage direction that describes what happens when the pilgrims' song is heard by the contest's attendees. In the original version for Dresden we find this: "Upon hearing the song, everyone's gestures change from passionate and threatened to mild and moved." In the Paris version this becomes: "Tannhäuser abruptly stops in his movements of passionate contrition, and listens to the song. A sudden sunbeam shines on him; he drops with convulsive ferocity to Elisabeth's feet, fervently and hastily kisses the hem of her robe and breaks then, stumbling in fantastic excitement, into a cry: 'To Rome!'" The calming effect of music on its audience's temperament in the earlier version ramps up to a full-blown magical naturalism in the later one: the "sudden sunbeam" is an external manifestation of an inner clarity that brings Tannhäuser to his knees. But at the beginning of act 3, following the intermission, we see Tannhäuser return from Rome without having experienced the hoped-for transformation and ready to give in again to the pull of the Venusberg. We might note that before the Paris premiere, Wagner dedicated one of his revisions of the score to magnifying Tannhäuser's moment of inner realization and decision, focusing on Tannhäuser alone instead of "everyone," amplifying the physical effect of hearing on his body, and roping in the sun's confirmation of the force and clarity of his epiphany—even though this decision ends up not producing the change he feels, in this moment, to be possible. In other words, a character's emotional reality, uncontradicted by the confidence of the orchestra, turns out not to be indexical of reality in the opera's world. The triumph of the chords that bring the second act to a crashing close after Tannhäuser's declaration of a new path is revealed, by the beginning of the third, to have incorrectly assessed the situation. Though Tannhäuser experiences these epiphanic moments of clarity as transformative and fresh, the opera's story ends up recording something else: the residue that these moments leave in the shape of the plot. While living in the unwritten middle, he repeatedly and confidently projects the shape of the next scene, which always turns out to be different than what he had imagined.

It is in these projections that we might detect an epistemic and affective form endemic to the contemporary compulsive subject. Wanting escape from what he feels caged by in his present life, Tannhäuser is struck by a thought that begins in the mode of "I should," which arrives as an impulse in both the imperative and subjunctive moods. This thought-event opens the concrete and too-determined realities of his life into the speculative realm of possibility while also implicating him as the author of the transformation that he might now inaugurate as the story's next act. When Tannhäuser cries "Nach Rom!" he is imagining a literal path before him that is also a metonym for a number of things: Rome means being cured of wanting things he thinks he shouldn't want, being free at last of shame, and being the kind of person who just wants x instead of wanting to want x.

But as the opera is about to reveal, the flood of clarity and purpose that comes with being struck with thought does not necessarily bear any relation to the activity that results from it. The causality that binds thought and consequence isn't automatically mimetic, as in the formal promise of phrases such as "believe it and it will happen." Instead, we can observe in *Tannhäuser* that the thought-event that clarifies the self's current purpose simply projects a template for living that can undergird the idea of having a direction for some time. But as we discover when the curtain opens again, though belief in a direction can be a deep relief, its effect is also to frame future living as the coloring in of an image that already exists in the projective thought. The resulting lived days are then measured according to how much or little they resemble the image and affect of the dream of change that they have been tasked with realizing. The future-opening image of the self's possibility thus frames living as the pantomiming of actions contained in the image, which only ends when the time of the present closes the gap with the time of the projection. One can see how living as reliving, as the realization and synchronization of a pre-idealized image, might lead to what Elissa Marder calls the modern addict's alienation from time.[21]

If the suffusing operatic aesthetics of the epiphanic moment reinforce the existence of a link between will and one's transformative potential, between thought and self-determination, between the intensity of a feeling and the degree of its truth, the intermediary unquoted time of the intermission demonstrates something else: the gap between the thought-event of self-determination and, perhaps later, the felt loss of the scaffolding it had once provided for living.

Addiction and the Event of Thought

Wagner's intensification of the romantic and magical-realist aspects of the act 2 finale—such that the sun itself reciprocates the inner clarity that strikes Tannhäuser—ends up producing a sharper deflation of the epiphanic scene's confidence when Tannhäuser returns in act 3, having failed to experience the change he had hoped for. This confidence normally crystallizes a claim about thinking, agency, and self-determination: even the contemporary subject who "knows" that addiction is a disease may nevertheless retain the belief, in their everyday engagements with compulsion and repetition, that change might stem from a self-determining impulse in which one is struck by the thought of how one could (otherwise) be. This thought takes shape as a flooding and propulsive feeling whose sense of momentum seems already to demonstrate the shaping and sovereign effect of thinking on one's circumstances. The thought-event of self-determination is a kind of epiphany, although it doesn't always have to be a shaking and thunderous event: it can be as quiet as the decision to embark on a new diet, or to be organized by a new motto, or to imagine a thing-to-be-achieved. Whatever the force of the impact, it is an epiphany if you are struck by a thought that contains the promise of a version of yourself free of a pattern that currently organizes the rhythms of your day. If mental health now requires a vigilant practice of self-noticing that has no clearly defined end, then health may never be achieved, but may exist only in visionary flashes colored in the subjunctive mood of "if only."

The third act's failure to realize the future promised in the affective atmosphere of the epiphany, however, aligns the opera with an alternate view of self-determination: one that understands the thought of how one might otherwise be not as the beginning of a path toward self-transformation, but which instead locates thinking itself as the symptom and site of the subject's compulsive repetition. This alternate tradition includes the published texts of Alcoholics Anonymous, whose literature insists repeatedly that ideation, or the arrival of a wonderfully clarifying thought that projects a future path free of threats, is not antithetical to addiction's unthought numbness and reflexiveness but rather is the very instrument by which addiction does its work. Here are just a few examples of the frequent occurrence throughout the Alcoholics Anonymous central text, known colloquially as the Big Book, of the event of *being struck by thought*:

> Suddenly *the thought crossed my mind* that if I were to put an ounce of whiskey in my milk it couldn't hurt me on a full stomach. (36)

As I crossed the threshold of the dining room, *the thought came to mind* that it would be nice to have a couple of cocktails with dinner. (41)

When I returned to the hotel *it struck me* a highball would be fine before going to bed. (41)

The event of thought enters the text both, as above, as the instigating moment of the compulsion's repetition, but also in moments of optimism that the cycle might be broken:

Nevertheless, *I still thought* I could control the situation, and there were periods of sobriety which renewed my wife's hope. (5)

As the whisky rose to my head *I told myself I would manage better* next time, but I might as well get good and drunk then. And I did. (6)

The alcoholic may *say to himself* in the most casual way, "It won't burn me this time, so here's how!" (24)[22]

It doesn't much matter, that is, if the thought that strikes the addict is in the transformative mode that declares disavowal of the addictive pattern, or in the equally optimistic mode that *this* time the return to the same object will somehow be less damaging than all the times before. What binds these different narratives is that the act of thinking, or of saying to oneself—as in *ad + dicere*, to say or declare, the etymological origin that echoes through the word "addict"—appears narratively at the very moment in which the addict's story enters the second act of addictive relapse.

Through its examples, then, the Big Book advances the idea that thinking is not automatically on the side of rational self-determination. Instead, it devotes much of its pedagogical energy to uncoupling what it variously calls "will power" and "self-knowledge" from any project of recovery:

I saw that will power and self-knowledge would not help in those strange mental blank spots. (42)

But the actual or potential alcoholic, with hardly an exception, will be absolutely unable to stop drinking on the basis of self-knowledge. (42)

These possessions are presented not only as unhelpful to recovery but also, in fact, as its primary obstacles. Take the way that the Big Book describes the mandate that a crucial component of recovery involves belief in a higher power: "The reader may still ask why he should believe in a Power greater than himself. We think there are good reasons. Let us have a look at some of them. The practical individual of today is a stickler for facts and results" (48). The Big Book not only frames a scientific and objective disposition toward the world as an obstacle in the path toward recovery, but also clarifies that this disposition is a historical formation, emblematized in the figure of the "practical individual of today."

In asserting a symptomatic connection between addiction and self-knowledge, AA thus reads addiction as an event in the history of the Enlightenment, as Ernest Kunst has argued.[23] If part of recovery requires the recognition that addiction is a disease of the body as well as the mind—an idea present in the Big Book as well as recent nonmoralizing and scientific accounts of addiction's chemistry—the insistence on seeing someone's addiction as an effect that flows causally from the will might itself be read as a symptom of the historical impulse to read the most selflike self as rational and self-determining. It is the Enlightenment, in the form of a fantasized echo of this idea, that keeps intruding into the space of recovery, dangling the tantalizing thought that the mind might be strong enough this time to overcome that which plagues both mind and body. In its figuration of this failure, we might consider addiction to be the Enlightenment's preeminent disease form.

This is how Mariana Valverde has historicized addiction in the West, reading alcohol addiction in particular as a case study in the ways that racial and gender differences, for example, were articulated and maintained as differences of a capacity for will—that is, of the mind's control over the body—as a defining property of the human's distance from the animal.[24] She writes that in North American and European societies, there is a "remarkable continuity" to be found in the discourses of willpower that dominate popular and scientific understandings of addiction since the eighteenth century, whether they are articulated within a religious conception of moral action or a capitalist individualist one of grit and self-making. The unwillingness to let go of the frame of willpower is especially striking when one compares addiction to other zones of knowledge, such as sexuality, which have repeatedly renewed their presumptions and models over the same period.[25] Writers such as Kuntz and Valverde, alongside mass pedagogical platforms such as AA, engage the conceptual project of historicizing the moment of quiet resolve and inner decision that leads, in Hollywood cinema, to the montage of self-transformation that is carried by the momentum of a song. The montage would be Enlightenment propaganda if it knew it were peddling something and if there were any sense that people needed to be convinced of it; most of the time, though, it just feels like the realism we want.

By contrast, Tannhäuser's epiphany at the end of act 2 offers a different aesthetic imagination of the relation between inner decision and external manifestation. Unlike the Hollywood montage, where the sound of your resolve becomes the soundtrack for the camera's temporal and spatial unencumbrance, following you through cuts in space and time, the opera does not show the scene from Tannhäuser's perspective alone. Instead, the scene is musically and generically in the third person: while Tannhäuser sings in an idiom that is shared by the other named characters and the orchestra, the pilgrims sing a chorale, a public-domain genre that could be written by anybody. We might say that the opera invites a consideration of the significance of sung style by its staging of a singing contest earlier in the act, which places the activity of singing in relief against ordinary operatic realism. Listening to the pilgrims' chorus is the instigating event that crystallizes hope and conviction for Tannhäuser, where "hope" means a projected subjectivity that scaffolds an image of the future that makes the present's ambivalence bearable. But the fact that the pilgrims sing a chorale is essential to the scene's theory of the kind of realism that epiphany represents. That the pilgrims sing in a generic style that exists outside of opera delaminates the kind of singing that Tannhäuser and the other named characters are doing *as* operatic singing, and specifically as Wagnerian; Abbate calls the music in the scene where we first hear the pilgrims "unperformed."[26] The idiom of the opera thus emerges from constituting the neutral idiom of the work into a specific style that exists in tension with another style, that of the chorale.

What does this stylistic difference indicate? As Tannhäuser listens to the chorale, the orchestra drops out. But when he is done listening, the orchestra kicks in again, and Tannhäuser sings in the way that opera characters do. He has grasped the idea of Rome and the need for penitence—that is to say, what is carried in the song's words. What he does not seem to absorb, however, is the form of life encoded in the way the pilgrims' words are sung. That form of life indicates a different concept of redemption that is not the result of a quest or the end point of a narrative, but that is lived, continuous, and cyclical, whose time is not the narrative time of operatic drama but the time of the chorale, of the breath and the collective. Tannhäuser hears the message and springs to his feet, but as soon as he sings "Nach—," picturing the thing he needs as ahead of himself somewhere, something to journey toward and to get, a failure to hear has already taken place.

Thus, it may be significant that "Nach Rom!," like the cries for the transformative promise represented by women, is also sung to a high perfect fifth. If, in Abbate's analysis, the repetition of a musical gesture across what appears to be an antithesis in the plot (Venus versus Elisabeth) reveals that something has gone unrecognized—that what feels like a new direction is simply a reorientation within a binary whose structure remains hidden from view—then the addition of "Nach Rom!" to the other cries may reveal that Tannhäuser's fantasy of women is undergirded by a deeper fantasy centered on narrative itself. This would include an inability to see past the idea that events are sequential, or that redemption is something that lies in the future as a goal, to be achieved as the high point of a plot. The desire for transformation by women and for transformation by religious redemption, despite how differently these feel to him, are also compulsions with respect to the same addictive object, which is the idea of nextness itself, the successiveness of acts, the linearity of plot. In other words, Tannhäuser is imagining change in the only way he knows how: as an operatic character in a three-act structure. The idiomatically and musically heterogenous staging of the act 2 finale thus offers a dense snapshot of both what is and isn't learned in its transformatively staged moment of hearing—a moment that also marks operatic style, the style of *Tannhäuser*, as occupying something smaller and more subjective than the whole of the opera's musical universe. Operatic idiom becomes a specific referent within the work's world, standing for the very thing that Tannhäuser wants to escape but cannot get himself out of.

The plot of *Tannhäuser* demonstrates what the structure of a life built on such projective moments might look like, unfolding through the elastic action of the thought-projection that drags the present forward to its shining vision, again and again. It doesn't much matter that none of the solutions he comes up with (whether emplotted in Venus, Elisabeth, the Virgin Mary, or Rome) ends up providing the satisfying something that he craves. Optimism may be what moves you out of yourself and into the world, as it does again and again for Tannhäuser, drawing him toward objects that seem to him to drip with transformative promise.[27] But it is also that the rhythm of craving and seeking becomes a kind of structure with which the self becomes identified. Helen Keane has argued that cigarette smokers are able to create a kind of time that is different from its shared and social form, a time that belongs, amid the normative demands of work and intimacy, just to you: "The temporal qualities of smoking are as central to its addictiveness as the pharmacology of nicotine.... People want 'time for themselves,' beyond the socially organized and solidified mappings of work and leisure.... The sameness of each act suggests a recursive and reversible time, a soothing contrast to the steady marching on of linear time towards death. . . . This makes addiction not the terrible cost of smoking, but rather an intrinsic part of its pleasure, ensuring as it does the predictable return of desire."[28] Though the normative and disciplinary social world thinks of the smoker as irrationally squandering the time of life, Keane sees them instead as traders of one form of time for another: the statistical future time of life expectancy for more time and pleasure in the present, in the form of a counterstructural improvisation amidst the suffocating demands of self-concern and self-management.

Keane describes smoking as the creation of a lattice of time that is overlaid onto the always advancing and metrically linear time of the civilized world. Addiction, then, isn't just a disease that stands in the way of achieving one's true and unfettered subjective form; rather, it generates subjectivity effects in the friction between its own metarhythm and the presumptively linear and shared time that characterizes the modern public.[29] The metarhythm of addiction is thus like an acetate sheet that is laid over the temporality of work and leisure, of conversation, of the rhythms of city and nature. It is a kind of electric field that only you can sense, and whose meaningfulness only you feel, though others might sense in your varying animations and vacancies that there is some other force pulling at you.

The sense that selfhood might be located as an effect of a rhythm is the common thread that the physician Gabor Maté has identified between himself and the patients with hard drug addictions with whom he has worked on Vancouver's Downtown Eastside. Maté is careful to distinguish what he calls his own addiction—to buying classical music CDs—from the experiences of his patients: the thousands of dollars that he regularly blows on records are cushioned by his salary and his social status as a doctor, which is celebrated rather than read as an indication of moral weakness. On his side of the social line demarcated by the war on drugs, the effects of his compulsion are mostly private and psychosocial rather than public and life-threatening. Yet, while his and his patients' behaviors are read and pathologized differently, what unites these experiences across the spectrum of compulsion is the way in which the addictive experience generates a rhythm that produces, in the addict's encounters with the world, effects of presence and absence, inside and outside, self and other.

Consider Maté's description of the psychosexual sphere that he shares with his wife, and of what happens to it when at least one of its members also inhabits an addictive metarhythm: "My relationship with Rae loses vitality. Because my internal world is dominated by obsession, I have little to say and what I do say rings hollow in my own ears. Because my attention is pulled inward, the interest I offer her becomes dutiful, rather than genuine. When I'm in one of my addictive cycles, it's almost as if I were engaged in a sexual affair, with all the attendant obsession, lying and manipulation. Above all, I'm absent."[30] Maté offers the sense that the self may be "absent" even when the physical body is not only present, but speaking. He is there, in the social time and scene of conversation, while also feeling the lunar ebb of the obsession whose current proportion of satiation and restlessness places him temporally somewhere between the last fix and the next one. It is these forces that locate him in the middle of a sequence that pulls his attention "inward," bleeding his words of their interiors and his objectively present self of its reality: his speech becomes "hollow" and his interest "dutiful." He imagines that, for a true and fully present form of subjectivity, interest would be "genuine" rather than obligatory, and speech's ultimate function would be not to transmit words but to imply the flickering presence of a self's thereness under their surface.

In Maté's language, we can see how a self emerges in the interstice between the recursive rhythm of compulsion and the shared and ongoing time of conversation with the partner. The self is not where the body or the mind is, exactly, but emerges instead as an effect of a rhythm that pulls him "inward" and away from an engagement with the outside world. Maté's way of parsing this scene of compulsion aligns with Jacques Derrida's observation that the "luminaries of the Enlightenment, identified essentially by the motif of publicity and with the public character of every act of reason, are in themselves a declaration of war on drugs"—that is, in the creation of a public defined by the sanitation and removal of any trace of irrationality and unthinking, a concept of the private necessarily came into existence as the pathologized counterspace of unreason.[31] Derrida's description offers a reversal of the moral order of cause and effect that has dominated the common sense of addiction since the eighteenth century. The normative view of addiction reads the addict's social and material estrangement from society as a consequence of their addictive habit, but the evacuation of unproductive pleasure and its temporalities from the space of the public makes it impossible, within the Enlightenment's discursive frame, to imagine an addict within the rational and objective forms of time that make up the public itself. Addiction, then, comes to be the name of that which definitionally cannot exist in the space of shared life.

In Maté's and Keane's descriptions, it is the friction between these forms of time that materializes the skin of a subjectivity. The history of the compulsive subject thus offers a way of conceptualizing the separation between self and world, and between private and public, as an effect of a rhythmic rather than a spatial difference. This stands in contrast to spatial zonings of privacy and publicity in common and juridical use, in which privacy is a property aligned with the inner spaces of marriage and home that protect citizens who benefit from these privileges from the panoptic demands of the state and the law.[32] Yet, as Maté's language in particular suggests, there exists, in such common phrases as "you seem absent," an acknowledgment of a use for the idea that one can be in public while, at the same time, not being there—that there is a notion of privacy that is not only zoned spatially, in the language of access and possession, but also can be carried with you across both public and private "space."[33] If the distinction between public and private emerged in part as a difference between competing forms and qualities of time, we can locate, in their rhythmic dissonance, the coeval emergence of a temporally constituted form of subjectivity.

In *Tannhäuser*, this temporal skin between an inside and an outside is represented aesthetically by the stretched-out form of the proto-leitmotif over the surface of the plot, which occupies the place of the compulsive repetition that Tannhäuser cannot shake; it is also represented aesthetically in the sound of operatic orchestral music and singing at the end of act 2, placed in contrast to a choral idiom that unfolds without beginning and end, and without animating arcs of narrative tension and resolution. In other words, "opera," and opera in the Wagnerian idiom, emerge as historical signifiers within *Tannhäuser*, shedding their metaformal protection as merely the genre and the medium of the work to become the aesthetic skin that records the trace of an emergent sense of self. If it is now the sound of opera that marks the inner world of compulsive repetition, we can remark that hearing and not-hearing, too, become historically indicative acts. The question of Tannhäuser's ability to hear, in his repeated declarations of purpose, the emergent form of the leitmotif—or the question of what he fails to hear when he converts the pilgrims' words into yet another quest to be won—comes to mark the line that separates the contemporary subject-oriented-toward-health from the subject-doomed-to-repeat.

Silence and World

The significance of hearing and not-hearing arises in Abbate's reading of *Tannhäuser* in a passage that describes the historical newness of the opera's representation of sound. Tracing the scene in which Tannhäuser first ascends to the upper world, Abbate writes that his arrival is greeted by an "operatic soundscape that was unprecedented in 1845 and would remain avant-garde well into the twentieth century":

In act 1 scene 3, Tannhäuser is transported from the Venusberg to the upper world, and when he arrives, *the pit orchestra drops out. Almost everything audible* during the next ten minutes comes directly from the stage: the Shepherd's song, his piping, the voices of the Pilgrims that approach and then fade away realistically, cowbells that imply unseen flocks, and finally tolling bells from the Wartburg tower and the Landgraf's hunting horns. *Aside from a tremolo wake-up call* when Tannhäuser comes to, and some discreet background accompaniment to the reprise of the Pilgrim's chorus, *the orchestra remains silent.*[34]

We might note in this description a trace of tension between what the critic senses in the scene and what the audiovisual facts of the scene seem to be. Abbate describes the orchestra as remaining silent, "aside from" a few appearances of music, instead of, say, a flatter assertion that there is just some orchestral music in the scene. This slightly circuitous phrasing seems to indicate that a description of silence is more true, or more usefully descriptive, than to say what is technically more accurate, which is that the orchestra does not, in fact, remain silent. The difference has to do with the status of music as evidence. Instead of furnishing proof that there *is* orchestral sound, the "tremolo wake-up call" and the "discreet background accompaniment" serve as exceptions in a reading of orchestral silence—that "the pit orchestra drops out" and, later, "the orchestra remains silent" (figs. 3.1 and 3.2).

I see this moment as the exposure of a fissure between the object of description—the thing that the critic senses in the work and attempts to put into language—and the methods and procedures of description available in the conventions of a discipline. For if it is plainly obvious that the orchestra does not remain silent in this scene, then this cannot be what Abbate means when she writes that "the orchestra remains silent." The task that remains for us, reading the critic's reading, is to ask what "silence" then could mean, if the term is no longer or not entirely being used as a merely technical description of music's absence.

FIGURE 3.1. "Discreet background accompaniment": a continuous stream of pizzicato eighth notes in the cellos. Wagner, *Tannhäuser*, act 1, scene 3.

FIGURE 3.2. A legato texture in the strings. Wagner, *Tannhäuser*, act 1, scene 3.

We might begin by noting a parallelism between critic and character: both Abbate and Tannhäuser, at different points in the opera, "cannot hear" something that is in some sense plainly there to be heard. And for both Abbate and Tannhäuser, the fullness of a sensory experience does not come from the ability to grasp everything; rather, it is the exclusion of certain elements that produces the experience of a totality. For Tannhäuser, the force of the epiphany he experiences at the end of act 2, the total certitude and body-collapsing impact of which are narrated graphically in Wagner's revised stage direction, can occur only because of what he cannot yet know about what it would mean to cease being an operatic protagonist and to absorb the form of life of the pilgrims in the opera's background. Similarly, it is only when the orchestral bits in act 1 scene 3 are carefully excluded that a definitive change of state from sound to silence can be claimed. In both cases, a certain experience of fullness or absoluteness is granted in part by excluding the perception of something that is there.

In fact, the scene's theatrical construction already destabilizes the normally implicit conditions of hearing and not-hearing that mark the relation between opera and its audience. As Tannhäuser emerges from the Venusberg and returns to the upper world, Wagner painstakingly notes the source and displacement of every sound in the landscape in which he arrives: faraway bells growing more distant, the sound of the pilgrims as they approach the front and then exit the left side of the stage (their voices continuing to recede long after they disappear from view), and offstage horns whose relative distances from one another are notated precisely in the score.[35] The scene's stage directions seem to be engaged in teaching the audience how to understand the relation of sound to fictive and actual space in the hall: "One hears the song of the old pilgrims, which come nearer along the mountain path from the direction of the Wartburg. . . . The shepherd, hearing the song, ceases playing the shawm and listens attentively." The pilgrims' song floats out from the back of the stage, pricking the shepherd's ears as well as the audience's ("man hört"), as if the shepherd were indicating, in his posture of listening, that the physical space carrying the sound past him and into the hall is continuous. The atypical porousness of the stage's boundaries seems to suggest that the opera's fictive space in this scene extends beyond the proscenium, and that offstage space is not at all abstract but rather a physical continuation of the stage space from which singers and instruments sound their locations.

What is the effect of these laborious and precise sonic and spatial indications? Typically, the presence of orchestral sound tells us, among other things, that what we hear and what the characters "hear" is not the same; characters in dramatic opera of this period do not usually ask about the overture that has just interrupted their day. But the elaborate choreography of a song that comes from the deep part of the stage and that the audience hears just as the shepherd at the stage's lip mimes an act of listening suggests that the audience has crossed a boundary. We are now "inside" the sound world of the opera—we could say, technically, that we are within its diegesis. The fragments of orchestral sound that we do hear, which are far fewer and more attenuated than is typical in this opera, may simply be the bits that break through from the other side that we have left behind. The listening shepherd now acts as the audience's surrogate. The transition from scene 2 to scene 3 is akin to a contemporary audiovisual device in which a camera zooms in on a painting or framed picture, and as the camera's frame draws flush with the frame of the image, the two-dimensional image dissolves into a three-dimensional one: now the camera is "in" the world that had only just before appeared as a flat object. Similarly, when the exceptional soundscape in Tannhäuser draws to an end and the orchestra "breaks" its own silence, returning to the normative aesthetic conventions of opera, its reassertion of a form of sound that exists "outside" the natural landscape of the scene pushes us back out of the frame and back into the position of the audience that exists in the space of the hall. To say that the orchestra drops out, then, might be a way of saying that the audience position projected by the opera at this particular moment is one that no longer has access to the "orchestra"—that is, to a formal position outside the fictional world of the work, marked by, among other things, one's capacity to hear the music emanating from the pit.

In other words, to call the orchestra silent in this scene might not be a reference to the presence or absence of notes played by its musicians. Silence might instead refer to a sense that the opera audience no longer occupies a privileged position of audition "outside" of the fictional world, with access to the orchestra's formal and narratorial frame, but has crossed over into the space of the fiction. At the same time, this space seems meticulously constructed to indicate that it is not an ordinary theatrical space, in which the proscenium marks a formal limit within the world and characters are capable of actions such as entrances and exits. Rather, the function of the proscenium in act 1, scene 3 seems closer to that of the frame in cinema, which simply demarcates the visible portion of a world that is theoretically unlimited and that extends in all directions around the bounds of the arbitrary frame. This is a kind of frame whose selective work is conventionally unnoticed by the characters, and therefore to whom the option of an exit from the world is unavailable.

It becomes even more significant that Abbate refers to some of the orchestral sound that is discounted from the scene as "discreet background accompaniment," a phrase more commonly applied to film music than to opera. It refers, specifically, to a kind of music that is perennially lambasted for providing mere filler and mood, as in Theodor Adorno and Hans Eisler's complaint in *Composing for the Films* that commercial film soundtracks are designed such that "the spectator should not be conscious of the music."[36] A less polemical description appears in Claudia Gorbman's *Unheard Melodies: Narrative Film Music*, which also stresses that a seminal feature of this kind of film music is for it not to be noticed. Gorbman describes a prototypical film experience in which "we" begin by noticing the underscore; at this point, "the story is perceived to inhabit a world strangely replete with musical sound, rhythm, signification . . . until, a few scenes or measures later, we drop off, become re-invested in the story again. Then the music is 'working' once more, masking its own insistence and sawing away in the backfield of consciousness."[37] What is the music doing when it is working? At the moment that we stop paying attention to it, we become "re-invested in the story." We might say that the music's work is to efface its own work so that it reappears elsewhere as a feeling of investment. The music's discreetness is not only to make itself unheard, but also to disavow its role in the production of investment elsewhere in order for this investment to feel self-produced between spectator and story.

Just as silence could be the description of what an audience hears when it passes through the membrane of a fictional world, leaving behind the ordinarily reassuring distance that it enjoys from the story's events, "not-hearing" in these descriptions is not just the opposite of hearing. It is also the description of a relation, present in the sensory construction of the twentieth-century film spectator, in which sensible foregrounds of experience now take on their meaning in relation to some idea of a background, and in which unawareness of music that is obviously there refers not just to inattention, but rather to an intensity of attention and absorption in an unfolding story. This is a relational and aesthetic mode, decidedly more cinematic than operatic, that structures the foregrounds and backgrounds throughout *Tannhäuser*: for instance, "sawing away in the backfield of consciousness" is an apt description of the Pilgrims' Chorus, which enters in act 1 and is implied to continue as the pilgrims roam, sometimes farther from and sometimes closer to the stage. When the operatic noise cuts out at the end of act 2 and the named characters hear the chorale, it is not because the pilgrims have just started singing; the pilgrims' *pianissimo* enters before the *fortissimo* of operatic noise cuts out, such that the effect is less of one genre interrupting the other than of one being peeled back to reveal the other. The chorale has been going on whether the characters could hear it or not.

The sense that these scenes construct an inner diegetic world, and that this diegesis is, moreover, closer to narrative cinema's relations of sound and audience than to those of opera, suggests that the modern spectator interpellated by the film soundtrack may not, in fact, be a historical effect exclusively of the technical and mechanical aspects of film. The presence of these structuring relations in an operatic soundscape suggests, rather, the existence of a more general subjective structure that is not tied to any particular medium, but that belongs more properly to the history of cultural forms, and that can be invoked in different audiovisual contexts. We could note, for instance, that though the diegesis in film is normally a term used to distinguish that which actually exists in a fictional world from that which does not, the term's definitions also often mobilize language that echoes descriptions of the modern therapeutic subject. For example, when Edward Branigan posits that the diegesis "is the implied spatial, temporal and causal system of a character—a collection of sense data which is represented as being at least potentially accessible to a character," or when Étienne Souriau delineates it by including "everything which concerns the film to the extent that it represents something," the idea of a character as a "causal system" distinguished by the sense data that it can access and make sense of, and of the boundary of a world marked by the fact that everything within it "represents something," are equally notions of the modern therapeutic subject as a kind of interpretive field, which moves through the world by translating external things into objects that have meaning within its ecosystem of impulses and symbols.

The modernity of this structure of self and world can be seen in the contemporary rise of talk therapy as a storytelling profession, in which the physician's work is achieved (it is often said) when the patient leaves with a different story than the one they entered with. Note what "story" means in this context. It refers not to a social and temporal world that includes a number of characters and records what happens to and between them, but to a psychically held interpretive framework, a narrative machine that sucks up events and spits out causation and consequence. One historical marker of modernity, then, is the size of story, which has shrunk from a collective form to something that you can carry around with you. It follows that the task of various talk therapies is, in some sense or another, to transform the individual from a character within the story into its *reader*, with the retrospective and pattern-identifying affordances that the term implies. This is clear in psychoanalysis in the idea of the immanence of the past in the present, but it is also present in contemporary therapeutic approaches that do not privilege the past, such as cognitive behavioral therapy, in which the focus is still to make the patient an objective or literate reader of their inner processes by tasking them with writing down or reporting on what they can witness within. In doing so, they become not only the grammatical object to whom the illness has "happened," but also a narratorial figure with respect to their "inner" world.[38]

This world takes form in *Tannhäuser* as the idiom of opera, which is the idiom into which the knight renders what he hears in the pilgrims' chorale—unaware, in the excitement of this discovery, that he has translated this missive from outside his world back into the pattern of despair and optimism that has always organized the shape of his life. *Tannhäuser* constructs a fictional world in which the significance of the language and existence of opera—which consists, among other things, of a linear plot in a multi-act structure, the existence of protagonists, thematic development, the structure of leitmotifs, and the technical complex of an orchestra and singers—is largely that the characters can vaguely sense something *outside* of its constitution of an ordinary atmosphere, and that this outside is where they pin the optimism of their future self-realization. It is as if "opera" peels back from "world" as the two become separate referents in the fiction's construction, which means that the whole of the fiction's world loses connection to operatic sound as the positive expression of its existence. Instead, "world" now refers to that which lies outside of the complex of opera, obscured and inaccessible except for occasional flashes when opera is quiet enough.

If Tannhäuser could hear the repetition in the leitmotif that threads together his moments of optimism, it would mean that he has become both a modern kind of music analyst and a modern therapeutic subject who is able to see the unfolding of his living from an objective, readerly position instead of simply living it as a character within the story. If he could hear and see these things, he might be able to grasp the thought that this time is actually *just like* the last time, which might mean that he could recognize, at least negatively, the trace of a different form of life that lies outside his current ecosystem of sense and interpretation. For now, though, sounds marked "opera" and "Wagner" thread through each new encounter with possibility, keeping the knowledge that their apparent differences are also just the return of the same old song. If Tannhäuser were to become healthy—if he could break free of the pattern at last—it would mean that he had found a way to give up his operatic being.

Coda: Audiovisual Aesthetics and the Problem of the Whole

To close, I turn to what implications this reading of silence in a passage of orchestral sound—and the historical unfoldings that such an aesthetic judgment allows to surface—might have for contemporary writing on audiovisual media. To trace in *Tannhäuser* the emergence of a modern sensory constitution of world—one in which the sensible foregrounds of one's experience no longer articulate the "world" but rather something closer to the intimate, hermeneutic, and affective sphere of the therapeutic "story"—depends in part on being able to see the analytic relevance of the word "silence" in a sequence of audiovisual description where operatic sound is objectively present. To read the emergent edges of a new shape of historical subject in the work thus bears to some extent on a question of musical analysis and its procedures, of whether the existence of some music is counted as there or not there. On one side of this difference falls an imagined form of the music analyst, a role characterized by the ability (or is it the responsibility?) of taking stock of all the music that exists in a given work and imbuing it with a positive analytic presence. That is, even if the analyst does not discuss every note, the assumption is that their professionalism consists, in part, in the fact that they have at least considered every note, an assumption that transforms into the particular kind of authority they claim in relation to the work.

This way of understanding the music analyst, which tasks them with the penetrating and omniscient sensory responsibility of hearing every note and drawing them into a field of interpretive legibility and sense, has implications not just for the "analyst" as a culturally imagined role but also for the imagined "relation" between music and other elements of an audiovisual work. Among film music scholars, in particular, my sense is that there is a kind of expert function, occupied by many of us some or much of the time, that is characterized by a hypersensory awareness and diligence directed toward the positive tracking of all instances of music, which are then asked the question of what sense they do or don't make in relation to the "rest of" the film. Any examples of this broad disciplinary tendency will obviously be selective; its sense has emerged for me in reflecting on the words and descriptions commonly used, say, in the teaching of film music to undergraduates, which perhaps reflects one kind of distillation of the world of habit and method that characterizes the procedures of a discipline.[39]

Consider, for instance, what might be conventional in this perfectly standard sentence about the history of film music: "Steiner came to Hollywood in 1929 and exerted great influence on the way of composing for films and on the use of musical elements from the classical repertoire, working along with specifically cinematic conventions to create or emphasize dramatic and psychological effects."[40] The vocabulary in this sentence—use, work along with, create, emphasize—is of a particular kind. These words are all meant to relate distinct elements that nonetheless coexist in a spatial plane. Musical elements from the classical repertoire are brought to cinema and used there; musical conventions operate alongside cinematic conventions; and music's presence "in" cinema is justified to the extent that one can attribute to it the creation or emphasis of dramatic or psychological "effects." Further clarification of how music is imagined to coexist with the other "elements" of cinema can be found in the introduction to *The Oxford Handbook of Film Music Studies*, whose first ten pages include these passages: "*The Oxford Handbook of Film Music Studies* charts the current state of, and prospects for, scholarly work focusing on one element of audiovisual aesthetic experience"; "Music's role over time has by no means been simple or obvious"; "Nicholas Cook's *Analysing Musical Multimedia* offered a framework for analysis of all manner of music's combinations with other media"; "forwards an initiative to explain why music is important to film and also how music functions in film, providing empirical grounding for practices of description and interpretation."[41] Amid the sunlit rationality and neat, quasi-military instrumentality of these descriptions (music is "one element" of audiovisual aesthetic experience; it has a "role" and a "status" in the soundtrack; it can be "combined" with "other" "media"; it is "important" to and has a "function" "in" "film"), one can hear that the role of the film music analyst—no less than the role of music itself—is being imagined in a very specific way. The verb "to chart," in particular, imagines its object as spatially plottable, reducible to maps, and observable from an unimpeachably objective height. It imagines the critic as a neutral figure who comes into the landscape from outside and can therefore dispassionately take stock of what there is to be seen and heard.

I use this source not because it is exceptional, but because it is not, and because of my sense that the overview to a collected volume is likely to draw out necessary efficiencies that are also drawn out in certain modes of teaching. These efficiencies tend to model the authority of the film music analyst on that of the surveyor, the writer of objective histories, the one who converts the world into elements that coexist in cartographic space. The model of knowledge that proceeds by isolating the "elements" of an audiovisual work to better investigate how they "work with" all the other elements remains a normative methodological assumption of present-day audiovisual scholarship. One can trace it in the common origin story that takes a version of Wagner's *Gesamtkunstwerk* as an aesthetic progenitor of commercial cinema's unified aesthetic system, elided with a contemporary rational-scientific orientation to knowledge in the modern disciplines of specialization and expertise.[42]

And yet, as the compulsion archive demonstrates, there is an alternate aesthetic tradition in which the "practical individual of today" who is a "stickler for facts and results" does not simply represent the truth of knowledge itself, but emerges as a historical disposition toward "knowledge" as an affective anchor that promises a certain kind of clarity and legibility. In this alternate tradition, Tannhäuser's epiphanies are understood not within the model of the satisfying copresence of aesthetic elements in an audiovisual whole; rather, this tradition offers a way to think of the flooding insights he experiences as existing in negative relation to tones and modes of the world that cannot, at present, enter his world of sense. This form of thinking about the audiovisual work is present in the concept of the unheard melody, in which the unheard names a crucial aesthetic relation for the contemporary film audience's sense of absorption in a fictive totality, and it is present in discourses of addiction, in which the compulsive subject's dream of self-determination and mastery—which might precipitate the aesthetic surplus of a number, or a song—is the very sound and tone of the place where the self is caught. I go to the addictive object because it allows me to keep going, to project the path of the self out a little into the future, and I can do so because what the addictive object offers is the enveloping focus of a single thing within the ongoing and the unfinished. But what any compulsive subject cannot grasp—at the risk of deflating the moment's aesthetic plenitude—is the form of the recurrence of the dream of freedom itself, which hovers just out of earshot as the pattern's unexposed secret.

To imagine the place of negative or nonadditive relations in the constitution of contemporary audiovisual wholes might yield different analytic languages. An archive of such language might place a film music text like Gorbman's alongside Adorno's "Music in the Background," which attempts to record a felt historical transition into modernity by tracking what happens to music and to listening under the life-structuring effects of the city. The essay describes the café as a place where music goes to disappear, since, in the intimate and laboring alienations of the work day, music's function might be less to provide attentive listening than to supply the ambience of company. These suffused backgrounds vaguely saturate and vitalize the city for those who pass through it, while also demanding next to nothing, including any mimetic relation of feeling; "the music scarcely touches their inner stirrings" but is rather "an objective event among, above them."[43] Inattention, the nonrelation of music to feeling, the dissolution of the composer, and the pointlessness of analysis and of formal listening are not descriptions of aesthetic failure; they are instead attempts to capture what is historical in the spatial and sensorial outline of an emergent subjective form.

Fidelity to the musical backgrounds of modern aesthetic experience, whether of the café or of the commercial film soundtrack, may require the imagination of a critical position that stays with the unheard and its implications, which would mean resisting the impulse to take up the objective position of the music professional who promises to see and hear all the notes and connections that the average consumer cannot. What methodologies and languages might come if we did not simply imagine the film music scholar in this sober mode of attention and readerly distance from their objects, but allowed them also to invent from the position of the compulsive subject? It might mean recognizing how formally limited the syntaxes for audiovisual description have been, and force the attempt to capture an experience, not of the *Gesamt*, but of fullness in contemporary life as an effect of what you can't absorb, of the modern's attachment to sensory plenitude as privacy, control over genre, and temporal sovereignty, of the desire not to replicate the world's totality but to reduce the world *until it can be felt*. It might mean to add to the aesthetic model of additive totalities by considering the totalities of *addiction* (see table 3.1).

When one declines the imagination of analysis as a bright light in a plottable space, or of knowledge as an extension of one's control over the elements within it, the neat connectivity found in verbs of interaction and effect dissolves into murkier descriptions that seem to imagine the writer as someone stranded, as if in the middle of a scene. For this kind of writing, the essay form becomes crucial for maintaining fidelity to a project of historical description, since the fragile affective emergences of the scene would evanesce under the professional desire to catalog all of its music into an analytic legibility. The difference between the essay and the

TABLE 3.1

TOTALITY BY ADDITION	TOTALITY BY ADDICTION
Work with	Forget
Emphasize	Hear but not absorb
Accompany	Distract/focus
Chart	Shut out
Combine	"Masking its own insistence and sawing away in the backfield of consciousness" (Gorbman)
Underline	
Refer	"The orchestra remains silent" [in a context of orchestral music] (Abbate)
Recall	
Represent	"The first characteristic of background music is that you don't have to listen to it" (Adorno)
Symbolize	
	"Its arcs glisten over the listeners until they sit there, abandoned once more, in the gray of their cigarette puffs. They are not an audience" (Adorno)

chapter or article is that the essay, at least gesturally, suspends the promise to add to something already in motion, instead beginning afresh out of a sense that there is something worth recording in this beginning that might have been missed or lost in the codifications of the things we already know.

Staying with the compulsive subject has, for example, allowed an articulation of addiction not just as an exceptional disease form, but also as a historical structure of sense-knowledge and sensation, and the ways in which these inform living within the impossible project of freedom. To be sure, proposing a broadly historical rather than a markedly social frame for addiction risks generalizing and diminishing the uneven consequences of current theory and policy on already scapegoated populations. And yet this risk could not even be taken without a prior separation of the category of the addict from some contrasting category of the nonaddict—that is, without an account of the desire to imagine a position free of addiction's temporal reach. The dyad of diagnosis and medicalization both promises and threatens affliction and freedom from affliction, obscuring a sense of the conflicting terms that animate the historical imagination of a life of value.

To generate new descriptions of addiction that are less individualizing, then, one might look anywhere that the concept helps to manage the conflicting demands of history and desire in the shaping of a life. For instance, if I am tempted to use the phrase "I'm addicted to this show" instead of "I love this show," what might the content of this difference be? I might be trying to say that desire is not enough to capture the intensity of my attachment—only a force unbidden or beyond my will can adequately express it. I might also be expressing embarrassment about the object of my desire: "I'm addicted to this show" might have, as a paraphrase, "I know I shouldn't like this show/I don't want to be the kind of person who loves this show, but. . . ." The phrase may thus be a way of protecting my desire: if I am addicted to something, there is nothing you can do to convince me to give it up, since it is not something that can be rationally chosen. In these scenarios, addiction is not a state that is contrasted with nonaddiction or sobriety, but rather appears as an in-the-moment improvisation of the wish both to remain recognizable as the kind of historical subject who aspires to self-determination and to make space, within the terms of its language, for forms of life-making and sustaining that fall outside of what the historical frame would recognize as such. The phrase tells us that sometimes we prefer *not* to have agency, and that language is a place where we manage the conflicting impulses not to become an erased subject of history while also letting desire (as if unsupervised) shape the contours of a life.

Recognizing that self-mastery is a much more ambivalent desire than it normally appears to be is particularly necessary at a time when the signifiers of "therapy" are increasingly used to index a particular kind of subject—that is, modern, civilized, and imbued with the narratological and readerly implications of a phrase like "self-aware." Without being untender about the benefits that talk and other forms of psychotherapy might afford any particular individual, we might also note that the mainstreaming of therapy as a signifier of enlightened subjectivity marks one of the latest unevenly distributed resources to differentiate a desirable, contemporary, commodifiable, and morally impeccable subject from an unaware and anachronistic population that is doomed merely to express, rather than overcome, the determinations of history. This concept of personhood functions both intramurally in the articulation of the advanced world's class structures and intermurally between the West and the symptomatic rest of the world, which is imagined still to be catching up to the West's standards of self-reflection, humane individualism, and concern for freedom. But, as this chapter has argued, the language and rhythms of addiction emerge to fill an expressive and formal void elided by the illuminating frame of ideal subjecthood, recording the place and the work of the unthought, unbidden, and ultimately untransformative in the shaping of the desired life.

✳ 4 ✳
The Soundtrack Is So Cliché

AMBIENT WESTERNNESS AFTER 9/11

Zooming Out, Fading In

The pilot episode of the television series *The West Wing* (1999–2006) closes with an audiovisual device that has become a nearly ubiquitous signifier for ending in popular cinema and television. We are in the White House, and President Bartlet has just wrapped up the day's business. As his staffers file out of the Oval Office, a string cue quietly enters the mix. As the cue rises, the president yells, "Mrs. Landingham! What's next?" Mrs. Landingham enters and begins to brief the president on the practicalities of the day, and as she does the cue keeps rising in volume as the camera slowly floats up and away, the two figures gradually receding against the backdrop of the Oval Office carpet. Mrs. Landingham is now saying something about a conference with Governor Thomas, but it's increasingly difficult to make out her words over the surging score, and one gets the sense anyhow that what she's saying doesn't much matter. What matters is simply that the next in "what's next" is taking place. When the details in the bustle of the day's concerns don't much matter, all that's left is the day as a texture and thrum of sound, heard at a distance where one is close enough to detect voices but not close enough to make out their meaning.[1]

This is a balance of film music, speech, and world sound that is often found at the ending of a scene or an episode: as the camera draws back from the protagonists' conversation, their voices grow indistinct as the widening frame lets in the hum of the city around them, eventually revealing the city block or the skyline as credits begin to roll. It is a balance distinct both from the underscore as a formally and metaphysically sited position that amplifies speech without damaging its sense, ceding priority to language, and from a sound mix in which music takes over in places where theme, atmosphere, and affect override the importance of language.

Instead, across popular audiovisual aesthetics, after the détente of the romance plot or the action plot, the zoom-out of the camera may produce, for a moment, a sound mix not of speech and music but, crucially, of *indistinct* speech and music, as the story ends and the camera relieves the protagonists of their protagonicity. This aural and spatial movement returns them to the fold of the society that surrounds them, implying that what we have just seen constitutes only a single story within the swirling mass of stories that take place every day. Instead of delivering genre's promise that satisfactions will be found via the formula's specific crises and resolutions, it seems to promise instead that after the genre plot is done and resolved, the social will once again be a place where *nothing happens*. Outside of the disturbances that induce narrative into existence, the social is imagined simply to be an ambience, a hubbub, an auditory middle distance in which the presence of others is experienced primarily as a texture without any particular specification of detail or genre. We might call this mix of indistinct speech and music the sound of the just-another-day, an aesthetic figuration of normal life as the thing that is interrupted by the happening of a plot—as in the cliché, "It was just a normal day, and then. . . ."

Normal life as an object of aesthetic figuration can take different forms and purposes, depending on the time and place in which it needs to be imagined. This chapter traces the audiovisual imagination of ordinariness in the United States in the early twenty-first century, particularly as it was narrated as an aspect of experience threatened by the rise of exogenous terrorism. As Elisabeth R. Anker has argued, melodrama became the de facto genre for US political discourse after September 11, 2001, since it seemed to offer a clarifying symbolic structure of innocent victimization and inhuman villainy. This was particularly potent at a time when the increasing tendency to model danger in terms of statistical probability produced, in Brian Massumi's words, a "threat-environment [that] took on an ambient thickness, achieved a consistency."[2] Though Massumi traces the phrase "war on terror" to US political discourse in the 1970s, he argues that 9/11 marks a "threshold" in which statistical threat transformed the experience and texture of the everyday into a zone defined by its vulnerability to the probability of unpredictable violence, which might strike in any ordinary space on any given day. In this sense, American ordinariness became a central part of the discourse and figuration of terrorism, since it was seen as the affective substrate that terrorism threatened to disturb and as the national possession that melodrama's heroic formulas aimed to safeguard and restore.

But melodrama, the major genre solution to unpredictable national violence in the early twenty-first century, was also unable to process fully all of the threats that would come to visit the national body. For instance, while conspiracy was a present but minor genre of 9/11—mostly derided by the mainstream as a niche and delusional view that the attacks were an "inside job," a plot by the US government—alongside melodrama as the major one, the symbolic landscape was rather different twenty years later, during the COVID-19 pandemic. Conspiracy in 2020 was no longer a minor genre, instead forcing acknowledgment by, and even adaptations in language and epidemiological strategy from, official channels of public health and authority up to the office of the president—a feat that the 9/11 conspiracists never managed to achieve.[3] As the immediacy of 9/11 has faded, then, different generic structures have emerged in the attempt to capture the affective experience of vulnerability for a national audience while at the same time contending with what its threats expose about the invisible texture of that nationality.

Popular films and television shows about terrorism after 9/11 were tasked with capturing and managing the affective experience of terrorism for the ordinary and unmarked subject in the West, which meant articulating, in some form, a sense of exactly what this subject stood to lose. As a result, these works become an archive of the invisible form of ordinary national belonging that typically, in historically unexceptional times, is imagined to operate in the background, beneath notice and representation. To be represented by a general form, rather than just an individual or universal one, is, of course, the province of minoritized subjects, but even traditionally unmarked subjects can have different unmarked components of their identity rise to salience in different circumstances.[4] For example, when the ordinary and unmarked American or (Western) European subject experiences, at the beginning of the twenty-first century, the threat of exogenous terrorism that emerges from the vague "over there" of the Middle East, this subject becomes interpellated not only as an American or European subject, but also as a subject of the "West." The threat of terrorism exposes the salience of an identity form that may not normally arise in the local encounters that make up ordinary experience, where this person's class, gender, or racial signifiers might be more significantly operative. The American subject who becomes a *Western* American subject might sense the affordance of the category, for instance, in a solidarity or relatedness with French citizens who become victims of a terrorist attack, as if the unpredictable and public acts of violence that became a mainstay of news reports in the West after 9/11 were all targeting one continuous body.

If the specter of exogenous terrorism after 9/11 necessarily conjures the "West" as an identity and an object, these audiovisual works figure

"Westernness" as the loss of an ambient, vague, and unspecified texture of the everyday that once offered protection from the damaging, linear effects of history. In these works, the everyday emerges as an aesthetic and aural form that exists outside of history's zone of narrative and consequence, and in which the appearance of terrorism as an ordinary-shattering event signals the subject's emergence from an intimate, unmarked, and ahistorical sphere into the collective time of historical event. The traumatic rupture for this subject is then not only the physical violence of the terrorist act itself, but rather the way in which its violence punctures the aesthetic protections of a fantasy of undisturbed dailiness. As I argue, the reason fear of the exogenous terrorist attack—in contrast to other kinds of fear—gripped the US national imagination so decisively after 9/11 was partly what such attacks revealed about the aesthetic imagination of the ordinary and unexceptional American life.

This chapter moves through a number of audiovisual works from US popular culture of the last twenty years, beginning with *The West Wing* as an audiovisual document of what history was supposed to feel like for the unmarked person at the turn of the century, before the decades in which attacks on the United States made this sense of implicit protection and its relation to history less tenable. It then moves to M. Night Shyamalan's *The Happening* as a film that records the generic form of unmarked US subjectivity in the post-9/11 era. Around this time, the genre of the post-9/11 terrorist film began itself to shift away from the unambivalent white melodramatic heroes of the 2000s out of the recognition of a new audience position that required both the management of its fear of the exotic terrorist and the reassurance that it was not racially intolerant. The general wane of melodrama across this body of works gives way to the rise of conspiracy as the dominant genre of later terrorist texts, a genre shift that also implies changes to the conditions of public visibility and self-identification in contemporary US political publics for minoritarian and nonminoritarian subjects alike. The tonal and generic shifts recorded in the popular media of terrorism thus track the ongoing attempt to manage and preserve the space, experience, and sound of an everyday protected from the narrative intrusions of history, even as this fantasy becomes less and less realizable. Finally, the chapter turns to Miranda July's *Kajillionaire* as a document that archives the aspiration to an ordinary and undisturbed American life as an aspiration to an aural middle distance. It is at this fantasized distance that the details of plot and genre blur into a hum that exposes the wish for life to consist of sounds and gestures that have been ground down into cliché, capturing the ambient promise of a historical form that starts to become perceptible at the very moment it begins to fade.

USA, the Backstage Musical: The West Wing

The West Wing, a show that was broadcast on American primetime television from 1999 to 2006, archives for the early 2000s a felt sense of ordinary life that emerges in relation to the nation as the place where history happens. The show's essential appeal is its promise to deliver, in episode after episode, the frisson that obtains in the interference zone between the banality of the everyday and the monumental significance of History. Characters on the show regularly marvel (and expect the show's audience to marvel) at their proximity to the nation's center, abstract and yet tangible—a proximity that is nowhere more evident than in the figure of Jed Bartlet himself, who is both an ordinary man and also the embodiment of the highest office in the land.

For example, when Charlie Young—a young man hired to be Bartlet's aide—first meets him, the president is about to deliver a nationwide address on a terrorist attack that had just claimed the lives of several Americans abroad. Young shares an intimate exchange with the president about the recent death of his mother when a background voice calls "Thirty seconds, please!" As this happens, the camera draws back to take in the apparatus of production—the teleprompters, the studio lights, the camera crews. In less than a minute, Bartlet transforms from the flesh-and-blood man shaking Charlie's hand into the image of the president of the United States that appears on screens around the world. As Charlie says, wonderingly, "I've never felt like this before"—to which a staffer responds, "It doesn't go away"—the camera pans from his face behind the cameras to a screen on which a news anchor is introducing the president's address, and then finally past this to the flesh-and-blood Bartlet himself, now live to the nation.[5]

The episode ends right when Bartlet begins his address—that is, right when the ordinary citizen's access to the production of the speech's content would begin. Whereas state aesthetics typically involve cutting out the backstage preparations surrounding an address—the hair and makeup, the line writing and rehearsal, the friendly and familiar bickering that we see Bartlet engage in just seconds before he goes live—in order to produce an aura of seriousness and composure that would befit the abstract immensity of its authority, *The West Wing* is interested in a different aspect of the aesthetics of citizenship: not its official public face, but the allure of being close to power, of feeling its heat near you, of the continual dissolve between man and office that *The West Wing* is nearly fetishistically attached to representing, captured in the play of embodiment and disembodiment that is the metaphysical anomaly of the president's body.

The backstage musical discovered that as much as contemporary audiences would be wowed by displays of body and machine that concealed the labor of rehearsal and technology in the production of seemingly magical effects, audiences would also thrill to the exposure of those tricks, enjoying the deflation and grounding of the magical effect as a secondary pleasure.[6] If the commodity's essential function is to make labor and the conditions of its production disappear, the backstage musical demonstrated that this trick came with a doubled magical form: the revelation of labor, of the ordinariness behind the sensation, as if to hide something was also to store an energy that could later be released. Thus, the modern spectacle is a kind of perpetual-motion machine of libidinal generation: labor is concealed to produce its products as a purely magical effect, but in the concealment this labor itself becomes energized as the secret of how it's made.

The West Wing understands this about the production of nation, too.[7] The feeling that Charlie has never had before is the surreal effect of being physically close to something abstract, of feeling the national and the historical as effects that seem to live tangibly in rooms and bodies. This is in marked contrast to another major US show about work in the 2000s, *The Office*, in which it is the slapstick deflation of the boss's and the organization's attempts to manifest symbolic presence and authority that makes the show's theory of the institution comic and not sentimental. Unlike *The West Wing*, in which Bartlet, as the president, functions as a vessel for History—signaled in his penchant for quotation and historical anecdote, his literary cadence in speech, his knowledge of Latin—that serves to clarify and ennoble the petty political squabbles and grudges in the ordinary life of professional politics, *The Office* focuses instead on how, in the absence of an institutional purpose that would give meaning and metavalue to the life of work (the characters work at a failing paper company), life's episodes become not divergences from the plot, but rather its point. The formal center of *The Office* lies in the inside jokes, pranks, and B plots invented by the workers to give narrative shape and intrigue to the living of days when the institution and History fail to provide that function. In this show, the dailiness of the daily is not something that needs rescue.

The West Wing has a different view of the little forms that people invent to induce absorption in the midst of the stultifying structures of work. The pilot episode establishes an affective dynamic: first, we are introduced to various members of the White House staff as they navigate the banal ordinaries of work, such as relationship drama, collegial bickering, and politics in the anti-utopian mode of the incremental change that meets resistance in the intractability of others. Then, at the end of the episode, the president walks in. The quippy Sorkinian repartée seems not so much to stop as dissolve as the figure of the president induces a shift to a quiet, ruminative mode: "Seems to me we've all been taking a little break. Thinking about our personal lives, or thinking about keeping our jobs. Breaks are good; it's not a bad idea to take a break every now and then. . . . Naval intelligence reports that approximately twelve hundred Cubans left Havana this morning. Approximately seven hundred turned back due to severe weather; some three hundred and fifty are missing and presumed dead. One hundred and thirty-seven have been taken into custody in Miami; they are seeking asylum." The camera peeks out through the backs of the staffers at the president, who stands in front of the *Resolute* desk. Then, as Bartlet looks up from the brief he's been reading, the camera pushes through the staffers and brings us close to the president. In the move from theater to the cinematic close-up, warm horns and strings now replace the room's silence as Bartlet shifts from the dry recitation of figures to the interpretation of their significance: "With the clothes on their backs they came through a storm, and the ones that didn't die want a better life, and they want it here. Talk about impressive. My point is this: break's over."

The West Wing offers many pleasurable national feelings, and it is no surprise that it became an antidote for political depression during the 2016 and 2020 election seasons.[8] But the show's most revealing pleasure is not that national problems might feel like screwball comedy rather than the constant dull shatter of crisis, such that if one could tune in to the nation's heart, one would find there a gregarious and bustling chatter, like the sound of an old radio show in the background; nor is it the utterly conventional sentimentality in which the refugee's and the immigrant's trajectory to the United States is taken as proof of the nation's inherent beneficence, and not as an effect of its ruthless hoarding and violent maintenance of precarity in what it considers to be the third world.[9] What makes ordinary life feel good in *The West Wing* is the idea that at the end of an ordinary day in which you have been absorbed in your petty squabbles and little private feelings, there exists a figure—call him the president—who can dawn a historical perspective into the intrinsic muddiness of the daily, giving the ordinary citizen (no less than the White House staffers among whom the camera places us) a feeling of purpose, or at least purposiveness. Hence, in Bartlet's language, "thinking about our personal lives" or "thinking about keeping our jobs" constitutes a "break" in the narrative time of life, whereas the feeling induced by brown bodies floating in the Gulf of Mexico induces for the show's interpellated citizen the feeling of narrative momentum.[10]

The show, in other words, pictures ordinary life as a zone of floating, ahistorical time, which exists in a dialectic with the nation—via its presidential avatar—as an entity that can deliver the vantage of the historical that is absent in the citizen's sense of the everyday, offering a deeper, more cumulative significance to living that otherwise risks becoming trivial, mere chatter. The sentimental scene of empathic politics, delivered in the cinematic aesthetic framework of the unheard melody—a gentle underscore that stays well below the primacy of voice, yet subtly amplifying and underlining it, such that its effect might in theory not even be noticeable—is therefore only one framework for the scene's pleasure.[11] If the structurally unsubordinated subject feels more connected to purpose in their own life via proximity to political suffering as what feels real about the world or history, it is in part because this connection offers another pleasure: history, as a sobering reality effect induced by world events, also implies the existence of an ordinary space that it interrupts and to which that subject returns, after the enigmatic force of the president's and the soundtrack's eloquence fades. The dyad in which history via the state induces narrative perspective and purpose in an ordinary life that is normally severed from it is governed by a patriarchal symbolic, which can be felt in Bartlet's gently patronizing tone ("Seems to me we've all been taking a little break") and its evocation of shame and gratitude among the staffers. *The West Wing*'s promise is that history would make sense, and belief in the nation and its progress would be possible, if only there were a Father sovereign enough to hold history for us as a horizon. In a world where such authority exists, the ordinary citizen is released, as it were, to enjoy the screwball antics of the everyday, taking pleasure in both their petty absorptions and in the occasional chastening effect of the dawning of historical perspective within their lives.

Event Without Content: The Happening

Released a few years later, *The Happening* (2008) continued and extended *The West Wing*'s formal interest in the atmospheric structure of US citizenship, but now in an ordinary permeated by terrorism's unspecifiable and unpredictable threat.[12] The film, uncharacteristically for the genre, acknowledges this absence of certainty: it concerns an unexplained "event" that strikes Central Park in New York City at 8:33 a.m. on an unspecified day. The event, which is how the film's characters often describe it, seems to be an airborne toxin that causes anyone it infects to commit dramatic and immediate suicide. Like *Taken*, another thriller released in the same year about the kidnapping of a white American girl by "third world" terrorists, *The Happening* attempts to articulate something about a collectively held post-9/11 atmosphere, primarily in the United States and Western Europe, for those whose sense of implicit safety in those areas of the world was marred by the appearance of exogenous terrorism (*Taken*, for example, is a French production with an Irish star playing an American role). If *Taken*'s title—in omitting the verb's subject and using only the past participle of "to take," as in the phrase "she was taken"—suggests that a crucial component of terrorist fear comes from what is unknown about its agents and their motivations, *The Happening* goes one step further by removing even the specification of the verb itself. A happening, after all, is a *something* wherein the subject, verb, and object all remain undetermined—and yet it is not nothing. Its only thingly presence lies in the naked form of eventness itself. All that the word specifies is that a mark has been made in the ongoingness of time, a beginning of a form that will (presumably) close at an unspecified point in the future, even though the conditions that determine the event's unfolding and end point are not yet known.

The movie, in fact, never satisfies the audience's desire for an explanation of its central event, right up to a final scene in which we see the still-unexplained happening spread to another central park, the Jardin des Tuileries outside of the Louvre in Paris, France. In refusing to offer any kind of answer to the question that the plot unfolds, the film smuggles the sensibility and formal interests of an "art" or "experimental" film into the body of a Hollywood blockbuster, whose basic contractual promise with its audience is to explain everything. By contrast, the "European" art film is, however reductively, typified by its eschewal of linear causation and direct explanation in order to shift the audience's perceptual focus onto the properties and effects of images and shots themselves—as in, for instance, *The Happening*'s occasional interpolation of disconnected shots of trees, grass, and bushes blown by the wind. These shots, however, function in the film as an aesthetic pivot between Hollywood and less overdetermined systems of signification, for while they are ostensibly showing something significant to the plot—the characters speculate that the toxin is being spread by the wind—and thus follow the narrative impulse of commercial filmmaking, they also operate under the plot's conditions of epistemic uncertainty. This is because the characters can only speculate that the toxin is carried by the wind, which means that their sense of the wind's significance to the happening emblematizes, in part, the desperate projection to attach significance to *something*—a desperation captured, perhaps as a poetic parable, in the cinematic attempt to photograph wind itself. The shots, moreover, are visually separated from the narrative sequences of the film: they float out of time and could appear in any order, and their length is dictated not by the necessities of the unfolding content of the shot, but by an implicit and invisible auteurial whim.

The Happening, in other words, is notable among American- and European-produced imaginaries of terrorism in the immediate post-9/11 period in that it is much more curious about terrorism's epistemic assaults than its physical ones. Consider the scene, immediately following the film's opening sequences on the attack in Central Park, in which we are introduced to the film's protagonist, Elliott Moore (Mark Wahlberg), a high school science teacher. Elliott is in the midst of teaching a class in a location marked on the screen only as "Philadelphia High School, Philadelphia." He speaks his first line in the movie: "Look, I don't know if you guys have heard about this article in *The New York Times* about honeybees vanishing?" Like a good Socratic pedagogue, he invites the class to speculate about the causes of the vanishing, offering encouragement and counterfactual arguments to their suggestions, which include disease, pollution, and global warming. Finally, he addresses Jake, a student who seems not to be paying attention. "You don't have an opinion?" Jake shrugs. "You're not interested in what happened to the bees." Jake makes a gesture that says "not really." Finally, after being pressed some more, Jake offers this reading: "An act of nature—and we'll never fully understand it." Jake is the only student to offer an answer to the question that does not affirm but places in question the epistemic framework of a high school science class, in which the scientific method offers the promise of the reassuringly known in the face of the world's material questions. And it is at this point that Elliott abandons the Socratic principle and offers the lesson's first unequivocal approval: "Nice answer, Jake. That's right. I mean, science will come up with some reason to put in the books, but at the end of the day it'll just be some theory."

What do we make of this scene's careful positioning immediately after the opening sequences of the attack? We might expect a commercial thriller, for example, to cut from the event to a medical bay, a laboratory, or a war room, places dedicated to providing solutions to national problems. But *The Happening* cuts instead to a protagonist who is involved not in manufacturing an answer, but rather in questioning (and in teaching how to question) the origins and procedures by which things like questions and answers, explanations and certainty, are generated. And what it shows is that these procedures do not come naturally or intuitively. At first the students exhibit no response to Elliott's bringing up the article about bees; they look bored or bemused, certainly not concerned, and do not instinctively show the need to "make sense" of the crisis reported in the news—a phenomenon in which the act of reporting itself elevates a happening in the world into a matter of concern, a thing that a certain kind of reader or citizen would respond to with care and attention. It turns out that this species of reader-citizen is something that must be trained: thus, Elliott first instructs them (in the process speaking the film's title) in the proper epistemic activity with which to respond to something reported in the news ("Let's hear some theories about why this might be happening") and also attaches the proper affective disposition of this ideal theorizing citizen when reading the news ("Scary, huh?"). We might see, in the film's following of a scene of public attack with a scene of pedagogy, the generational transmission of the construction of a national character that we might call the dyad of the informed/concerned citizen. This is a model of virtuous, ethical, and involved citizenship that attaches the objectivity effects of information circulated in the news—often backed by a sense of "science"—to an affective mode of worry for the world that often masks its own shaping desires as a selfless concern for others.[13] We might think of the concerned citizen as crucially organized by both senses of the word "concerned": an anxious demeanor attached to a formal extension of the self into the world under the governing impulse of interest or an involving responsibility.[14]

The concerned citizen is someone who might, for example, speak Elliott's opening line: "Look, I don't know if you guys have heard about this article in *The New York Times* about honeybees vanishing?" Spoken by a white, middle-aged science teacher to a group of diverse kids at "Philadelphia High School," the line strikes me as enacting a subtly satirical typification, further accentuated by the joke of the subject who becomes anxious over an article they did not even read but merely "heard about." The informed/concerned citizen modeled by Elliott at the beginning of the film might be someone who reads a mainstream and intellectually prestigious newspaper like *The New York Times* in order to enjoy the sensations both of feeling informed and feeling concerned, a play that begins (1) with a feeling of panic about a crisis or injustice reported by the newspaper that is at the same time (2) soothed by the same newspaper's affective promise to make the world sensible and bearable, offering a reassuring authority built on the foundations of objective reporting, academic expertise, and scientific finding.[15] These figures of "knowledge" appear throughout the film: as Elliott joins a mass exodus from cities on the East Coast, he regularly encounters television screens—hastily conjured and plugged in by diner owners, or found in private or abandoned homes—on which an array of experts appear: a professor of statistics from Carnegie Mellon, a chief medical correspondent, a professor in the department of botanical toxicology at the University of Chicago, and a variety of quietly urgent professional news anchors. These authorities float different explanations: one describes a neurotoxin that flips the brain's innate "preservation switch," while another suggests a cover-up by the government (we're told that the Central

Intelligence Agency has offices in the northeast). Yet even after the attack seems to subside in the United States, these figures of knowledge are not able to provide the satisfying answer that their audiences—no less than the audiences of commercial genre film—expect at the event's narrative close. In withholding the answer to its central mystery, *The Happening* instead foregrounds the play of knowledge, along with the institutions that formalize it and derive their cultural authority from it, as an epistemic activity and dynamic that springs up in the wake of an event without explanation.

The Happening was widely derided by critics and audiences as a bad and forgettable thriller. I wonder, however, if we could also locate some of its signifiers of badness—for example, dialogue that lacks precision and nuance, broad acting, cliché, and a general lack of the precisely observed that typically indicates a work of uniqueness and quality in the middlebrow register of US film reception—as elements in a comedy of nonspecificity. Is the location tag "Philadelphia High School, Philadelphia" supposed to be funny, for example? Or the scene that opens with the punch line of a construction worker's joke, right before this ordinary workday moment is interrupted by the toxin's attack—a punch line that is incomprehensible without the joke's missing first half, as if signaling that one should insert here a "generic construction worker joke"? Or the way in which Wahlberg and Zooey Deschanel's acting, rather than performing in the valued idiom of the implication but underspecification of complex depths, instead seems often and simply to pair the reading of a line with a corresponding facial affect, the embodied equivalent to an instruction like "man responds with horror to scene"? These moments invite us to recognize a dispersed aesthetic effect across *The Happening*'s surface not as the failure to achieve a convincing realism via specificity, but rather as the achievement of specific and pointed references to generality. What is more—as in "Philadelphia High School, Philadelphia," where the generality of the reference inflects the self-seriousness of the thriller into the modes of comedy and satire—the film's play with generality and type is also where it does its political thinking, as I will argue. This is in contradistinction to the overt register of thriller seriousness, where a focus on the apocalyptic toxin that simply targets the human body tends to erase social and political difference.

Consider two shots that, like the film's occasional and decontextualized shots of wind, seem not to have any connection to the plots unfolding around them, and therefore seem most acutely to expose the presence of a directorial consciousness. As Elliott is packing his bags to flee Philadelphia, the film inserts a close-up shot of the day's *Philadelphia Inquirer* on his desk, whose headline reads: "KILLADELPHIA—Murder Rates Soaring" (fig. 4.1) Later, as Elliott and other escapees take refuge in a planned community filled with unoccupied model homes, the camera lingers, as they escape, on a billboard on the outskirts of the neighborhood (fig. 4.2):

YOU *Deserve* THIS!
FUTURE SITE OF CLEAR HILL COMMUNITY
1,340 NEW DELUXE HOMES
$300,000 AND UP

FIGURE 4.1. "KILLADELPHIA" headline. M. Night Shyamalan, dir., *The Happening* (2008).

FIGURE 4.2. "YOU *Deserve* THIS!" billboard. M. Night Shyamalan, dir., *The Happening* (2008).

These shots exist in a film that is otherwise careful to exclude explicit commentary on matters of, for example, class or race, even though the narrative arc absolutely depends on such matters (for example, one way to describe the film is that it produces an epidemic in order to facilitate the white protagonists' adoption of, and marital healing by, a little brown girl—on which more later). We might ask about the particular placement of these references, not in the film's overt registers of narrative, dialogue, and plot, but rather in frames that barely register for the film's characters (a newspaper lying on a table, a billboard they run past in a panic) while being heavily visually emphasized for the film audience. Why, that is, interpose a reference to murder rates in Philadelphia at a moment when the characters are occupied with a spreading neurotoxin?

Just moments before, Elliott and his wife, Alma (Deschanel), had been consuming the news in its televised form, watching as the network's chief medical correspondent explained that "our brains come equipped with a self-preservation mechanism to stop us from harmful actions.... This new neurotoxin is basically flipping the preservation switch, blocking the neurotransmitters in a specific order, causing specific self-damaging and catastrophic effects." Or, as Alma then pithily summarizes, "It makes you kill yourself. Just when you thought there couldn't be anything more evil that could be invented." It might appear as though the newspaper headline and the medical expert on TV express a tonal difference in their approach to reporting: one sensationalizing, the other responsible and factual. It would then be Alma, the news report's consumer, who draws a melodramatic conclusion from the facts. Yet, as Alfred Hitchcock suggested, a filmmaker who aims for a melodramatic effect must employ a realist style—or, as he put it, "I use melodrama because I have a tremendous desire for understatement in filmmaking."[16] In his view, a sensational style, like that employed by the "KILLADELPHIA" headline, draws attention to its own sensationalizing desire and thus deprives its audience of the opportunity to infer its own affects (think of the utterly inflaming effect of the sober, restrained tone of true crime reporting, for example). Hitchcock's paradigmatic example of a modern melodramatic form was, in fact, the newspaper, which he believed "deals to a great extent in melodrama" with its coy use of "simple statement."

We might read the shot of the newspaper, then, relegated to the commentary space of a directorial aside, as a shot meant not to contrast but to expose the sensationalizing desires hidden in the TV news reporter's affective claim simply to present the neutral objectivity of facts. At the same time, the unprompted and unexplained insertion of a reference to an affect that a white middle-class subject in Philadelphia might experience in encountering a newspaper headline about soaring murder rates in their own city (but not in their neighborhood) suggests that the panic we see gripping the characters in the plot of this thriller is not only an appropriate response to a terrifying situation, but also part of a political species of response that exposes the salience of their class and their whiteness. This is not to say that there isn't value in reading the news, any more than to say that sometimes one might wish to see a doctor. But there is a difference between seeing the doctor as simply knowing, on one hand, and, on the other, recognizing that the play of anxiety/assurance generated in the figure's midst depends on an epistemic relationship in which the invention of the doctor as a figure of authoritative knowledge could not exist without a coeval historical invention of the "body" as a site of epistemic mystery, conveniently expressed in the language of "medicine," in which the doctor happens to locate its expertise.[17] It is, of course, typically the subjects who benefit the most from the institution's assurance effects who have a hard time recognizing the latter.

The film's exposure of a type of citizen-subject affectively and epistemically constituted by the national crisis event and by the news continues in its most conceptually brilliant sequence, in which Elliott, Alma, and a few children take temporary refuge in a newly constructed suburban model home, staged to approximate the look of real life with fake books, plastic houseplants, and tables replete with fake food. As Elliott sits down to the dinner table with one of the children, Josh, who's joined his group, the following exchange occurs:

JOSH: Why is this happening?
ELLIOTT: I don't know for sure, Josh. I read this article about the coast of
    Australia—it said they found large quantities of a primordial bacteria.
    It hadn't been around for billions of years, it just appeared in the water.
    It's toxic to humans, fishermen who come into contact with it are
    dying . . . it feels kind of similar to that, with the bees disappearing? I
    mean, I don't know, it feels like a pattern.

As he says this, his brow creased in consternation, he picks up a prop glass filled with plastic wine, swirls it, and gives it a sniff (fig. 4.3).

Elliott's modeling of an informed subject who "feels" out patterns and explanations in order to mitigate the uncertainties of the world is lampooned by the scene's setting as merely the familiar replication of a type: the middle-class cultural subject who, deprived of actual usable power, opts instead for the compensatory sovereignty of "knowing" what is true in the world, a way of grasping at some feeling of control that Elliott had

FIGURE 4.3. Elliott sniffs a glass of fake red wine. M. Night Shyamalan, dir., *The Happening* (2008).

earlier called "theory." And yet *The Happening* is careful, in each of these sly and metadiscursive moments, not to dissipate the overall affects of worry and urgency in the characters' response to the putative terrorist attack, instead offering opportunities for the audience to see the film's characters and their affective attunements as elements of a political type only in the peripheral zone of directorial comment. If the film's plot models melodrama as the orthodox emotional response to national threat—such that it became almost a civic duty after 9/11 to inhabit an emotional orientation of fear, opposition, and hatred toward "terrorists" along with concomitant feelings of pride, sentimentality, and attachment to the wounds and vulnerabilities suffered by "America"—*The Happening* acknowledges the normative demand of this response to terrorism in its overt text while creating, in the directorial space of the side-eye, an interpretive zone in which the serious, concerned, and anxious response of the subject terrified by terrorism is reinscribed with its political modifiers.

The Happening, from its title onward, articulates terrorism's exposure of a class identity anchored in its possession of facts and its control of interpretation, from staging a scene of classroom interpretation immediately after the opening "attack" to its sketches of the generality of a subject of knowledge whom the terrorist event throws into a desperate need to *know*. Yet the epistemic undoing that characterizes the affective life of post-9/11 terrorist discourse in the United States is not one that affects all who live in the general ambit of the nation equally. What promoted terrorist fear after 9/11 into a national ambience was not the kind of terrorist attack aimed at punishing and terrifying a specific group already scapegoated and minoritized within the cultural mainstream—a population made vulnerable by virtue of religion, gender, sexuality, age, or race, for example. Rather, it was a form of exogenous terrorism whose precise fear effects are tied to the attack's apparent neutrality about such identity differences, instead targeting anyone who happens to be located in a particular public place at a particular moment on an ordinary day. *The Happening* follows this view: its mysterious attacks begin in Central Park and then move to the Jardin des Tuileries, the public garden outside the Louvre Museum in Paris, France. These are urban locations of identity's dispersal rather than concentration; they are public and tourist squares where, in theory, the identities or group saliences of the act's victims are relatively unpredictable. The imagery of terrorism after 9/11 is drawn from an imagination of public spaces and infrastructures: post-9/11 fear conjures up shopping malls, highways, parks, concentrated downtown hubs, subways, trains, and public services such as the postal service (the lacing of letters with anthrax delivered by US mail in October 2001 was cited in the Homeland Security Act of 2002, along with the plane hijackings, as the grounds for the establishment of the permanent Department of Homeland Security).[18]

But even when a terrorist attack directed against the West appears to be relatively indifferent to the precise complement of its victims, simply targeting an accessible public space, it is nevertheless an identity attack—but not an attack *on* a particular identity, that is, on a specific group that is already vulnerable to violence on the basis of a collective mark. The apparently indifferent and random terror attack is, rather, an attack on identity itself as a social difference machine. It is an attack that targets those who thought identity would be a protection against violence, and so the terrorist attack attacks the concept of identity itself—class identity, racial identity, sexual identity, and so on—as an originary way of separating and reinforcing those who are normally and those who are exceptionally subjected to violence. The rise of cities and the demands of increased production that necessitated the importation of ethnic difference, which is then regulated as part of a class system that is segmented spatially in time and place, creating zones of value and risk, are part of this history.[19] Unlike the attack on an already vulnerable group, which only confirms the correct distribution of violence in society—in a way validating the original purpose of class/race/sexual segmentation and segregation, spatially and culturally—the terrorist attack attacks this very segmentation, rupturing the hard work performed by the middle class to distinguish itself from those below in every domain of their existence: in their taste in food and decor, in their commitment to "health," in their anxious concern for the "world," in their tone of voice, in their moral and intellectual pride—all of which are meant, ultimately, to validate their protection in a good life free of the ordinary violence that they know happens elsewhere, every day, to other people. Although in the film's overt text Elliott is ostensibly an everyman, an empty vessel into whom any subject anxious about terrorism can project themselves, it is the film's peritext that shows that this character is general rather than universal: it is a sketch of a subject whose claim to security in the world comes at a critical and interpretive distance, who is used to historical events' happening elsewhere (via the mediating distance of a newspaper, for example), and who presumes that the trappings of middle-class life are meant to protect him from what hurts in history.

The terrorist attack's charging of public space with the intensity of threat thus operates in relation to the affective promise of the suburban home as a guarantee of safety. We might think of the domestic horror film—whose affective locus is captured in phrases like "the call came from inside the house"—as the genre that complements terrorism's symbolic capture of public space. The horror film in which the evil force encroaches on the suburban house as a symbol of protection and safety is an expression of the anxious underside of the dream of upward mobility, of the magical protective circle that heterofamilial home ownership is supposed to extend, in the latter half of the twentieth century, to the subject who wins at life, instead of being defeated by it.[20] Even the teenage sex-slasher films that emerged in the 1970s, in which the threat of violent death looms over the suggestion of nonreproductive, nonmarital sex, can be seen as part of the disciplining apparatus of productive and reproductive citizenship. The terrorist threat is the negative image of the domestic horror film: whereas the latter exposes what is anxious in the middle-class good-life dream of retreat to the privacy of the home, the former captures what becomes of its obverse, public life: of the role that infrastructures and imaginations of the public play in the symbolic apparatus of the wanted American life.

Thus *The Happening* follows a long narrative arc from the dense publics of the city to, eventually, the radical isolation of the nuclear family. As Elliott and Alma, along with Elliott's colleague Julian (John Leguizamo) and his daughter, Jess (Ashlyn Sanchez), join in a mass exodus from the East Coast, trying to outrun the widening edge of the mysterious epidemic, it becomes clear that the toxin, whatever its origin or epidemiology, appears to be drawn to *concentrations* of people. Or, as a soldier they encounter along the way explains it, "They're attacking populations. We need to go where there aren't that many people." When a realtor in the group mentions an undeveloped area nearby that isn't recorded on maps, the soldier says, "There's no significant population there. That's our safe zone." In the threat environment of terrorism, what matters is the presence not of people but of populations, as the line graphs and dots on abstract maps they encounter in news reports along the way seem to demonstrate.[21] Identifying the concept of the population itself as the toxin's target, Elliott and his coterie attempt to flee any place where they might be counted in a numerical aggregate: the movie's itinerary takes them from concentrated urban centers to arterial roads that lead to small towns, from which country paths lead them further still into undeveloped lands. At the end of the story, they come across a house where a reclusive old woman lives. She's off the power grid, without even a radio to receive news of the world, and the film implies that her rejection of the outside world is the reason for her survival. But when the toxin arrives even here, the owner succumbs to the wind, leaving only a domestic triangle: Elliott, Alma, and Jess, the little brown girl whose parents had succumbed to the toxin along the way.

The film thus draws a line from its opening in two different "publics"— the public park and the public school—to the cadential triad of the nuclear family, which finds itself in an anachronistic and spatially removed relation to the rest of society. In the toxin plot's final sequence, before the deflation of the film's coda, Elliott is in the main house and Alma and Jess are holed up in a springhouse in the yard where, the owner had explained to them, "they used to hide people from slave chasers." The springhouse is notable for a "speaking tube" that connects it to a room in the main house, which transmits voices in a way that makes it seem "like you were in the same room." From the distance of the two houses, Elliott and Alma talk and reminisce, freed, as in the psychoanalytic hypothesis, of sight's anchoring effects on the here and now. Elliott then declares that if they are going to die, he wants to die with her. He walks out of the house and into the wind. Alma, holding Jess's hand, also walks outside and toward Elliott. As they draw together and touch, the wind whipping around them, the string underscore reaching elegiac heights, the slow coming-together of bodies in space quasi-allegorical, the film cuts to an empty shot of landscape, tagged with a location and time stamp (fig. 4.4).

What is the effect of the clinical noting of time and place here, as if the moment were being tagged by a metatextual figure, archiving it for later retrieval? We will eventually hear Elliott speculate, some moments later, that "the event must have ended before we went out there." But at the moment that the film audience sees the time and location stamp, this is not yet evident. The stamp implies that something worth noting happened at precisely 9:58 a.m., without specifying anything about what it might be. Without an explanation, it induces only the feeling of eventness, of a shift into the space of recorded history and memory, sensed, perhaps, as one would sense a shift in the direction of the wind.

FIGURE 4.4. Time and location stamp, stamping nothing. M. Night Shyamalan, dir., *The Happening* (2008).

This final stamp—which seems to stamp nearly nothing in the film's representational register—captures instead what terrorism's threat reveals about how the ordinary American subject imagines aesthetically their relation to history, as well as the distance between historical event and the banality of the everyday. The terrorist threat that suddenly introduces risk into the very crannies of the ordinary that were supposed to be history-free zones of nonevent exposes the presence of protections that had until now been implicit. Suddenly nowhere is safe, not the streets, not the parks. Suddenly the subject emerges from the cocoon of that juridical and affective inheritance known as privacy. Ironically, the middle-class white subject now finds himself a statistic, or at least statistical; we might see the casual and parenthetical reference to slavery as a gesture that momentarily brings the shadow of political history over the toxin plot. Like the romantic subject who might say or feel, when love's plot finally picks them up as one of its protagonists, that "it's finally *happening* to me," the film shows that the subject formed from terrorism also lives across the line of before and after: a before that is not timeless but outside of the official sequentiality of the time of history, in which one lives one's ordinary life, and an after in which that ordinary life on the peripheries of history is now thrown into the arena of event, of the space that rises to the notice and accounting of the news. Romantic and terrorist narratives after the fact often start the same way: "I was just minding my business when, out of the blue . . ."; "the day started out like any other. . . ." The historical interrupts not only because it is sudden, but also because it introduces linear time as such, the time of plot, into the comfortingly familiar idling of something that is thought of as the ordinary or the everyday. The subject feels the shift between two time states, the "just-another-day" of life before the event and the public world of collective, historical time that makes a mark in the official record (even if the tradition of announcing one's engagement or wedding in the newspaper wanes, modern romantic subjects are still inclined to say "I have news" when reporting on romantic events).

While, in *The West Wing*, the intrusions of history were still distant enough to feel ennobling, as in the president's speech that figures, in its spreading underscore, the filtering of political event into a sense of larger purpose and connection that the ordinary citizen might enjoy and then leave behind as they return to their everyday world, *The Happening* shows historical event to be much closer to the ordinary American and much less reliably mediated and interpreted by official canons of knowledge and authority. The exogenous terrorist attack's agnosticism of time and space, in taking the fantasmatic whole of "America" as its target, now threatens to interrupt the ordinary citizen's sense of the everyday at any given moment. Under such conditions, theory might emerge as a frantic interpretive activity that attempts to install knowledge and foreknowledge as stable anchors against the predictability that has been stolen from the future—for, as the film's coda implies, no one knows when or where history will strike again.

Personhood and the Cliché: Non-Stop

In the atmosphere of the always possible statistical threat that permeated the mainstream US sense of a privileged ordinariness in the early twenty-first century, melodrama surged both as an in situ resource for interpreting the always unfinished story of the present and as a popular commercial idiom that delivered, in the span of a sitting, symbolic resolutions that remained necessarily deferred in the actuality of political experience. But in the attempt, in both professional politics and popular narrative entertainment, to propose melodrama as a form of logic still capable of processing contemporary crises, gaps emerge in the application of genre to problems in the present that expose historical presumptions about the relations between subjectivity, interiority, virtue, and expression. Even if we take melodrama's basic structure to have remained unchanged since the eighteenth century, a genre or a mode's endurance depends on its ability to continue to deliver affective and material explanations for historical conditions and crises as they emerge over time—conditions that, in different times and places, are liable to produce different stresses, and different kinds of stress, on different parts of the formula.[22]

Consider certain observable shifts in the mode as melodramatic political discourse became coarticulated with the closed narrative forms of melodramatic audiovisual entertainment in the post-9/11 United States. A week after the Sandy Hook Elementary School shooting on December 14, 2012, Wayne LaPierre, CEO of the National Rifle Association, broke his organization's silence by delivering some remarks at a media event in Washington, DC. In doing so, he introduced a line that would travel the subsequent decade in American professional politics, passing nearly verbatim from speech to speech:

> Now, we must speak . . . for the safety of our nation's children. Because for all the noise and anger directed at us over the past week, no one—nobody—has addressed the most important, pressing and immediate question we face: How do we protect our children right now, starting today, in a way that we know works? The only way to answer that question is to face the truth. . . . The only thing that stops a bad guy with a gun is a good guy with a gun.
> WAYNE LAPIERRE, *December 21, 2012*[23]

> And President Trump has urged leaders across America to follow the example of states like Indiana, and allow qualified school personnel, on a voluntary basis, to carry concealed weapons. Because the quickest way to stop a bad guy with a gun is a good guy with a gun.
> VICE PRESIDENT MIKE PENCE, *May 4, 2018*[24]

> We know that the only way to stop a bad guy with a gun is a good guy with a gun. Now, I wanted to be a little bit more original than to use a phrase that you probably heard a thousand times. But what's a better phrase than that? We can't do better. How simple is that?
> PRESIDENT DONALD TRUMP, *April 26, 2019*[25]

As the line circulates, its freshness starts to take on the contours of a conventionality, eventually becoming what Donald Trump calls "a phrase." And so, when he amends the phrase by introducing it with the words "we know," he might be claiming, as LaPierre did, that we know the phrase's logic to be true, that it describes a solution that "we know works." But in the semantic world of professional politics, where repetition carries an authorizing force, Trump could also be invoking his audience's memory of the phrase itself, which it has "probably heard a thousand times." Hence the note of impatience that can also be carried in "we know," as in "we know, *we know*"—a response, sometimes frustrated, sometimes abashed, that claims to place the work and meaningfulness of knowing in the past.

But in politics and elsewhere, the apparent confidence of canned wisdom cannot entirely mask a temporal relation to knowledge that is much more precarious and unstable. Trump declares that "we know that the only way to stop a bad guy"—as in, because we already know it, you don't need me to say it again. But this confidence is undermined by the stark fact that the phrase does still need to be repeated at event after event, that its work of insisting a reality into existence is not yet finished. The potency of the phrase lies in the fact that it does not really originate with a speaker but is born from the trail it leaves as it travels across its many invocations, transforming repetition (I've heard this before) into common sense ("We know . . ."). But repetition alone doesn't make a phrase real. While the phrase claims to describe the world as it exists, it must also remain hypothetical, because the politician only needs the phrase's anchoring when the problem that it addresses is still ongoing and unfinished. When clichés are offered as wisdom, they seem to promise that a situation's outcome is knowable and predictable. Yet a cliché is also only needed in situations where it might turn out not to be true. What is tired and repeated in the cliché is not only a failure to be original but a resource, as if it were trying to lend its own predictable and unsurprising form to the unknowable situation it addresses.

One place where the solutions proffered in political phrases can be tested in advance of their (perhaps never fully realized) implementation in the world is narrative cinema, since its task is to produce fictional worlds in which an idea can be followed through to its end while governed by the genre's laws of realism and consequence. For instance, "the only way to stop a bad guy with a gun is a good guy with a gun" is essentially a plot description of the 2014 action-thriller *Non-Stop*, released two years after LaPierre first introduced the phrase.[26] In the film, Liam Neeson plays Bryan Mills, a US air marshal who must thwart a terrorist plot on a plane in mid-flight. In a pivotal scene, Mills finds himself accused by the plane's passengers of having masterminded the plot, in part because of a live news report piped into the cabin that exposes his apparently shady past, which includes a dishonorable discharge due to alcoholism. With the plane's consensus turned against him, Mills delivers a speech that ends: "Everything you've heard about me is true. I've lost my family, my job; I'm an alcoholic . . . I'm not a good father. I'm not a good man. I am not hijacking this plane. I'm trying to save it. And I will save it if you work with me." When the "I" appears in the speech, a warm string tone enters softly in the soundtrack. The effect on the people in the cabin is immediate: a passenger who had been holding Marks under the barrel of his gun hands him the weapon, transforming him, quite literally, into a good guy with a gun. The passengers who had just moments before suspected Marks of being a terrorist now suddenly take him as their leader, without discussing amongst themselves or even making eye contact with one another to confirm their collectively changed tune.

What happens when the film attempts to demonstrate the truth of the political phrase in narrative time? It turns out that the film uncovers a problem that the political speeches cited earlier do not anticipate: in the suddenness and chaos of a terrorist threat, how does one determine if the "guy" with a gun is good or bad? The melodramatic formula of good and bad guys has always depended on the expectation that virtue is an intrinsic and essential state (that is, one is either good or bad, authentic or deceptive), and that political and social repair depend on the capacity for this state to be known, both by oneself and by others. This is an expectation that is complicated, if not entirely unprecedented, in scenes of contemporary terrorist threat, where the audience for a public event is united not by their shared membership in a court, or their national or political affiliation, but simply by their unpredictable copresence in the time and place of an attack. In the crisis temporality of terrorist response, after all, there is little time for deliberation or for the inconvenience of different views. Though we might say, following the plot, that Marks's speech manages to persuade a mistrustful crowd that is undecided about his virtue, persuasion would require the possibility of the other's failure to be persuaded—otherwise, we would have to call it something else, such as mind control. It would be more accurate to say that the speech replaces the scene where the passengers would have to confront the question of Marks's goodness or badness, of whom to trust; the speech removes or circumvents knowledge of others as an epistemic problem. The melodramatic fantasy of the good guy who reliably rescues us from the bad guy presumes another, more essential fantasy: of the transparency of the inner self, of virtue as something knowable, decisive, and automatic.

In the application of genre to the uncertainties of the political present, the film stumbles upon, or uncovers, the salience of an epistemic and historical question: how does one demonstrate one's virtue, or determine the virtue of others, in the forms of stranger-encounter that comprise contemporary US publics? It is in the very place where this question emerges that the film mobilizes a cliché, which fuses two kinds of expressive trope that are ubiquitous in contemporary public aesthetics: the confessional disclosure of one's identity and story of hardship and suffering, emblematized in the self-identifying formula "I am an x," and the utterly banal and familiar swell of a sentimental music cue. This cliché, the sentimentally underscored self-disclosure, crystallizes a vernacular theory of difference, structural disadvantage, self-identification, and merit and can be found dispersed across popular entertainment and advertisements that hope to hitch a ride on its empowering swell.[27] At the same time, it is a kind of aesthetic object whose very generality presents a methodological conundrum for film music analysis, or at least approaches to film music that focus on detailing the musical specificities of cues—their instrumentation, their form, their harmonic and melodic content, or their references to concepts, persons, objects, or other music within and beyond the film. There is instead a sense in scenes of sentimentally underscored self-disclosure that the particular musical details, beyond a general lyrical swell, don't much matter, or rather that they are not something that will lead to an understanding of what matters most—in fact, that what is important about the function of music in such scenes is not anything that can be found through musical analysis.

The sense that the analytic particularity of the cue is not what is most essential to its function in the scene also suggests that its purpose will not primarily be mimetic—that is, to index specific feelings, atmospheres, moods, or elements in the fiction's world. Instead, the cliché's appearance at a moment that exposes epistemic stresses on the melodramatic formula within the film's plot indicates a different aspect of the soundtrack's function. To prove that the good guy with the gun is the "quickest way"—in Mike Pence's version of the phrase—to neutralize unpredictable public violence, what is needed from film music is its epistemic promise to make virtue a knowable and sensible thing, rendering it as a vibration that others can sense from and in you, setting aside for good the question of your goodness. The political salience of film music's evocation of feeling in the scene is therefore not primarily its specification of *what* or *which* feeling. Rather, it is the soundtrack's operation as a technical infrastructure for an epistemically accessible interiority.

Two strains of film music writing that have engaged the idea that the audiovisual structure of commercial film music reflects an outline of the subject that encounters it come from psychoanalysis and the materialist critique of mass culture. Yet psychoanalytic approaches to the film underscore generally presume a universal narrative of subject formation and tend to lack language for the historical emergence of specific subjective forms. At the same time, the strain of film music analysis that inherits a Marxist material critique of mass culture often presumes an ideal subject who can see through and resist the indoctrinating and homogenizing forces of mass entertainment. This frame for thinking about film music and ideology, in lacking a language for conventional pleasure that leads anywhere other than damage, also fails to recognize one of its own historical presumptions, which is its implicit placement of the independent and critical subject at the end point of theory.[28]

These approaches relate the particular force of commercial film music to certain totalizing schemas of modern subjectivity, namely those of psychoanalysis and the commodity form. But the vague and sentimental bath of film music that enters with Marks's confession isn't a simple assertion of the subject's universality, even if it marks the fantasy of affective convergence in a body politic. Rather, its invocation of a minoritarian trope of self-identification evokes the tension between originality and type, between truth and strategy, and between authenticity and the copy that striates contemporary questions in politics and aesthetics. It is a tension that is evident, for example, when Trump grudgingly and reluctantly opts for "a phrase that you probably heard a thousand times" because, as he admits, he "can't do better." This is a matter of some anxiety for Trump, a speaker whose aesthetic appeal is rooted in an idea of spontaneous and unscripted authenticity. Yet in spite of his commitment to originality as a subjective ideal, Trump seems to expose that there are times when the contemporary political subject might want to be a type rather than an original, when a canned phrase might do something that a new and interesting one could not.

In particular, the line "I'm an alcoholic" raises the question of the kind of audience that the passengers in the cabin represent, and therefore of the kind of speech act that addresses them. We might ask, for example, if the connotatively powerful phrase "I'm an alcoholic" suggests that the film here imagines Marks's fellow Americans to be a collective, like Alcoholics Anonymous—a group of strangers united by one difference. In this context, to say "I'm an alcoholic" is to speak to a room that is presumed to include similar others, such that the declaration of a particularity is simultaneously a gesture of joining. Or—if we consider the passengers' suspicion of Marks until he puts his sins into speech, performing his self-awareness and repentance to a body with the power to decide his fate—might he not be saying the words to an identified in-group, but rather exposing himself to a normative world in which his difference shows up as a detail that must be confessed? What kind of public, what genre of group, are the people who are formed into a collective by a terrorist attack?

It is this essential anxiety about public life in the contemporary United States that the invocations of melodrama in this section's opening speeches are meant to assuage. When you are out in the still-possible stranger spaces of the early American twenty-first century (before total privatization, before the complete defunding and rezoning of public parks, in the intermixing zones of planes and trains, or the unchosen family of in-person work) and a terrorist event shifts your sense of the day from a background ongoingness to something that is happening, what will the strangers around you be to you? Are they united by the empathic presumption that all persons under the umbrella of a subordinating force will share an inner felt sameness, and therefore belong a priori to an affective community? Or are they a normative public to whom one has to declare one's difference in order not to present a threat (as in the nation-state question "Anything to declare?")?

In other words, to dismiss the underscored scene of speech as simply an overused and predictable aesthetic trope is to misunderstand the demand of knowledge that it exists to address. To accuse something of being a cliché is to express the wish that it were more original, which is to say more attuned to the freshness of the instance, instead of forcing its details into a premade container of sense. Yet the challenge to which the self-declarative statement implicitly responds is not only a challenge of specification; it is also epistemological. Film music as a modern technical apparatus of feeling exists not only to explain or express what a character or an audience is or should be feeling at any moment, but also to address and resolve the epistemic problem of interiority and feeling as knowable by others in the first place.

Feeling's utility, then, lies not only in its specifying and differentiating function among a range of feeling states, in the way that early silent-film piano scores would categorize cues according to mood and situation; nor is it only something felt by individuals or found floating in a room, as tone or charge. In *Non-Stop*, it is also a solution invoked by the film when melodrama is called up yet again to be the narrating form of a contemporary crisis, but that—in its attempt to anticipate and neutralize the future terrorist happening—encounters the question of the stranger in contemporary American public worlds. In response to this question, feeling enters as a concept and a promise about interiority and its capacity to be known, rendered, and felt, which allows its hero to overcome the question of conviction and proceed to the third act's solution. Feeling as a metonym for subjectivity has always performed this epistemic function in melodrama and sentimentality, but the particular stresses of the terrorist threat on the time and space of modern encounter further expose the burdens of signification placed on feeling, at the fissures where genre meets the historical situations that it is supposed to clarify.

The Happening, in fact, offers a figure for thinking of film music's work not as mimetic or representational, but as addressing the epistemic anxiety of the interiority of its subjects. The figure is a mood ring. We first encounter it when the camera lands on the newspaper with the headline "KILL-ADELPHIA"; just above it, slightly blurred, is a smaller headline that reads "THE POWER OF MUSIC." The mood ring, lying next to the newspaper, is what draws Elliott (and the camera) to the newspaper as he picks it up and puts it on. He will later explain to Jessi, the little girl, in a quiet moment during their escape from the city, what the ring does: "You know that everyone gives off energy, right? It's scientifically proven. They've got these cameras that can record what color you are when you're feeling different things. People that are angry give off a different color than people that are sad. You see this ring? This ring can supposedly tell you what you're feeling. Let's see what you're feeling right now." Jessi puts the ring on, and Elliott tells her that the ring's yellow means that she's about to laugh. Of course, she does. We see here that Elliott, whose dopey literalness is so often the film's way of capturing subjectivity's intense typification and unoriginality, now demonstrates a rare moment of irony. He tells Jessi one thing, that the mood ring—like the popular cinematic soundtrack itself—is purely denotative, a passive medium meant to illustrate in color the different things that people might feel. Yet this explanation of the ring's function is merely a ploy; in reality, he uses the mimetic alibi to induce in Jessi the unambiguity of laughter. Up to this point Jessi's face has been blank, not expressing much; Alma had told her earlier that they were both people who didn't like to show their emotions. We might imagine how a child might feel in this moment, which is to say that we might imagine the distance between what a child "feels" internally and the capacity for its expression or translation into public language. And yet the ring's real power turns out to lie not in its representative capacity, its one-to-one mapping of feelings to colors (as Alma later asks, "What's the color for love?"). Rather, Elliott uses it as a tool to produce the specificity of a feeling by naming it, and thereby securing the emotive capacity of the one who expresses it. The cliché of film music is less a failure to achieve the originality demanded by subjectivity than an assurance that the interiority of others is still knowable and available in the stranger spaces of contemporary life, that something like the recognition of an other's inner world is still durable enough as a fantasy to circumvent terrorism's reformulations of space and time. The relief the ring provides, for the one who beholds it, is the promise that the inner life of others, no less or more than of oneself, is as certain and knowable as color.

Even a derivative commercial thriller like *Non-Stop*, then, is unable simply to be a vehicle for an ideological formula like the phrase about the good guy. Even this debased aesthetic object must still attempt to realize the truth of the phrase in narrative time, clothing it in the specificities of backstory, setting, character, and plot. The film runs the ideology's formula like a string of computer code, and in so doing it snags in places that then prompt improvisations in the film's form to keep the genre's symbolic sequence intact. It is in these improvisations and compensations that the genre's relation to its historical context can be detected, for it is in these moments that the gap between the present and the genres that exist to make sense of it can be felt.

Race After the "Postracial" Terrorist Film

It has been my claim so far that as terrorism took root in the mainstream imagination of the United States around the turn of the millennium, it exposed and expressed, in the cultural objects that attempted to take stock of it, everydayness as an aesthetic form sheltered from the external world where news, event, and history take place. What was exceptionally gripping and threatening about terrorism as a form of violence was its threat, in taking the West as its object, to what we might broadly call "identity" as a mechanism of the distribution of violence, separating out zones of society where protections and vulnerabilities can compound and aggregate. Thus, the terror attack that targets public space and public infrastructure, in its apparent indifference to the *kind* of victim it will produce, shatters the exemption that some citizens assume protects them from being considered part of a population at risk. In cultural documents that attempt to capture atmospheres of citizenship around and after 9/11, such as *The Happening* and *The West Wing*, some characters encounter historical event as an interruption of private life figured as a zone of unmetered, absorbed, and ahistorical intimacy, a zone whose existence relies on institutions such as the nation to be the bearers of historical responsibility and memory.

Something seems to shift in the status of institutional authority, however, between the American crises of 2001 and 2020—between the terrorist attacks by foreign actants and the COVID-19 pandemic that "enters" the nation from abroad. This shift shows up in certain movements in the life of genre. For one, whereas melodrama was *the* major genre of the US reception of the 9/11 attacks, melodrama was a comparatively minor genre—though still present, in the demonization of China as the infiltrating agent, for example—in US discourse around the COVID pandemic. By contrast, conspiracy, which was a minor genre in 2001 (emblematized in phrases such as "9/11 was an inside job"), became a major genre during the pandemic, as the antistate position solidified around identity forms such as the "anti-vaxxer" in numbers nonnegligible enough to pressure national bodies into ceding official language and strategy to the conspiracists.

The difference in the weight borne by each genre could certainly be a response to the different aesthetic qualities of each crisis, from the spectacularity of plane crashes to the shadowy insinuations of a virus. Yet whatever the reasons for this genre shift, it bookends a phase of national history in which the authority assumed by president and nation in the melodramatic narration of 9/11 arrives, twenty years later, at another national crisis in which the implicit authority of the official can no longer be assured of the same guarantees. This shift corresponds to changes in the aesthetic figuration of conspiracy theory, too. In the early 2000s the images most often associated with conspiracy theorists included tinfoil hats and walls plastered with evidence, question marks, and the taut strings and lines between them that show the work of thinking and interpretation.[29] This was a figure not of ignorance (far from it) but rather of "craziness"; its neurodivergence was seen as a conduit of "genius" that allowed this figure to see through the indoctrinations of the mainstream. In this archetype, the aim was usually not to engage with the world, but to retreat from it or to bring it to an end. The conspiracist of the 2000s was an end-times figure who siloed themselves from society in order to see through the current organization of world, and whose existence was a portent of the world's next form. It is quite a contrast, I think, to remember how social it could look to be a conspiracy theorist in 2020: if the conspiracy theorist in 2001 invokes the prepper who bunkers down in the hope of weathering the end of the world, in 2020 it is the figure of the group that bands together with those who still retain their minds to exit the bunker and feel their strength against a hopelessly infected population.[30]

We might call these two archetypes the "academic" and the "activist." Though the activist figure seems less defeated, its aims are also more modest: the antistate actors who attacked the US Capitol on January 6, 2021, spurred by the theory of a stolen election, had no plan to bring down the existing structure of power so that they could institute their own, but rather wanted just to feel themselves against it a little, to hijack the official's presumption of being untouchable. The contrarian position that delights in its contrarianism, after all, in a way acknowledges and affirms the centrality of the place of power. It is here that the more recent form of conspiracy theorist invokes the figure not of genius but rather of ignorance, in Eve Sedgwick's sense, which refers not to an actual lack of knowledge but rather to a cunning and deliberate posture that protects one's desire to remain the same while placing the burden of responsibility on the one who "knows."[31] As conspiracists destabilized the official and objective status of facts, the phrase "I believe in science," which emerged as a response and a defense of rationality and medicine, in effect conceded that the conspiracists were successful in shattering the possibility of objective truths by removing science into the domain of faith. In an ironic twist, the graduation of conspiracy theory from an isolating to a social genre in 2020 forced the conspiracists' opponents back into the language and mode of the earlier form of conspiracy—of which an emblem might be the phrase, found on an iconic poster in the 1990s alien conspiracy television show *The X-Files* (and then later the subtitle of one of its spinoff films), "I Want to Believe."

In popular film, meanwhile, this shift in the respective statuses of melodrama and conspiracy could be felt in the fact that the hero played by Liam Neeson in the 2014 film *Non-Stop* could no longer automatically assume the role or appoint himself in it, unlike the terrorism-fighting protagonist he had played in *Taken* six years earlier. In *Taken*, Neeson's Bryan Mills (who shares initials, as well as a vaguely generic-sounding English name, with *Non-Stop*'s Bill Marks) is an ex–government agent whose meticulous habits and overzealous concern for safety might have served him well in crisis situations, but that cause him to flounder in ordinary civilian life, especially in his relationships with his ex-wife and daughter, who call his tendencies paranoid.[32] Emasculated by his ex-wife's new husband and pitied by his daughter, the movie sees him withdraw into the comfortable but static social sphere of his ex-military brotherhood, where, it seems, he is content to live out his days. The movie sees him as an object both of pity and of admiration, a martyr figure who is denied the approval of women that would reconnect him to narrative and life but whose voluntary celibacy we are supposed to understand as noble because it is undertaken in the name of national sacrifice (consider the mix of pity and pride one imagines an audience is supposed to feel when his ex-wife tells him, "You sacrificed our marriage in service of our country").

But when terrorists kidnap his daughter, he undergoes an abrupt and total transformation. Suddenly his need for complete control, his lack of flexibility and feeling, and his rigid inability to adapt and change are no longer signs of his social underdevelopment and causes of his social martyrdom; now, in the unfolding emergency, they are assets. Once shunted to the social periphery, he is suddenly again at its center, needed and looked up to by his ex-wife and her husband. We might observe how the brown threat of exogenous terrorism restores and revivifies the white male subject to the center of things, in a world, perhaps, where his traditional strength and his zealous control were cultural commodities that seemed to be on the way out. It would not be an exaggeration to describe the effect of brown men on white men as erotically energizing, as we see Neeson's listless body spring gorgeously into kineticism.

Mills's former employment with the government unites him with Bartlet as figures of national paranoia, which the appearance of terrorism justifies and ratifies retroactively as a necessary and sensible mode. In the *West Wing* episode "Mr. Willis of Ohio," when Bartlet's daughter, Zoey, chafes against her inability to have a normal life under Secret Service scrutiny, her father excoriates her by detailing with painful precision the things that *could* happen if she were kidnapped by terrorists (an eventuality that would come to pass later in the series).[33] Paranoia segues neatly into condescension: he then tells her, in the ennobling tones he had earlier used to relate the Cuban refugee crisis to his staffers, that the life she has not chosen as his daughter is a privilege for which she should not hesitate to pay the price of her privacy. Chastened, Zoey smiles, now seeing things from her father's point of view, and offers him a quiet "You're right" and "I'm sorry." In other words, neither *The West Wing* nor *Taken* has a concept that, for example, young women might have a particular epistemic access to the threats of the public world. Instead, both see the daughter figures as wanting simply to have a good time—that is, to not be encumbered by history—and as impatient with their fathers' risk calculation and insistence on the dangers of the world ("Mom says your job made you paranoid," Mills's daughter says to him, to which he replies, "It didn't make me paranoid. It made me aware"). It is the brown threat, in both cases, that converts the male impulse to control and protect young women into a legitimate and sensible response, for which the daughters express gratitude that someone had held this awareness of the world in the face of their desire simply to have fun in it.

As Jonathan Kay discovered in his study of what he calls the "age of conspiracy" after 9/11, conspiracy theorists diverged wildly in their accounts of what happened that day, but what they agreed on is that the *official* account could not be trusted.[34] The kind of implicit authority that Bartlet and Mills are able to claim in the 2000s as avatars of the state is thus precisely the kind of authority that conspiracy theorists sought to undermine. In *Non-Stop*, however, the terrorists turn out to be American citizens who were disappointed by the insufficiency of the state's security measures after 9/11; their aim is to execute a terrorist attack during a flight on which a US air marshal—literally an official of the state—is a passenger. The villains in *Non-Stop* are therefore related to conspiracy theorists in their desire to undermine the implicit authority of the official as a stabilizing social force. Their aim, too, is not to replace it with a better official form but simply to shake it a little, exposing its institutional solidity as an invention masquerading as an essential truth.

The modification of the terrorist figure between 2008 and 2014 thus expresses another challenge that the commercial terrorism film had to address. In the more immediate aftermath to 9/11, the Manichean framing of an America united in its feelings of hurt and anger at the terrorists and their heinous acts rendered readings of imperialism or racism inapposite, coincidental, or perhaps even accurate but excusable in the face of the heinous moral breach that the attacks represented. In *Non-Stop*, however, we might see the film's ideological task differently: to continue to process, for its intended audience, existence in an atmosphere of terrorist threat (and of the exposures of identity that such attacks threaten) while also managing this audience's desire not to feel racist. *Non-Stop*'s strategy is simply to remove brown people from the still-intact terrorist symbolic; in fact, the character who bears the strongest whiff of alien threat is Marks himself (at one point a talking head on the news notes that "this guy wasn't even born in the US. He could be IRA, for all we know").

In *The Happening*, by contrast, the racial and imperial underside of terrorist fear is managed by the white parents' immaculate conception of a brown child. We learn in the film's coda that Elliott and Alma have adopted Jess after the toxin removed her parents from the picture. Yet in the final scene with these characters, we watch the couple embrace after Alma gets a positive result from a pregnancy test. As in romantic comedy, pregnancy is used as a signifier of a future after crisis, but the fact that we never see the biologically conceived child also means that the film leaves open the reading of an inverted sequence in which the biological conception at the end pertains to the child whom the couple has already adopted. We might read, in the film ending's oddly meticulous focus on the conditions of reproduction, an acknowledgment that part of what made terrorist fear after 9/11 so quickly become the tenor of national culture was the white West's apprehension of the increasing permeability of its borders to the encroaching brownness of the world. The retroactive, biological birth of the brown child by white parents may thus be seen as a kind of symbolic attempt to incorporate and make sense of the inevitable loss of the West's white intactness.

These films' different solutions to the problem of racism in the terrorist text further demonstrate a shift from the early 9/11 period, in which the melodramatic formula could rely on the epistemic clarity of innocent Americans and evil outsiders. If, in *The West Wing*, the implicit authority of the state sheltered a texture and atmosphere of everydayness that the citizen could imagine inhabiting, the waning force of this authority over the next decade produced shifts in the symbolic status of the citizen, no less than that of the audience. For example, *Non-Stop* still invokes the figure of brown threat: as Marks moves through the airport, we see, through his professionally suspicious POV, a man wearing a kufi. He looks at many other people, and kinds of people, but the effect of the shot of a brown man in indicatively Muslim headdress in a film about terrorist attacks on a plane is to trigger, regardless of the audience member's "personal" views, awareness of a certain generically racist line of speculation.

Let us call this trope the brown herring, and add it to the archive of a US liberal aesthetic mode. The brown herring is a device in which a narrative invites a racist or otherwise unenlightened inference from its audience before then disavowing the reference in the subsequent plot, thus attributing the racist thought to the audience rather than to the production of its own form. The brown herring seems to acknowledge the husk of a defunct subject position, once endemic to the question of terrorism, but now necessarily disavowed in the film's construction of a subject position that wants to be able to experience its fear of terrorism as a threatening agent, while at the same time being protected from considering its own racism (and, of course, both of these positions obscure the possibility that one might understand the entirely valid fear of terrorism as inseparable from the fear of the crumbling of one's invisible subject protections). The symbolic structure animating *The West Wing* and *Taken*, in which the white man is innervated by the brown threat to a young white woman, is thus transferred to a different set of locations in the postracist terrorist cultural text (figs. 4.5a and 4.5b).

In the face of the virtuous citizen's complex need both to retain and disavow their sense of the threat of the encroaching brown world, the virtuous symbolic of race and gender that animates the melodramatic response to 9/11 now transfers into the spectatorial relation between the aesthetic text and its audience. The film introduces a brown figure, only to remove it from consideration, at which the audience might breathe a sigh of relief—thank goodness, the terrorist won't be a brown man, which would spoil, or at least complicate, the catharsis of the hero's achievement. Or the audience might feel shame, as if they had initiated the thought of terrorism, rather than this thought's having been an effect of film technique. In both triangles, the brown figure enters into a relation with some passivized figure (the film audience/white women), after which the agent in control (the film/the white man) neutralizes the inciting agent, producing an affective response in the passive figure of chastisement, perhaps relief, perhaps gratitude.

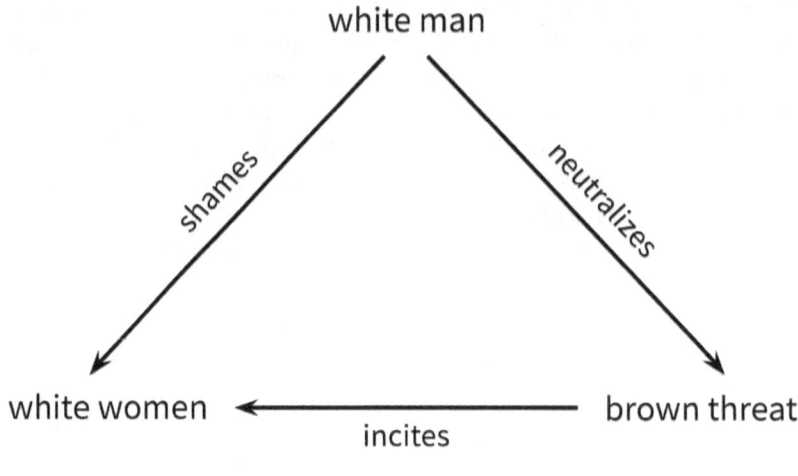

FIGURE 4.5A.

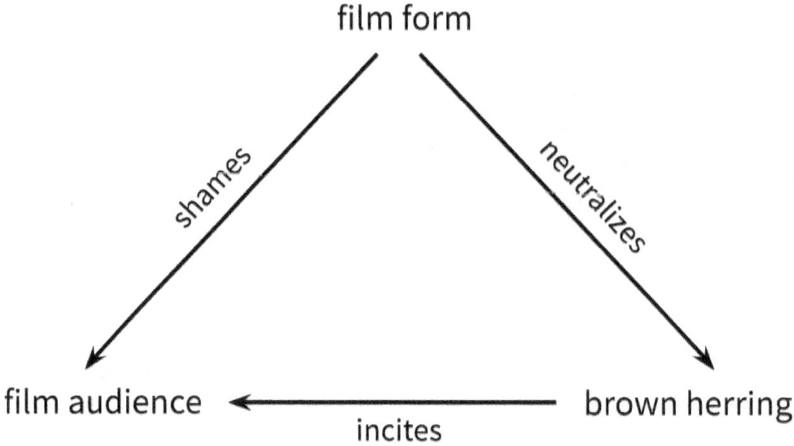

FIGURE 4.5B.

The postracial terrorist text therefore preserves an energetic economy in which brownness retains its position and function, even if the alignment of virtue with specific identity positions is more muddled than before. The loss of these dependable certainties is reflected elsewhere, too, such as in the death of Marks's daughter before the start of the plot. The unrecoverable daughter figure makes this terrorist narrative elegiac and melancholic rather than heroically redemptive, as does the portrayal of the terrorists as patriotic (if perhaps misguided) American citizens who were themselves victims of the 9/11 attacks. Moral binaries of good and evil are still necessary for surviving and managing public life, but their conferral is no longer automatic or clear. Rather, this conferral now hinges on a matter of speech, which is no longer in the sovereign mode of President George W. Bush's remarks after 9/11 ("Make no mistake: The United States will hunt down and punish those responsible for these cowardly acts") or in *Taken*'s best-remembered lines ("I will look for you, I will find you, and I will kill you"),[35] but rather come in an autobiographical confessional mode that locates the self at the juncture of a series of types ("I've lost my family, my job; I'm an alcoholic . . ."). It is as if the unassailable certainty of a villain, which had sustained the sense of US innocence and victimization in the period immediately after 9/11, could only avert the imperative to look inward for so long. As this version of Liam Neeson's hero finds that he can no longer assume, but must earn, the authority to act on behalf of the nation, the speech that earns this authorization is one that mobilizes autobiography in the general mode. What his audience recognizes, what they see and hear in him that is enough to dispel the stain of the outsider, is an invocation of domestic and personal experience broad enough that anyone, in theory, could see themselves in his shoes. Melodrama's recognition of the needed American hero, in other words, becomes possible only through the texture and the sound of generality—that is, through an encounter with the details of the other's life at a distance where its singularities seem to blur into common property.

Hold Music, General Forms, and the Lyric Ordinary: Kajillionaire

Kajillionaire is about Old Dolio Dyne, a twenty-seven-year-old white American woman who, along with her parents, Robert and Theresa, manages to live in present-day Los Angeles via a seemingly endless repertory of grifts and scams.[36] A particular focus of theirs is the kind of financial device that, in the face of the capitalist problem of fully extracted populations, shifts its focus instead to the extraction of time: sweepstakes, payment plans, trial periods, vague refund policies. But they also see the potential for profit in state-funded social programs and in grifting from ordinary civilians in the fuzzy zones of the social contract. If the corporation in this era arrogates the legal rights and status of personhood, this is a nuclear family conceived as a corporation, a body constituted merely by shared financial interests: when Melanie, a Latina woman who later becomes Old Dolio's love interest, first meets the family, she assumes that they are merely business partners and asks how they know each other.

Also, the film proposes hold music as a way of thinking about film music. Throughout the film, the first few instrumental bars of Bobby Vinton's "Mr. Lonely" are used as an underscore cue, floating across the plot without connecting to the entry of the voice until the very last scene, framing the entirety of the film in the anticipatory space of anacrusis. The first time the opening of "Mr. Lonely" is used in the soundtrack, Old Dolio has just attended, as part of a grift, a prenatal class titled "Positive Parenting," where she happens to learn that it might be normal to feel and want to feel nurtured by one's mother. The cue comes in as she walks out of the session and into a golden sunset, a color palette the movie always turns to whenever Old Dolio gets close to tenderness—or what her mom calls the province of "false, fakey people"—and that stands in contrast to the cool industrial blues of the airports and community centers that provide the settings for the family's grifts, and of the commercial office space they rent as a place to sleep. But this scene, which features the song's first emergence in the soundtrack, cuts immediately to Old Dolio lying later that night in the office cubicle that serves as her bedroom, a cut that also cuts out the song's higher and lower frequencies. We learn that we're listening to the flattened bandwidth of hold music piping through her phone.

The classic audiovisual trope in which a nondiegetic cue is revealed to issue from a diegetic source not only suggests a material origin for a specific cue, but can also indicate a particular medium that grounds the imaginative appearance of film music in an era of material culture. Periods of film have alternately grounded the symbolic imagination of film music's material origin in the nineteenth-century orchestra, the record player, and the radio, among other technical sources.[37] If *Kajillionaire* suggests that its inheritance of the convention of music appearing from outside the film's world is now secured or tethered by hold music as a fantasmatic cultural and material origin, what would this be suggesting?

Hold music is corporate profit maximization rendered as musical duration; it measures the precise temporal intervals that result from the calculus that weighs customer satisfaction against the least possible expenditure of resource. Neither unheard nor meant to be listened to, hold music invites a mode of partial attention in which listening is directed primarily toward monitoring the continued presence of something, which is the continued presence of an absence, before someone picks up. Meanwhile, the person on hold might cultivate their own partial and efficient practices, picking up a task that would be productive even if interrupted—folding laundry, a phone game—and that leaves enough room in the attention to register the hold music's interruption by silence, or a voice.

Hold music, in other words, is usually heard at an aural and attentional distance at which the details don't much matter. What matters is simply that there is a sonic layer there where nothing would otherwise be, a presence whose purpose is merely to assure the one on hold that there is a presence, and specifically a presence that registers an absence, and that is also recessed enough in aesthetic importance and demand that living can more or less continue, so long as the hold music's continued presence in the barely attended background assures the person that they have not been abandoned. The movie also suggests that hold music is *all* the music that Old Dolio listens to—that it's primarily because of the existence of hold music that she's familiar with music at all. Late in the film, when Old Dolio is allowing Melanie to introduce her to gestures of love that she knows from romantic pop culture but has never herself experienced, she begins to dance for Melanie by first calling a commercial line and putting their hold music on speakerphone. "They never pick up," Old Dolio explains.

Kajillionaire thus links its central family to hold music as a historical and material formation, and at the same time to a critique of the American dream that sees its class and heterofamilial ambitions as a fused jumble of incoherent promise. When Old Dolio fails to notice a new security camera in the post office where they regularly steal packages, an exchange takes place in which the father adopts a tone that aims to humiliate desire, which turns out to be a central affective tactic by which this family stays together:

ROBERT: Once your face is in their system they got you. Fines, 401k, home equity. But maybe you want all that, I don't know. Me, I prefer to just skim.
OLD DOLIO: So do I.
ROBERT: Do you? Oh, that's interesting. Because most people want to be kajillionaires. That's the dream. That's how they get you hooked. Hooked on sugar, hooked on caffeine, ha ha ha, cry cry cry! Mother-daughter getaway. How the fuck does that help us get the rent? Come on, think!

Kajillionaire locates itself in the genre of the heist movie—at different points, Melanie whispers that she feels like she's in *Ocean's Eleven* and *Mission: Impossible*—but detaches itself from the narrative cumulation of the rags-to-riches plot. If the heist movie imagines that there is some improbable amount of money—say, a kajillion dollars—that would put to an end the strangling mathematics of money, the pacing of rent, the decimal of gas, the climbing price of serotonin, the father instead names "skimming" as a way of staying afloat, especially in historical periods where traditional phrases that imagine success as a punctuated event—such as arriving, securing a future, making it—feel as comically implausible as the economic bracket of the film's title. To fail to "think," for the father, is to be lured in by an ideological and material complex so enmeshed that his account of it appears as a modernist collage of financial ambition, home ownership, nuclear family sentimentality, ordinary substance dependence, and intense emotionality itself as the co-imbricating branches of a normative system. Seen this way, bleeding relationality of its sentimentality and conceiving of the social as a space of pure transaction could well feel like protection enough.

But it is also that this family, which aims to distance itself as much as possible from the ordinariness that "most people" inhabit, thus enables the film to give this ordinariness an aesthetic and conceptual figuration. A striking example comes in a set piece from the center of the film. Melanie invites the Dynes to the home of one of her clients, an old man named Abe, in order to steal his checkbook. As they enter, Abe's voice floats in from an unseen bedroom, telling them to "make yourself at home." The mother pours herself a glass of water from the tap. "That's it," the old man calls from the other room, "Just be how you are at home. Just a normal day around the house." When Old Dolio later enters his bedroom to look surreptitiously for the checkbook, Abe gives her both unsolicited encouragement and notes on their performance: "It sounds good. Maybe some silverware clinking. Or play the piano."

To pull off the grift, in other words, Melanie and the Dynes must become actors in a scene directed by Abe. And what they are directed to do is to produce the sound of "a normal day around the house," even though none of them—Abe, Melanie, or the Dynes—can know exactly what normality or a house sounds like for any of the others, apart from the few specific instructions that Abe gives to Old Dolio. At the end of his life, Abe's last wish, it seems, is to become or to play the director, and what he chooses to direct is the sound of a normal family, heard from the distance of a hallway's length and through a half-closed door.

What do Melanie and the Dynes—the latter of whom have never been a normal family—end up producing when called upon to produce the sound of a normal day? There is the sound of getting a glass of water. Plates clinking on a counter. The TV, without beginning or end, tuned to sports. Recaps of the day asked and answered. Queries about hunger and food, in such a way that it doesn't even occur that there might not be any. At the piano Melanie begins to play an endlessly looping melody over an Alberti bass, the sustaining pedal bleeding the harmonies a little together into soft watercolor edges. The melody is a wandering, quasi-modal line that belongs to the kind of film or hold music that finds something of use in what Erik Satie found in the European classical tradition. As the camera floats away from Melanie at the piano, the endlessness of the piece suffuses the scene as the Dynes, on the set of a living room furnished in tired styles from the end of the last century, playact the dad-and-family tropes from sitcoms of the same era, but as if attempting to reconstruct the syntax of a dead language. Golf happens to be on. Old Dolio asks, "He just scored?," to which Robert replies, "Oh, he scored a one-holer." The barely remembered idioms of sports talk point to their function: what matters is not the content of what is said, but rather that sports allow for an oblique intimacy, an object of mutual absorption that facilitates being alongside in time as a way of being with.

When these characters who have never experienced the normal American family attempt to reconstruct the sound of that normalcy, they turn to the endlessness of hold music, the foley of domesticity, and the hollowed-out phrases of sports and predictable intimacy. ("You know, I think I will mow the lawn tomorrow." "You said that last weekend." "Did I?") The soundscape is one of iteration, of bad acting, and of language so ground down that all that remains is the husk of cliché. As in *The Happening*, the movie draws out and formalizes the generality of the subject that thinks of itself as merely normal, an aesthetic and habitual container that contains this lifeform from history's happening. And it works: Old Dolio senses in this soundscape of generic forms the kind of life she aspires to have. What she aspires to is, crucially, not a grandiose dream of freedom or total absorption in love, but merely the sound of life at a middle distance. It is an aspiration that focuses its normative ambition on the backgrounds rather than the foregrounds of experience, locating there a wish for sensuous fullness that's mostly there to fill the space, since an absence might disturb the mind into questions (is there someone there?). In this ordinary, there are no endings, only interruptions of the general thrum that places life both far and near enough to bear—form at a distance where it softens into ambience.

EPILOGUE
Where Nothing Happens

The accounts that fill these chapters often begin with someone who senses something missing in the fabric that embeds them in the world. Perhaps the runway of an older dream has run out, and now they find themselves suffering from plot withdrawal, like a cartoon animal whose legs pump uselessly in the air. What changes things is the arrival of a thought, perhaps taking form as a sense image, that seems to breathe the consecutiveness of narrative back into the experience of living. The idea could be a fuzzy fantasy, as it is for the romantic protagonists in chapter 2, of the world's sound dimming in response to a look across the room, a scission of foreground from background that seems also to release narrative from time as a montage gathers the future ahead into a single formal movement. It could be a jolting vision of animating purpose, of finally being that which one has never managed to be, as in chapter 3. Or, as in chapter 4, the desire to be nationally ordinary might take shape as a desire to encounter the detail of the world at a middle distance, where the inciting effects that could come from familiar and unfamiliar encounters fade out to leave behind only the general contours of ambient forms: the sound effects of domesticity, the background hubbub of a city where nothing happens, and the worn comforts of old phrases whose outlines have far outlasted their original sense, a displacement of content into form that seems to promise a life sheltered from the vulnerabilities of plot.

In this book, these moments of mediated sensation and imagination are almost always conventional, both in the trajectory of an individual life and as the expression of a collective aesthetic inheritance. As observed in chapter 3, the person who is struck by the clarifying and animating thought has almost certainly been struck by this same thought before and almost certainly will be again, even though it is crucial in the moment of the idea's reappearance that it feel like both the first time and the last time it will be needed. Conventionality doesn't feel conventional when it finally happens to you, as Berlant writes; to see conventionality as only a failure of originality or improvisation or agency or thoughtfulness is to mistake its ambition.[1] The subjects who want to be subjects within love, or ordinary national belonging, or who imagine that the aim of subjectivity is to master it and comprehend it find themselves, in the shadow of the aspiration, in an everyday that falls far short of the symbolic and narrative coherences that these fantasies promise. It is this disappointing difference that makes them long for an interpretive horizon, which might take the form of a sensory infrastructure, that could someday restore significance to the unredeemed and unaccumulating parts of existence, drawing them finally into the sunlit space of the representable.

"Someday" is the generic wish not only to be within narrative but also to be after it and in some sense above it, in a readerly position that might be figured as the narrator, the analyst, or the editor. It is the dream of a vantage point after the story from which everything that has happened and will happen can be seen, and from which significances and connections can be drawn that necessarily remain opaque in the midst of living. My claim is that normative fantasies of belonging also embed, as a structural component, a positional or spatial fantasy of taking up the place of the narrator in the text in which you are also the character, a claim that also highlights what is desirable about the epistemic fantasy of encountering, absorbing, and mastering knowledge itself. In the latter, the dreamed-of arrival that "someday" marks is often rendered as an epilogue, which announces an end to the indefinite sequentiality of a book's chapters while also implicitly promising an overview of what has come before. The epilogue, then, is located not only after but also a little above the body of the text, a position that the reader who encounters it might experience as a clearing of density into air, as the tensely stretched surface of the text's body now releases into a province of writing in which both the reader and the writer find themselves stranded with the question: "what happened (here)?"

In texts whose endings are structured around this passage, ending is also a kind of surfacing, a rise in epistemic level over the mystery whose threat had instigated the adventure. And yet, in the examples in this book, the promise of the view from the end, when it is imagined from the muddled middle, offers both a fantasy of ending that allows the person to go on while also interposing this fantasy in the referential place of "living" itself. The comforts of personhood operate similarly to the comforts of theory, in the sense that to take up the promise of either is to enter the binding between what is unfinished in the present and an image of knowing as a homecoming. And yet, for the figures in this book, the comforts that become isomorphic to the feeling of living will someday give living back as the task they're left with. After the work comes unworking as the necessary activity for uncovering the trail of your interest again.

The narratives that this book has traced generally elide what comes after the punctuating gestures of the kiss, the death, or the documentary shift to text that describes what happened to the film's real life people after the end of the story. Nevertheless, there is often still a little something. In the narrative structures of mass television and film, there is often an epilogue, after the intrigue of the plot has been wrapped up, in which nothing of importance remains to happen. Love's question has been answered, or the villain apprehended, or the bomb defused, or the championship won. And yet, the resolution of the tension that called the representation into being does not align perfectly with the end of representation as such. There is an interval, a gap of a few or five minutes, where we can sense the atmosphere and thrum of life after genre. They are minutes in which the pressure of plot finally lifts from the world, and it's as if you can see it for the first time in its natural state of repose. Characters return to the daily activities they might have been engaging in at the start of the story and before this dailiness was interrupted by the plot's crisis. Sometimes this release of tension is given a physical counterpart in the world, as in *Rear Window* (1954), whose events take place during a heat wave. Heat is the plot's accelerating agent, opening the neighbors' windows to one another and drawing them into mutual implication. When the intrigue is resolved, the heat dissipates—the first shot of the epilogue is of a thermometer, registering a cool seventy-two degrees Fahrenheit. The camera now makes its final rounds, giving a glimpse into the apartments of each of the characters who had been drawn into the complications of the plot and who are now allowed to return to the separateness of their lives. There is a sense that this is how the world will now be, forever; anyway, there is nothing left to monitor, which is why the film can end. By contrast, the heat wave that stretches across *Do the Right Thing* (1989) is still in effect when the film ends, as the voice on the radio reminds us just before the credits roll. In this film, heat is not merely an expression of the pressure that narrative exerts on a world, although it does precipitate the narrative; its atmospheric figuration is located both within the story's pattern and outside of it, which means that the end of story itself cannot clear the air, remove the conditions that set these narratives in motion.

Mostly, though, the epilogue allows one to sense the kinds of futures that genre promises to deliver, or perhaps to leave behind, after the ravages of the plot. After all, the story had to go through all that it did to earn this brief glimpse of peace and possibility, which the credits capture by cutting it off, like the shutter of a camera. But what is this photograph of—after the aspirational achievements of love, of self-knowing, of citizen-belonging, of theory, are done?

Artificial Intelligence

Steven Spielberg's *A.I. Artificial Intelligence* (2001) is about a little boy mecha named David who is programmed to serve as a surrogate child for a human family.[2] His incapacity to interpret mood and tone, or to read the cues that differentiate seriousness from the irony of play, however, leads to his expulsion from the protective circle of nuclear domesticity, outside of which he finds the world to be an unrelenting horror. In this retelling of the Pinocchio story, David spends the rest of the film trying to become a real boy, since he thinks that this will finally make the mother, Monica, love him. The film's final act takes place across a temporal cut of some two thousand years, and after the extinction of human life. Artificial life forms are still around, and they see in David the last remaining record of his long-disappeared world. They tell him that they can reconstruct his mother from a lock of hair that he still has with him, but only for one day, after which Monica will never be resurrectable in any form again.

The movie's final sequence is simply this final and ordinary day that David spends with Monica, ending as they go to bed and as the lights in the windows of their home, also recreated from David's memory, go out one by one. It is a day whose ordinariness is located in the fact that nothing dramatic happens in it: David and Monica make breakfast, draw pictures, and celebrate a birthday. That David would have endured the horrors of the plot and waited thousands of years just to experience this brief and ordinary day has made the film's coda available to antinormative critical reading. Annalee Newitz, for example, sees in the film's identification of the family space as good and the stranger world as bad the kind of conventional affective misrecognition that keeps people attached to conventionality and from becoming interested in alternatives that do not yet benefit from the familiarity effects of forms eternally repeated. In particular, they note that the ragtag band of robot sex workers and discarded older models that shelter David along the way are far more compassionate to him than the family, whose traumatic expulsion of him from their midst becomes the instigating force of the Pinocchio plot. As Newitz writes,

> It would seem that synthetic families made up of prostitutes and animals might serve children better than ones populated by human kin. That one could tease such a reading out of *A.I.* may be one reason why Steven

Spielberg tacked on his infamously hokey "David spends the day with mommy" ending.... When robots of the far future find him, they resurrect Monica for one happy day of traditional family bliss in a scene that suggests David has ascended to some kind of mecha heaven. This is the robot's reward for enduring abuse, the murder of his friends, and emotional enslavement: one day with mommy.³

The critique notes, to modify a phrase from Freud, the economic problem of normativity: how can love or family or nation be the object of such continuing idealization in the face of all the evidence and testimony otherwise, which its subjects have somehow learned to recite as an affirmation of their ongoing fidelity to its ideals, and not as an exit letter?⁴ The final line thus focuses on sentimentality's absurd math, aiming to deromanticize conventional suffering and the liveness that comes with it. In this reading, to cling to the husks of normative femininity, heterosexuality, and the family is to miss all the uncanonical beauties that might be found outside of the frame: politics in the subjunctive mood.

And yet: is David's final day with Monica really just an ordinary day of "traditional family bliss"? "One day with mommy" seems to name a child's experience of childhood. And yet several differences distinguish David's last day with Monica from the ordinary experience of a child. For one, David knows in advance that it is the only day he will get. The day is less an example of ordinarily lived ordinariness than of much rarer experiences of the intensified awareness of ordinariness: for instance, one final day together before a break-up, or a last tour of one's haunts around town before a move, or a last day before planned death. During days like these, the rehearsal of one's habitual gestures is likely to become theatrical, since the attempt to inhabit the ordinary consciously can have the effect of turning the ordinary into a performance. The person who repeats its gestures will be both a participant in the scene and also its observer, placed at a remove by their inescapable awareness of its significance. The fantasy of being fully present to ordinariness is a fantasy precisely because ordinariness and sharp aesthetic awareness are almost definitionally antonymic.

Another difference from the ordinary experience of childhood is that it is David, the child, who must keep his greater knowledge of the world beyond the scene from Monica. Before Monica is reanimated, the future artificial intelligences tell David that he cannot reveal the day's significance or the conditions by which it came to be to Monica, since "she would become frightened and everything would be spoiled." David must therefore participate in the day with Monica as if they were both equally present in it, while also keeping both his greater knowledge and the very fact that there *is* such knowledge a secret. (Monica: "What day is it?" David: "It is . . . today.") If these descriptions suggest that when David returns to the scene of childhood, he can only do so by returning in the epistemic position of the parent—that is, as the one who participates in the scene while maintaining frames of knowledge and awareness that must remain hidden—the movie also suggests that Monica now reappears in the position of the child. The difference in their epistemic positions shows up in, among other places, a little smile that crosses Monica's face when David tries to show her something of the adventure that he has been on, painting her pictures in the hope that their abstractive effect might allow her to absorb truths that he cannot explicitly tell. But Monica has no way of understanding the wider world that precedes her. When David shows her what is essentially a plot summary of the movie *A.I. Artificial Intelligence*, rendered in storyboards that recapitulate the film up to this point, Monica's expression remains blank.[5] And then, as if suddenly becoming aware of how this blankness must look, she turns up the corners of her mouth, but without the orbicularis oculi engaging the muscles around the eyes that would produce the appearance of a real, a genuine, smile.

This is, in fact, a smile we have seen before: it appears throughout the first act of the film on David's face, in scenes that are meant to show the alienating threat of his robotic affect. Monica is now a replica, in a sense, though not exactly a robot. And with this smile, the film aligns her with the robot's original way of expressing emotion, that is to say, by replicating it. What Monica's capacity for the smile reveals is that the difference between the robot and the pattern of a real human life is not located *in* this difference—that is, in the programming or the machinery. The robot smiled this way because this smile has always been a part of human life. What does the smile that doesn't reach the eyes say? It is a smile that can come because it's the best one can muster in the moment, such that its mechanicity reveals an inner state that a more human performance would conceal. For David at the beginning of the film and Monica at the end, the smile says: I don't fully understand, but go on. It acknowledges that my understanding of a scene feels deficient, which means that someone else must have a fuller understanding that has not yet been disclosed to me. At the same time, the smile may be meant to forestall the moment's transformation into a *thing*, since I may not want to bring a perturbance in my inner life into explicitness or a demand for satisfaction at this very moment; I am willing to be a character with imperfect knowledge in this scene if it means that the scene can continue.

The lyrical quality of the final day is thus both riven and made possible by a foundational epistemic difference, one that inverts David and Monica from their original occupations of the positions of parent and child. David can't talk about a past that exists before Monica's experience and comprehension, and he can't talk about the future, since he knows, in a way that Monica can't, what the future brings. Like a parent relating to a child, he can only be there with her in the present, and it is only under these conditions that the ordinariness of the day can be returned to at all. As in the fantasy of childhood that remembers it as a time free from concern, this ending requires someone to take up, quietly and in the background, the work of concern, of minding the scene as if from the outside while also participating in it, and keeping this role in the shadows to themselves.

That David can only get the child's day with mommy by returning in the epistemic position of the adult suggests that to dream of and aspire to normative forms of personhood is already to interpose a narratorial distance and dislocation between oneself and the dream. The desire for a norm is as much for the specific norm itself as it is for a general place from which one can enjoy the assurance of reliability that any repeated thing provides. Genre is not only about pleasure but also about knowing that pleasure will be right where you left it; this is how Berlant talks about love.[6] It is then the failure of this pleasure to be right where you left it that generates its world of talk, suspicion, aspiration, strategy, humiliation, and surprise—its lived experience. When faced with the threat of living without the liveliness you know, though, a new thought of personhood might flash up and again secure you in the position of its reader or narrator, such that in the structure of this thought one is both inside the dream's representation and watching oneself inside it, as if from an unseen spectator space in the dark. This position outside is what the dream costs, and what it promises.

Acknowledgments

I could never answer the question about the work's audience, and then I remembered that I began by writing for Elizabeth Alvarado, Woo Chan Lee, and Zachary Loeffler. They and so many others have given me the scarce gift of close reading and the more diffuse one of permission, without which nothing would have happened. Tristan Bates, as a developmental editor and a friend, kept the book going in crucial stretches when I couldn't alone. Sometimes, writing is the name for what precedes it, and because Nadia Chana knows this too, writing and living have been much less lonely. Patrick Fitzgibbon modeled heart and linguistic joy. Uncountable ideas in this book, and especially the epilogue, came in the space and the delight that talking with Tien-Tien Jong has brought me for a decade. Marcelle Pierson has said sane things to me about writing since graduate school, some of which I've absorbed. It's hard to measure the atmospheric effects of a partner, but Victoria Thurmond has taken me out of myself and tethered me to reality for many years; she also made the line diagrams in chapter 4. Speaking of atmosphere, Duck the dog was physically closer to the book than just about anyone else, having slept under the desk during most of its writing. Gratitude for cheerleading and support from my parents, Jenny Shang and Sanmin Wang, and my brother, Andy Shang, whose own fervencies for theory remind me (comfortingly) that I'm not so original, in the end. And I'm happy for the company of Chloe Blackshear, Lee Veeraraghavan, Yun Emily Wang, and Shirl Yang, who are also trying to come up with a life.

I can't thank enough the series editors, David J. Levin and Mary Ann Smart, whose trust in the book became the book. It also owes much to the other mentors who helped incubate the initial project into existence: Berthold Hoeckner, Martha Feldman, Dan Morgan, and Lauren Berlant. Marta Tonegutti and Kristin Rawlings at the University of Chicago Press were so thoughtful and sensitive to the needs of a first-time writer, and I also thank the staff and the board at the press for their belief and help. I benefited enormously from the anonymous readers' precious gifts of attention and paraphrase, much of which directly contributed to the book's shape and arguments. Special thanks are owed to the conveners and readers at the Humanities Center at Pitt, who offered sharp incitements for the chapter on love. As research assistants, Candace Burgess provided needed help with sources and musical examples, and Echo Davidson proofed the entire manuscript in the last stretches, making finishing it that much more imaginable. I'm grateful to have Jonathan de Souza and Martha Sprigge as friends and path-clearers, and Rika Asai for sustaining company. For invaluable gifts of recognition and precedent, I thank Carla Nappi. I have learned so much about affect and mentorship from Olivia Bloechl, and I owe a great deal to my colleagues, the staff, and several chairs in the music department at the University of Pittsburgh, who all ambiently and directly provided the space and the support that the book needed to come into being.

Between the footnotes and the acknowledgments, academic convention doesn't quite allow for the recognition of work that—at last—opens a place for you in the future. Here I would like to mention Stanley Cavell and Lauren Berlant, one of whom I never met and one whom I had the fortune of knowing after the writing had already made its mark. They made me a writer, by offering not a discipline or even a set of questions, but more fundamentally a way of becoming interested in the world that I can no longer quite separate from the sound of my own thinking. May you also find those who give you permission to write.

Parts of chapter 1 were originally published in a different form as "The Voice of Feeling: Liberal Subjects, Music, and the Cinematic Speech," in The Oxford Handbook of Voice Studies, edited by Nina Eidsheim and Katherine Meizel (Oxford University Press, 2019).

Notes

Introduction

1. Leonard Bernstein, "I Hate Music! A Cycle of Five Kid Songs for Soprano" (New York: Warner Bros., 1943).

2. For a suggestion that the spectacularity of children could be a beginning for film theory and philosophy, see Stanley Cavell, *The World Viewed: Reflections on the Ontology of Film* (Cambridge, MA: Harvard University Press, 1979), 20.

3. Hortense Spillers, "Mama's Baby, Papa's Maybe: An American Grammar Book," *Diacritics* 17, no. 2 (1987): 65.

4. Immanuel Kant, *The Metaphysics of Morals*, trans. and ed. by Mary Gregor (Cambridge: Cambridge University Press, 1996), 186. Italics in original.

5. Stanley Cavell, "Knowing and Acknowledging," in *Must We Mean What We Say? A Book of Essays* (Cambridge: Cambridge University Press, 2015): 220–45.

6. Lauren Berlant, "The Subject of True Feeling: Pain, Privacy, Politics," in *Cultural Pluralism, Identity Politics, and the Law*, ed. Austin Sarat and Thomas R. Kearns (Ann Arbor: University of Michigan Press, 1999), 49–84.

7. This book's understanding of the development of capitalism and liberalism in relation to aesthetics is owed to writers across many traditions of thought, including theorists of the public sphere, mass-mediated print, screen, and stage cultures (especially in relation to melodrama and sentimentality), and of sexuality, emotion, voice, interiority, and other central components of modern identification that are transformed as they encounter markets of consumption and circulation. This work permeates the book, but I cite specific writers and traditions in the places where their scholarship has been especially salient. On the specific matter of pain as an imaginative resource for a modern, Western conception of the human, see Eric Hayot, *The Hypothetical Mandarin: Sympathy, Modernity, and Chinese Pain* (Oxford: Oxford University Press, 2009) and Saba Mahmood, *Politics of Piety: The Islamic Revival and the Feminist Subject* (Princeton, NJ: Princeton University Press, 2005).

8. The phrase "moral community" comes from Mary Ann Warren's founding introduction of the personhood concept into bioethical discourse on abortion. Note, here, that morality becomes thinkable via an elision between a species and an unmarked (US) national concept: "What sort of entity, exactly, has the inalienable rights to life, liberty, and the pursuit of happiness?" Mary Ann Warren, "On the Moral and Legal Status of Abortion," *The Monist* 57, no. 1 (1973): 43–61. For a snapshot of current discourse on personhood in bioethics, see the articles collected in *The American Journal of Bioethics* 24, no. 1 (2024).

9. Sylvia Wynter, "Unsettling the Coloniality of Being/Power/Truth/Freedom: Towards the Human, After Man, Its Overrepresentation—An Argument," *The New Centennial Review* 3, no. 3 (2003): 264. On the effects of this elision within European musical and intellectual history, see Olivia A. Bloechl, *Native American Song at the Frontiers of Early Modern Music* (Cambridge: University of Cambridge Press, 2008).

10. Jacques Rancière, *The Politics of Aesthetics: The Distribution of the Sensible*, trans. Gabriel Rockhill (London: Continuum, 2004).

11. For work that forwards an account of Western humanism in order to leverage a critique of academic disciplinary methods, particularly in the humanities, see Kandice Chuh, *The Difference Aesthetics Makes: On the Humanities "After Man"* (Durham, NC: Duke University Press, 2019) and Alexander Weheliye, "After Man," *American Literary History* 20, no. 1–2 (2008): 321–36.

12. For a beginning into this area of thought, see J. L. Austin, *How to Do Things with Words*, ed. J. O. Urmson and Marina Sbisà (Oxford: Oxford University Press, 1975); Cavell, *Must We Mean What We Say?*; and Eve Kosofsky Sedgwick, *Epistemology of the Closet* (Berkeley: University of California Press, 2008).

13. Fredric Jameson, *The Political Unconscious: Narrative as a Socially Symbolic Act* (Ithaca, NY: Cornell University Press, 1981), 1, 89–136.

14. This is the central insight of Raymond Williams's essay "Structures of Feeling," which has enabled and conceptually grounded a great deal of affect theoretical work of the past and current generation. In particular, the recognition that any historical moment is caught at the juncture of newer and older interpretive horizons and codifications of collective experience, including ones that still await naming, opens a conceptual place for the felt—which might or might not yet have precipitated articulable feelings—in historical work, as a concept that has allowed some theorists to register the tremors and figurations of emergent collective experiences. Raymond Williams, "Structures of Feeling," in *Marxism and Literature* (Oxford: Oxford University Press, 1977), 128–35.

15. Lauren Berlant, *Cruel Optimism* (Durham, NC: Duke University Press, 2011), 15. Italics in original.

16. For affect as a vibratory potential that is useful analytically precisely because it travels outside of political and social significations, see, with different emphases, Brian Massumi, *Parables for the Virtual: Movement, Affect, Sensation* (Durham, NC: Duke University Press, 2002) and Teresa Brennan, *The Transmission of Affect* (Ithaca, NY: Cornell University Press, 2004).

17. Jonathan Culler, *Theory of the Lyric* (Cambridge, MA: Harvard University Press, 2015), 1.

18. Jessica Gabriel Peritz, *The Lyric Myth of Voice: Civilizing Song in Enlightenment Italy* (Oakland: University of California Press, 2022).

19. Foucault, *Order of Things*, 350–51. For a deft summary of the implications of this epistemic shift for academic knowledge production, with a focus on empirical and social scientific approaches, see Patrick R. Grzanka, "Queer Survey Research and the Ontological Dimensions of Heterosexism," *WSQ: Women's Studies Quarterly* 44, no. 3 (2016): 131–49. On sexuality in the modern episteme (since the late nineteenth century), see Sedgwick, *Epistemology of the Closet*.

20. Michel Foucault, *The History of Sexuality*, vol. 1, *An Introduction*, trans. Robert Hurley (New York: Pantheon Books, 1978), 33–34.

21. For the argument that modern listeners tend to project modern metaphysical ideas about the voice indefinitely into the past, see Gary Tomlinson, "Modern Opera," in *Metaphysical Song: An Essay on Opera* (Princeton, NJ: Princeton University Press, 1999).

22. For the idea that poetic lyric theory has tended to see the genre as historically engaged only before the modern period, see Arthur Z. Wang, "Situation, Occasion, Encounter: Claudia Rankine's *Citizen* and Lyric Theory in the Historical Present," *Contemporary Literature* 60, no. 4 (2019): 518–20. On the dissolution of the lyric promise of voice in the later twentieth century, see Marcelle Coulter Pierson, "The Voice Under Erasure: Singing, Melody and Expression in Late Modernist Music" (PhD diss., University of Chicago, 2015).

23. Claudia Rankine, *Citizen: An American Lyric* (Minneapolis, MN: Graywolf Press, 2014). Arthur Z. Wang makes the argument that Rankine's book develops formal containers of situation, encounter, and occasion to capture experiences that fail to rise to the legibility of an "event." Wang, "Situation, Occasion, Encounter."

24. Min Hyoung Song, *Climate Lyricism* (Durham, NC: Duke University Press, 2022).

25. Michel Foucault, *The Order of Things: An Archaeology of the Human Sciences* (New York: Vintage Books, 1970), xix.

26. Here I am thinking of Althusser's description of the institution as something that disciplines and entrains a collective meaningfulness while also presenting these meanings simply as a way of life. Louis Althusser, "Ideology and Ideological State Apparatuses (Notes Toward an Investigation)," in *Lenin and Philosophy, and Other Essays*, trans. Ben Brewster (New York: Monthly Review Press, 2001).

27. For a sense of the tension between the very possibility of "minority" knowledges in academic study and of minority representation in mass culture—as these knowledges and representations became consolidated, particularly in the decades after the sixties, both within and outside of universities—and alternate possibilities of activism and theory that this positive appearance forecloses, see Chandan Reddy, *Freedom with Violence: Race, Sexuality, and the U.S. State* (Durham, NC: Duke University Press, 2011), and Lisa Duggan, *The Twilight of Equality? Neoliberalism, Cultural Politics, and the Attack on Democracy* (Boston: Beacon Press, 2003). For the argument that mass representations of a socially subordinated group are not representations *of* that group, but rather, in their underdescriptions of their subjects' complexity, allow the promise of generic belonging, see Lauren Berlant, *The Female Complaint: The Unfinished Business of Sentimentality in American Culture* (Durham, NC: Duke University Press, 2008).

28. This argument is developed further in Dan Wang, "☺ [What Is an Asian American Style?]," in *The Routledge Companion to Gender and Affect*, ed. Todd Reeser (London: Routledge, 2022), 79–89.

29. James Buhler and David Neumeyer, "Music and the Ontology of the Sound Film: The Classical Hollywood System," in *The Oxford Handbook of Film Music Studies*, ed. David Neumeyer (Oxford: Oxford University Press, 2014), 30.

30. For the idea that (especially) uninvited speech "expos[es] the body of the other as vulnerable to address," see Judith Butler, *Excitable Speech: A Politics of the Performative* (New York: Routledge, 1997), 12–13.

31. The following scene, in fact, thematizes the productivity of epistemic mystery within the love or the sexual plot. It is the next day, and Mary is back at work, taking dictation from Jim as his secretary, when he confesses to her that he cannot remember

anything that happened after ten o'clock the previous night—that is, he has no memory of scene we have just watched, erasing the period in which, as Mary says, she felt that he finally "saw her." The camera focuses on Mary's face as this erasure registers, before she repeats, ironically and in the midst of taking dictation, "I cannot understand the change in your attitude." In other words, what Mary recalls in recalling the previous night is the way in which the ordinary epistemic opacity of the other generates the life of interpreting, guessing, speaking, correcting, wishing, disappointing, and surprising that love or sexual relation might open in its subjects.

32. On the detective novel as a model for the "epistemic frenzy" that love induces in its subjects, see Lauren Berlant, "Love, a Queer Feeling," in *Homosexuality and Psychoanalysis*, ed. Tim Dean and Christopher Lane (Chicago: University of Chicago Press, 2001), 434–35.

33. Writers on liberalism have attended to the centrality in its political imagination of the individual's capacity to form and articulate preferences; see Alasdair MacIntyre, "Liberalism Turned into a Tradition," in *Whose Justice? Which Rationality?* (Notre Dame, IN: University of Notre Dame Press, 1988). On the increasingly marketized development of this necessity in neoliberalism, particularly as a way of accessing one's own identity in love and sexuality, see Eva Illouz, *Consuming the Romantic Utopia: Love and the Cultural Contradictions of Capitalism* (Berkeley: University of California Press, 1997).

34. Buhler and Neumeyer, "Music and the Ontology of the Sound Film," 29–32.

35. Ann Cvetkovich, *Depression: A Public Feeling* (Durham, NC: Duke University Press, 2012), 122; Rachel Sherman, *Uneasy Street: The Anxieties of Affluence* (Princeton, NJ: Princeton University Press, 2017), 12–13; and Takeo Rivera, *Model Minority Masochism: Performing the Cultural Politics of Asian American Masculinity* (Oxford: Oxford University Press, 2022), xxxiv. All italics in the original texts.

36. Within the European art music tradition, a classic text is Lydia Goehr, *The Imaginary Museum of Musical Works: An Essay in the Philosophy of Music* (Oxford: Oxford University Press, 2007). Within postcolonialism, see Dipesh Chakrabarty, *Provincializing Europe: Postcolonial Thought and Historical Difference* (Princeton, NJ: Princeton University Press, 2000). For an account that aims to provincialize Western ideals of agency, interiority, and political action, see also Mahmood, *Politics of Piety*.

37. Elissa Marder, "Trauma, Addiction, and Temporal Bulimia in *Madame Bovary*," *Diacritics* 27, no. 3 (1997): 49.

38. Fredric Jameson, "Realism and Utopia in *The Wire*," *Criticism* 52, nos. 3–4 (2010): 367–68.

Chapter One

1. See Jeffrey Kallberg, *Chopin at the Boundaries: Sex, History, and Musical Genre* (Cambridge, MA: Harvard University Press, 1996). For a study of the work of genre in cultural contexts that valorize originality, such as Europe in the nineteenth century, see Matthew Gelbart, *Musical Genre and Romantic Ideology: Belonging in the Age of Originality* (Oxford: Oxford University Press, 2022).

2. This is the approach taken in Culler's study of lyric poetry, in which the aim to derive a common set of generic features that extend from ancient Greece to modern poetic production is meant to show that "lyric forms are not confined to one historical period but remain as possibilities in different eras." Culler, *Theory of the Lyric*, 4.

3. In the tradition of Marxist literary criticism extended by Jameson, for example, one way to read works that disturb genre categorization is to see them as registering a strain between the emerging experiences of their contemporary worlds and older genre formulas that are no longer entirely capable of processing them. See Jameson, *The Political Unconscious*.

4. See Peter Brooks's idea that melodrama is "central to our modernity" and an "inescapable dimension of modern consciousness," or Linda Williams's that "[m]elodrama is still the best, and most accurate, description of the serious narrative and iconic work performed by American mass culture, broadly conceived," or Christine Gledhill's description of "a central nineteenth century paradigm and a formative influence on twentieth century mass culture," or Fredric Jameson's that "an end of melodrama . . . threatens to become the end of mass culture itself," or Sheetal Majithia's that "melodrama reproduces itself in structures of feeling that pervade the social arena at large." Peter Brooks, *The Melodramatic Imagination: Balzac, Henry James, Melodrama, and the Mode of Excess* (New Haven, CT: Yale University Press, 1976), vii–viii; Linda Williams, *Playing the Race Card: Melodramas of Black and White from Uncle Tom to O. J. Simpson* (Princeton, NJ: Princeton University Press, 2001), 12; Christine Gledhill, *Home Is Where the Heart Is: Studies in Melodrama and the Woman's Film* (London: BFI Books, 1987), 14; Jameson, "Realism and Utopia in *The Wire*," 367–68; and Sheetal Majithia, "Rethinking Postcolonial Melodrama and Affect," Modern Drama 58, no. 1 (2015): 1–23.

5. Richard Curtis, dir., *Love Actually* (Universal City, CA: Universal Pictures Home Entertainment, 2014), DVD.

6. It is significant for the film's understanding of gendered national subjectivity that one of these men is the prime minister—the most powerful man in Britain—whose summoning of resources as he pursues his former assistant, including security detail and a full motorcade, provides the material expression of the momentum that his desire can produce in the world. The next section explores further the logic by which a head of state, in his very exceptionality, becomes the general model of a liberal political subjectivity.

7. MacIntyre, "Liberalism Turned into a Tradition," 336.

8. Henri Bergson, *Time and Free Will: An Essay on the Immediate Data of Consciousness* (New York: Macmillan, 1910), 100.

9. James Chandler, *An Archaeology of Sympathy: The Sentimental Mode in Literature and Cinema* (Chicago: University of Chicago Press, 2013), 12; and Elizabeth A. Povinelli, *The Empire of Love: Toward a Theory of Intimacy, Genealogy, and Carnality* (Durham, NC: Duke University Press, 2006), 188.

10. Berlant, "The Subject of True Feeling," 53.

11. Tim Walker, "Colin Firth Was the Third Choice to Play George VI in *The King's Speech*," *The Telegraph*, last modified August 25, 2016, https://www.telegraph.co.uk/news/celebritynews/8269816/Colin-Firth-was-the-third-choice-to-play-George-VI-in-The-Kings-Speech.html.

12. Tom Hooper, dir., *The King's Speech* (United Kingdom: UK Film Council, 2010), DVD.

13. Geoffrey Rush, director's commentary, *The King's Speech*.

14. Berlant, "The Subject of True Feeling."

15. Berlant proposes, in contrast to the trauma/reparation model of pain, the idea of subordinate experience as shocking but not surprising, ongoing, and everyday. Ibid., 77–84.

16. Hooper, director's commentary, *The King's Speech*.

17. Special thanks to Kiri Miller for pointing out that the voice produces absorption not only in the act of listening but also as a choreography, a bodily attunement and mimeticism as audiences huddle around the sound of the voice.

18. Sara Ahmed, *The Promise of Happiness* (Durham, NC: Duke University Press, 2010), 122.

19. Tom Ford, dir., *A Single Man* (Culver City, CA: Sony Pictures, 2010), DVD.

20. Hans Ulrich Gumbrecht, *Production of Presence: What Meaning Cannot Convey* (Stanford, CA: Stanford University Press, 2004), 136.

21. On film music's facilitation of spatial translocation to an elsewhere via the affective experience of being transported, see Berthold Hoeckner, "Transport and Transportation in Audiovisual Memory," in *Beyond the Soundtrack: Representing Music in Cinema*, ed. Daniel Ira Goldmark, Lawrence Kramer, and Richard Leppert (Berkeley: University of California Press, 2007), 163–83.

22. Stanley Cavell, "Performative and Passionate Utterance," in *Philosophy the Day After Tomorrow* (Cambridge, MA: Belknap Press of Harvard University Press, 2005), 185.

23. By contrast, Christopher Isherwood's novel, upon which the film is based, constantly reminds the reader of how fractured George's subjectivity is. There is no moment of presence to cap off a life before death takes hold, only a failure of the body at a moment that could have been any other. The film's end, then, might be an instance of what the book calls, in another context, an "almost indecently melodramatic situation." See Isherwood, *A Single Man* (London: Methuen, 1964), 157.

Chapter Two

1. Hemangini Gupta, "Modern Love," in *Gender: Love* (Farmington Hills, MI: Macmillan Reference USA, 2017), 227–41. See also Yunxiang Yan, *Private Life Under Socialism: Love, Intimacy, and Family Change in a Small Chinese Village, 1949–1999* (Stanford, CA: Stanford University Press, 2003).

2. One way to read a paragraph like this one would be to imagine that the romantic subject in India is a belated form that, in its mimesis of the West, aims at one day fully becoming Western. This is, as Chakrabarty writes, the historicist view in which the European form is the marker of a global "present" against which all other cultures are paced and timed. And yet the imitation does not necessarily follow the original, as Judith Butler argues about homosexuality: as a "belated" imitation, it can also be said to produce heterosexuality as the fantasy of a prior essence, since the concept of an "original" can only follow from the copy. See Chakrabarty, *Provincializing Europe*; and Judith Butler, "Imitation and Gender Insubordination," in *The Lesbian and Gay Studies Reader*, ed. Henry Abelove, Michèle Aina Barale, and David M. Halperin (New York: Routledge, 1993), 307–20.

3. James Baldwin, "On Being White . . . and Other Lies," in *The Cross of Redemption: Uncollected Writings*, ed. Randall Kenan (New York: Pantheon Books, 2010), 135.

4. Illouz, *Consuming the Romantic Utopia*.

5. Foucault, *History of Sexuality*.

6. Lauren Berlant and Michael Warner, "Sex in Public," *Critical Inquiry* 24, no. 2 (1998): 547–66.

7. Povinelli, *The Empire of Love*.

8. bell hooks, *All About Love: New Visions* (New York: William Morrow, 2000); and Eugenie Brinkema, *Life-Destroying Diagrams* (Durham, NC: Duke University Press, 2022), 289–369. On love as fidelity to the recurrence of a form, see also Berlant, *The Female Complaint*, 14–15.

9. See Berlant, "Love, a Queer Feeling."

10. *Saturday Night Live*, "Weekend Update: Romantic Comedy Expert—Saturday Night Live," YouTube video, 3:37, published October 26, 2014, https://www.youtube.com/watch?v=YxruI7Y7kww.

11. Stanley Cavell, *Pursuits of Happiness: The Hollywood Comedy of Remarriage* (Cambridge, MA: Harvard University Press, 1981).

12. Noah Baumbach, dir., *Frances Ha* (New York, NY: IFC Films, 2013), DVD.

13. Giorgio Biancorosso, *Situated Listening: The Sound of Absorption in Classical Cinema* (Oxford: Oxford University Press, 2016), 163.

14. Alice Wu, dir., *Saving Face* (Culver City, CA: Sony Pictures Home Entertainment, 2005), DVD.

15. On the way in which sounds in the "fantastical gap" between the world of the story and its outside both complicate and reinforce the idea of a line between them, see Robynn J. Stilwell, "The Fantastical Gap Between Diegetic and Nondiegetic," in *Beyond the Soundtrack: Representing Music in Cinema*, ed. Daniel Ira Goldmark, Lawrence Kramer, and Richard Leppert (Berkeley: University of California Press, 2007), 184–202.

16. Rick Famuyiwa, dir., *Brown Sugar* (2002; Los Angeles, CA: Searchlight Pictures, 2003), DVD.

17. Roger Michell, dir., *Notting Hill* (1999; Universal City, CA: Universal Pictures Home Entertainment, 2007), DVD.

18. Clea DuVall, dir., *Happiest Season* (2020; Culver City, CA: TriStar Pictures), Hulu.

19. Foucault, *History of Sexuality*, vol. 1.

20. D. A. Miller, "Secret Subjects, Open Secrets," *Dickens Studies Annual* 14 (1985), 17–38.

21. See Sianne Ngai, *Theory of the Gimmick: Aesthetic Judgment and Capitalist Form* (Cambridge, MA: Harvard University Press, 2020).

22. On the mythic symbolization of the child within heterosexuality, see Lee Edelman *No Future: Queer Theory and the Death Drive* (Durham: Duke University Press, 2004).

23. See Northrop Frye, *Anatomy of Criticism* (Princeton: Princeton University Press, 2015).

24. Dean Smith, "The 365 Day Proposal," YouTube video, 15:44, January 18, 2015, https://www.youtube.com/watch?v=ECRqF4BHkGk&t=183s.

25. Hayden White, *Metahistory: The Historical Imagination in Nineteenth-Century Europe* (Baltimore: The Johns Hopkins University Press, 1973), 6.

26. Duggan, *Twilight of Equality?*, ix–xxii.

27. Berlant, "The Subject of True Feeling," 52.

28. See Sam Hart, "Box Office Breakup," *Reuters*, February 14, 2023, https://www.reuters.com/graphics/USA-FILM/akveqmlarvr/.

29. Tamar Jeffers McDonald notes that while radical sex comedies from the 1960s and '70s stress the importance of sexual fulfillment for both men and women,

'90s romantic comedies saw an "Ephronesque turn" in which the desire for sex was either returned to its primary association with men or was deemphasized entirely. McDonald, "Homme-Com: Engendering Change in Contemporary Romantic Comedy," in *Falling in Love Again: Romantic Comedy in Contemporary Cinema*, ed. Stacey Abbott and Deborah Jermyn (London: I. B. Tauris, 2009), 151.

30. Berlant, "The Subject of True Feeling," 60–61.

31. Ann duCille, *The Coupling Convention: Sex, Text, and Tradition in Black Women's Fiction* (Oxford: Oxford University Press, 1993), 3.

32. Reddy, *Freedom with Violence*, 15.

33. David M. Halperin, "Queer Love," *Critical Inquiry* 45, no. 2 (2019): 403.

34. Soraya Roberts, "RomCon: Our Failure to See Black Romantic Comedies," *Longreads*, November 9, 2018, https://longreads.com/2018/11/09/romcon-our-failure-to-see-black-romantic-comedies/.

35. Here I am in dialogue with Stanley Cavell's theory of film genre, in which new works sometimes discover new ways of belonging to a genre, while older traits once deemed essential to belonging turn out to be inessential. Cavell doesn't specify any kind of formal link between the traits that disappear and the ones they're replaced with, only that new features "compensate" for the absence of old ones while also clarifying them. In my reading of the remake, I am suggesting that the shape of new entries to a genre can emerge via the effort to trace new causal paths through the parts of a story that no longer "speak" in a new historical time. Thus, new traits are not only replacements of the old ones (as if traits sometimes just lose their urgency), but are formal inventions that preserve the shape of old traits in their creative avoidance of them. See Cavell, *Pursuits of Happiness: The Hollywood Comedy of Remarriage* (Cambridge, MA: Harvard University Press, 1981), 27–30. I learned this way of reading a series of texts around their displacements from Barbara Johnson, "The Frame of Reference: Poe, Lacan, Derrida," *Yale French Studies* 55–56 (1977): 457–505.

36. Ernst Lubitsch, dir., *The Shop Around the Corner* (1940; Burbank, CA: Warner Home Video, 2002), DVD.

37. Nora Ephron, dir., *You've Got Mail* (1998; Burbank, CA: Warner Home Video, 1999), DVD.

38. Povinelli, *The Empire of Love*, 175–76.

39. Robert Z. Leonard, dir., *In the Good Old Summertime* (1949; Burbank, CA: Warner Archive Collection, 2017), DVD.

40. Theodor W. Adorno, "Music in the Background," in *Essays on Music*, ed. Richard Leppert (Berkeley: University of California Press, 2002), 508.

41. For Jameson, the melodramatic polarization of good and evil operates dialectically in relation to the emergence of single, universalizing concepts of the subject. It is when a dominant social order begins to crumble, and along with it its normative legislations of proper and improper, right and wrong, normative and aberrant, that determinations of good and evil become interpersonal, since they can no longer be secured by one's status within a central authority. But these periods in which goodness and badness are not guaranteed in advance but must continually be professed, witnessed, and affirmed performatively will once again be upended when there emerges some new, unified, and homogenizing concept of universal subjectivity (Jameson's example is the rise of a universal feudal class in twelfth-century Europe), since the universal frame seems incompatible with melodramatic scissions of good and evil.

In moments such as these, Jameson suggests, classical literary romance's scenes of recognition attempt to solve this conundrum via scenes of "semic evaporation." Jameson, *The Political Unconscious*, 105–6.

Chapter Three

1. Jonathan Metzl and Anna Kirkland, *Against Health: How Health Became the New Morality* (New York: NYU Press, 2010).

2. Mimi Khúc, "The Revolution is in the Heart," TEDxUMD, University of Maryland, February 18, 2017. Video of lecture, 17:10, https://www.mimikhuc.com/projects/the-revolution-is-in-the-heart.

3. Jonathan M. Metzl, "Introduction: Why 'Against Health'?," in *Against Health: How Health Became the New Morality*, ed. Jonathan M. Metzl and Anna Kirkland (New York: NYU Press, 2010), 7.

4. Ibid.

5. Bob Fosse, dir., *Cabaret* (1972; Universal City, CA: Universal Pictures Home Entertainment, 2013), DVD.

6. Berlant, *Cruel Optimism*.

7. See Terence Cave, *Recognitions: A Study in Poetics* (Oxford: Clarendon Press, 1990).

8. See Mariana Valverde, *Diseases of the Will: Alcohol and the Dilemmas of Freedom* (Cambridge: Cambridge University Press, 1998).

9. Howard Markel, "The D.S.M. Gets Addiction Right," *The New York Times*, June 5, 2012, https://www.nytimes.com/2012/06/06/opinion/the-dsm-gets-addiction-right.html.

10. Valverde, *Diseases of the Will*, 94–95.

11. On the success of the disease/infection model in Western medicine, and in contrast to other ways of modeling nonnormative bodily states, see Georges Canguilhem, *On the Normal and the Pathological* (Dordrecht: D. Reidel, 1978).

12. Eve Kosofsky Sedgwick, "Epidemics of the Will," in *Tendencies* (London: Routledge, 1994), 133.

13. Ibid., 140.

14. See Northrop Frye, *Anatomy of Criticism* (Princeton, NJ: Princeton University Press, 2000), 38.

15. Carolyn Abbate, *In Search of Opera* (Princeton, NJ: Princeton University Press, 2001), 118.

16. Reinhold Brinkmann, "Tannhäusers Lied," in *Das Drama Richard Wagners als musikalisches Kunstwerk*, ed. Carl Dahlhaus (Regensburg: G. Bosse, 1970), 199–211, cited in Abbate, *In Search of Opera*, 264.

17. Abbate, *In Search of Opera*, 118.

18. The very undecidability between reading vertically for metaformal meaning and laterally for emergent musical processes is a common theme in contemporary musicological writing on the leitmotif. As Arnold Whittall observes, for example, "Most commentators on Wagner express reservations about motif-labelling while finding it difficult to discard the activity altogether." Whittall, "Leitmotif," in *Grove Music Online*, 2001, accessed May 22, 2024, https://www-oxfordmusiconline-com.pitt.idm.oclc.org/grovemusic/view/10.1093/gmo/9781561592630.001.0001/omo-9781561592630-e-0000016360. Matthew Bribitzer-Stull describes the motive as a formal figure that unifies different

scales and levels of a structure: "But whereas the concept of theme intersects with various tonal levels, themes themselves are conceptually surface-level entities. Varied repetitions of motives, however, may occur on deep structural levels, helping to unify the surface of the music with its tonal background." Matthew Bribitzer-Stull, *Understanding the Leitmotif: From Wagner to Hollywood Film Music* (Cambridge: Cambridge University Press, 2015), 46.

19. For a critique of the leitmotif as a mnemonic aid, see Theodor W. Adorno, *In Search of Wagner*, trans. Rodney Livingstone (London: Verso, 1991), 31.

20. All references to *Tannhäuser* are from Richard Wagner, *Tannhäuser: In Full Score* (New York: Dover, 1984). My translations.

21. Marder, "Trauma, Addiction, and Temporal Bulimia in *Madame Bovary*."

22. *Alcoholics Anonymous: The Story of How Many Thousands of Men and Women Have Recovered From Alcoholism*, 4th edition (New York City: Alcoholics Anonymous World Services, 2001); my italics.

23. Ernest Kurtz, *Not-God: A History of Alcoholics Anonymous* (Center City, MN: Hazelden Educational Services, 1979).

24. Valverde, *Diseases of the Will*.

25. Ibid., 14.

26. Abbate, *In Search of Opera*, 125.

27. Berlant, *Cruel Optimism*, 1.

28. Keane, "Smoking, Addiction, and the Making of Time," in *High Anxieties: Cultural Studies in Addiction*, ed. Janet Brodie and Marc Redfield (Berkeley: University of California Press, 2002), 132–33.

29. For an argument that aligns this form of public time to the modern "West" as a historical, geographical, and capitalist formation, see Helga Nowotny, *Time: The Modern and Postmodern Experience*, trans. Neville Plaice (Cambridge: Polity, 1994).

30. Gabor Maté, *In the Realm of Hungry Ghosts: Close Encounters with Addiction* (Berkeley, CA: North Atlantic Books, 2008), 138.

31. Jacques Derrida, "The Rhetoric of Drugs," in *Points . . . : Interviews, 1974–1994*, ed. Elisabeth Weber (Stanford, CA: Stanford University Press, 1995), 228–54.

32. On the history of privacy in Anglo-American common law, see Reva B. Seigel, "'The Rule of Love': Wife Beating as Prerogative and Privacy" (1996), *Faculty Scholarship Series*, paper 1092, http://digitalcommons.law.yale.edu/fss_papers/1092. See also Berlant, "The Subject of True Feeling." For effects of a spatial concept of the public on theories of illness and political subjectivity, see Johanna Hedva, "Sick Woman Theory," accessed October 12, 2022, https://johannahedva.com/SickWomanTheory_Hedva_2020.pdf.

33. On conceptualizing privacy and publicity not only as physically demarcated zones, but also as governed by conventions and affects that, for example, grant unmarked heterosexualities a kind of "right-to-privacy-in-public," see Duggan, *Twilight of Equality?*, 52–53.

34. Abbate, *In Search of Opera*, 124; my italics.

35. "Sämmtliche Waldhörner hinter der Szene links ziemlich entfernt und verschieden verteilt; die Hörner in C der Bühne zunächst; die Hörner in F etwas zurück und tiefer, die Hörner in Es am entferntesten und tiefsten" (All French horns behind the scene at left somewhat distant and split up; the horns in C initially on the stage; the horns in F somewhat back and deeper; the horns in E-flat the deepest and furthest back).

36. Theodor W. Adorno and Hans Eisler, *Composing for the Films* (Freeport, NY: Books for Libraries Press, 1971), 5.

37. Claudia Gorbman, *Unheard Melodies: Narrative Film Music* (London: BFI, 1987), 2.

38. For an account of CBT's development in relation to other talk therapies, see Marvin R. Goldfried, *From Cognitive-Behavior Therapy to Psychotherapy Integration: An Evolving View* (New York: Springer, 1995).

39. On discipline as a collection of habits, see Royal S. Brown, "How Not to Think Film Music," *Music and the Moving Image* 1, no. 1 (2008): 2–18.

40. José Cláudio Siqueira Castanheira, "Timeline Philosophy: Technological Hedonism and Formal Aspects of Films and Music Videos," in *Music/Video: Histories, Aesthetics, Media*, ed. Gina Arnold, Daniel Cookney, Kirsty Fairclough, and Michael N. Goddard (London: Bloomsbury, 2017), 216.

41. James Buhler and David Neumeyer, "Overview," in *The Oxford Handbook of Film Music Studies*, ed. David Neumeyer (Oxford: Oxford University Press, 2014), 1–14.

42. On the use of the *Gesamtkunstwerk* as an origin figure for the saturating aesthetic experiences of modern entertainment, see Carolyn Birdsall, *Nazi Soundscapes: Sound, Technology, and Urban Space in Germany, 1933–1945* (Amsterdam: Amsterdam University Press, 2012). For the view that many interpreters of Wagner and cinema have been tempted into the idea that the latter more perfectly realizes what Wagner could do only imperfectly, with his limited historical technologies of stagecraft, see Michel Chion, *Music in Cinema*, ed. and trans. Claudia Gorbman (New York: Columbia University Press, 2021), 292–94.

43. Adorno, "Music in the Background," 507.

Chapter Four

1. *The West Wing*, season 1, episode 1, "Pilot," directed by Thomas Schlamme, written by Aaron Sorkin, aired September 22, 1999, in broadcast syndication, Warner Home Video, 2021, DVD.

2. Anker, *Orgies of Feeling*; and Brian Massumi, "The Future Birth of the Affective Fact: The Political Ontology of Threat," in *The Affect Theory Reader*, ed. Melissa Gregg and Gregory J. Seigworth (Durham, NC: Duke University Press, 2010), 62. See also Kathleen M. Woodward, *Statistical Panic: Cultural Politics and Poetics of the Emotions* (Durham, NC: Duke University Press, 2009).

3. Jeff Mason, "Attacking Anti-Vaccine Movement, Biden Mandates Widespread COVID Shots, Tests," *Reuters*, September 10, 2021, https://www.reuters.com/world/us/biden-deliver-six-step-plan-covid-19-pandemic-2021-09-09/.

4. On the argument that minoritarian literature always ends up being a reflection of collective experience, see Gilles Deleuze and Félix Guattari, "What Is a Minor Literature?", trans. Robert Brinkley, *Mississippi Review* 11, no. 3 (1983): 13–33.

5. *The West Wing*, season 1, episode 3, "A Proportional Response," directed by Marc Buckland, written by Aaron Sorkin, aired October 6, 1999, in broadcast syndication, Warner Home Video, 2021, DVD.

6. On the backstage musical and spectacles of privacy, see Desirée J. Garcia, "'What's Happened to Chorus Girls?': Domesticity and the Postwar Backstage Musical," *Cinema Journal* 61, no. 5 (2021): 31–58. See also Allison Robbins, "Doubled Selves: Eleanor Powell and the MGM Backstage Musical, 1935–37," *Journal of the Society for*

American Music 7, no. 1 (2013): 65–93; and Rick Altman, *The American Film Musical* (Bloomington: Indiana University Press, 1988).

7. On reading the nation as a body capable of sensory effects, see Lauren Berlant, "The Queen of America Goes to Washington City: Harriet Jacobs, Frances Harper, Anita Hill," in *Feminisms: An Anthology of Literary Theory and Criticism*, ed. Robyn R. Warhol and Diane Price Herndl (New Brunswick, NJ: Rutgers University Press, 1997), 931–52.

8. Maxine Wally, "WTV Club: Watching The West Wing to Escape From 2020 Politics," *W Magazine*, August 22, 2020, https://www.wmagazine.com/culture/the-west-wing-season-one-w-tv-club-quarantine-binge-watch; and David Sims, "Bartlet for America, Forever," *The Atlantic*, May 10, 2016, https://www.theatlantic.com/entertainment/archive/2016/05/west-wing-nostalgia/482022/.

9. For example, Reddy writes of "what is empirically proven and well known of all US wars abroad: they are one of America's most successful tactics for recruiting so-called 'immigrants'" (*Freedom with Violence*, 14). See also Michael Hudson, *Super Imperialism: The Origin and Fundamentals of U.S. World Dominance* (London: Pluto Press, 2015).

10. I am imagining here not a subordinated but an ordinary subject position within the interplay of what Gayatri Chakravorty Spivak called "time" and "timing" as names for different positions of experience within an objective, linear, and narratorial conception of a unified world-time. See Spivak, "Time and Timing: Law and History," in *Chronotopes: The Construction of Time*, ed. John Bender and David E. Wellbery (Stanford, CA: Stanford University Press, 1991), 99–117.

11. Claudia Gorbman, *Unheard Melodies: Narrative Film Music* (London: BFI, 1987).

12. M. Night Shyamalan, dir., *The Happening* (Century City, CA: 20th Century Fox, 2008), DVD.

13. For more on strategies of concern and empathy as ways of masking one's own desires, see Linda Alcoff, "The Problem of Speaking for Others," *Cultural Critique* 20 (Winter 1991–92): 5–32. On empathy as objectification, see Lauren Berlant, Sadhana Bery, Rizvana Bradley, Jane Caflisch, Lori Gruen, and Saidiya Hartman, "A Diagnostic On Whiteness: The Empathy Conundrum," June 30, 2018, https://onscreen.thekitchen.org/media/a-diagnostic-on-whiteness-the-empathy-conundrum.

14. By "citizen" I am referring not only to the legal status sponsored by the state, but also to an affective and normative orientation to the state that often governs the normative citizen's sense of proper belonging to the legal category—a way of being that seems to invoke a nationally imagined ideal. See Lauren Berlant, "Citizenship," in *Keywords for American Cultural Studies*, ed. Glenn Hendler and Bruce Burgett (New York: NYU Press, 2014).

15. C. Riley Snorton has brilliantly explored how the mainstream press's self-understood project simply to clarify and explain is, necessarily, also an epistemically aggressive act when directed toward minoritized populations, which occupy the epistemic condition of "the unknown/the knowable" within the project of public knowledge. See Snorton, *Nobody Is Supposed to Know: Black Sexuality on the Down Low* (Minneapolis: University of Minnesota Press, 2014), and "Who's Out in Hip Hop?," *Souls* 16, nos. 3–4 (2014): 283–302.

16. Alfred Hitchcock, "Why I Make Melodramas," *Film and Stars* (1937), accessed October 15, 2022, https://the.hitchcock.zone/wiki/Film_and_Stars_(1937)_-_Why_I_Make_Melodramas.

17. Michel Foucault, *History of Sexuality*, vol. 1, *An Introduction*, 1st American ed. (New York: Pantheon Books, 1978), 15–49.

18. US Congress, House, *Homeland Security Act of 2002*, HR 5005, 107th Congress, introduced in House November 22, 2002, https://www.dhs.gov/sites/default/files/publications/hr_5005_enr.pdf.

19. See Sherman, *Uneasy Street*, 6–7.

20. Berlant, *Cruel Optimism*.

21. On the origin of the concept of the population as a form of state knowledge and control in the European eighteenth century, see Foucault, *History of Sexuality*, 25–35.

22. On the idea that genre captures and manages the political contradictions of a given historical moment, see Jameson, *The Political Unconscious*.

23. "NRA: Full Statement by Wayne LaPierre in Response to Newtown Shootings," *The Guardian*, December 21, 2012, https://www.theguardian.com/world/2012/dec/21/nra-full-statement-lapierre-newtown.

24. "Vice President Remarks at NRA's Annual Leadership Forum," *C-SPAN*, May 4, 2018, https://www.c-span.org/video/?444682-101/vice-president-pence-addresses-nras-annual-leadership-forum.

25. "Remarks at the National Rifle Association Institute for Legislative Action Leadership Forum in Indianapolis, Indiana," *GovInfo*, April 26, 2019, https://www.govinfo.gov/content/pkg/DCPD-201900243/html/DCPD-201900243.htm.

26. Jaume Collet-Serra, dir., *Non-Stop* (Universal City, CA: Universal Studios, 2014), DVD.

27. On the use of this trope in the meritocratic genre of US reality television, see Susan Schuyler, "Reality Television, Melodrama, and the Great Recession," *Studies in Popular Culture* 37, no. 2 (2015): 43–65.

28. For a survey of psychoanalytic and Marxist literature in relation to film music theorizing, see Caryl Flinn, *Strains of Utopia: Gender, Nostalgia, and Hollywood Film Music* (Princeton, NJ: Princeton University Press, 1992). The classic text that reads Hollywood film music as a commodity deracinated from the authentic production of culture is Adorno and Eisler, *Composing for the Films*. For the argument that possibilities of a less commodified and easily capturable subjectivity can be found in the (sometimes accidental) ruptures of film musical spectacle, see Amy Herzog, *Dreams of Difference, Songs of the Same: The Musical Moment in Film* (Minneapolis: University of Minnesota Press, 2010).

29. These dispersed figures in popular culture could be comic, as in the conspiracy board created by Charlie Day's character in the television series *It's Always Sunny in Philadelphia*, which appeared in an episode that aired on October 30, 2008, and which would subsequently enjoy life as a meme of theory's connecting drive; or they could be apocalyptic, as in the scribbled notes and diagrams of Richard Kind's character in Joel and Ethan Coen's 2009 film *A Serious Man*.

30. Woo Chan Lee offered the wonderful observation that the zombie genre is a melodramatic form in which the other is not evil, exactly, but brainless, making it a key genre for politics in the polemical mode. These two responses to a "brainless" mainstream can also be found in two different modalities of the zombie as political metaphor: the one in which one escapes with loved ones, and the one in which a ragtag band of mercenaries stages an attempt at counterattack. See also Slavoj Žižek, "Madness and Habit in German Idealism: Discipline Between the Two Freedoms," accessed May 3, 2024, https://www.lacan.com/zizdazedandconfused.html.

31. Eve Kosofsky Sedgwick, "Privilege of Unknowing: Diderot's *The Nun*," in *Tendencies* (London: Routledge, 1994), 23–50.

32. Pierre Morel, dir., *Taken* (Century City, CA: 20th Century Fox, 2008), DVD.

33. *The West Wing*, season 1, episode 6, "Mr. Willis of Ohio," directed by Christopher Misiano, written by Aaron Sorkin, aired November 3, 1999, in broadcast syndication, Warner Home Video, 2021, DVD.

34. Jonathan Kay, *Among the Truthers: A Journey Through America's Growing Conspiracist Underground* (New York: Harper, 2011).

35. George W. Bush, "Remarks by the President Upon Arrival at Barksdale Air Force Base," September 11, 2001, https://georgewbush-whitehouse.archives.gov/news/releases/2001/09/20010911-1.html.

36. Miranda July, dir., *Kajillionaire* (Universal City, CA: Universal Pictures Home Entertainment, 2020), DVD.

37. As Tony Thomas writes, "Music until then had not been used very much for under-scoring—the producers were afraid the audience would ask, 'Where's the music coming from?' unless they saw an orchestra or a radio or phonograph." Thomas, *Music for the Movies* (South Brunswick: A. S. Barnes, 1973), 34. On the record player as a material and fantasmatic origin for film music in classical Hollywood cinema, see Berthold Hoeckner, *Film, Music, Memory* (Chicago: University of Chicago Press, 2022).

Epilogue

1. Berlant, *The Female Complaint*.

2. My thanks to Tien-Tien Jong for introducing me to the Newitz passage. The thoughts in this section came in the space of a recorded conversation we had about the film, and I cite it here to acknowledge the itinerary of this writing. Tien-Tien Jong and Dan Wang, *Watching Film*, podcast audio, October 9, 2023, https://open.spotify.com/show/3U99UNB78X28wsCeILBsy1?si=27f5a71694744482. Steven Spielberg, dir., *A.I. Artificial Intelligence* (2001; Hollywood, CA: Paramount Home Media Distribution, 2015), DVD.

3. Annalee Newitz, *Pretend We're Dead: Capitalist Monsters in American Popular Culture* (Durham, NC: Duke University Press, 2006), 147.

4. Sigmund Freud, "The Economic Problem of Masochism," in *The Standard Edition of the Complete Psychological Works of Sigmund Freud*, trans. James Strachey (London: Hogarth Press, 1961), 19:159–70.

5. Thanks to Tien-Tien Jong for the sharp insight that David's paintings resemble storyboards for the film.

6. Berlant, "Love, a Queer Feeling."

Bibliography

Abbate, Carolyn. *In Search of Opera*. Princeton, NJ: Princeton University Press, 2001.
Adorno, Theodor W. "Music in the Background." In *Essays on Music*, edited by Richard Leppert. Berkeley: University of California Press, 2002.
Adorno, Theodor W. *In Search of Wagner*. Translated by Rodney Livingstone. London: Verso, 1991.
Adorno, Theodor W., and Hans Eisler. *Composing for the Films*. Freeport, NY: Books for Libraries Press, 1971.
Ahmed, Sara. 2010. *The Promise of Happiness*. Durham, NC: Duke University Press.
Alcoff, Linda. "The Problem of Speaking for Others." *Cultural Critique* 20 (Winter 1991–92): 5–32.
Alcoholics Anonymous: The Story of How Many Thousands of Men and Women Have Recovered From Alcoholism. 4th ed. New York: Alcoholics Anonymous World Services, 2001.
Althusser, Louis. "Ideology and Ideological State Apparatuses (Notes Toward an Investigation)." In *Lenin and Philosophy, and Other Essays*, translated by Ben Brewster. New York: Monthly Review Press, 2001.
Altman, Rick. *The American Film Musical*. Bloomington: Indiana University Press, 1988.
Anker, Elisabeth R. *Orgies of Feeling: Melodrama and the Politics of Freedom*. Durham, NC: Duke University Press, 2014.
Austin, J. L. *How to Do Things with Words*. Edited by J. O. Urmson and Marina Sbisà. Oxford: Oxford University Press, 1975.
Baldwin, James. "On Being White . . . and Other Lies." In *The Cross of Redemption: Uncollected Writings*, edited by Randall Kenan. New York: Pantheon Books, 2010.
Baumbach, Noah, dir. *Frances Ha*. DVD. New York: IFC Films, 2013.
Bergson, Henri. 1910. *Time and Free Will: An Essay on the Immediate Data of Consciousness*. New York: Macmillan.
Berlant, Lauren. "Citizenship." In *Keywords for American Cultural Studies*, edited by Glenn Hendler and Bruce Burgett. New York: NYU Press, 2014.
Berlant, Lauren. *Cruel Optimism*. Durham, NC: Duke University Press, 2011.
Berlant, Lauren. *The Female Complaint: The Unfinished Business of Sentimentality in American Culture*. Durham, NC: Duke University Press, 2008.
Berlant, Lauren. "Love, a Queer Feeling." In *Homosexuality and Psychoanalysis*, edited by Tim Dean and Christopher Lane. Chicago: University of Chicago Press, 2001.

Berlant, Lauren. "The Queen of America Goes to Washington City: Harriet Jacobs, Frances Harper, Anita Hill." In *Feminisms: An Anthology of Literary Theory and Criticism*, edited by Robyn R. Warhol and Diane Price Herndl. New Brunswick, NJ: Rutgers University Press, 1997.

Berlant, Lauren. "The Subject of True Feeling: Pain, Privacy, Politics." In *Cultural Pluralism, Identity Politics, and the Law*, edited by Austin Sarat and Thomas R. Kearns. Ann Arbor: University of Michigan Press, 1999.

Berlant, Lauren, Sadhana Bery, Rizvana Bradley, Jane Caflisch, Lori Gruen, and Saidiya Hartman. "A Diagnostic on Whiteness: The Empathy Conundrum." June 30, 2018. https://onscreen.thekitchen.org/media/a-diagnostic-on-whiteness-the-empathy-conundrum.

Berlant, Lauren, and Michael Warner. "Sex in Public." *Critical Inquiry* 24, no. 2 (1998): 547–66.

Bernstein, Leonard. "I Hate Music! A Cycle of Five Kid Songs for Soprano." New York: Warner Bros., 1943.

Biancorosso, Giorgio. *Situated Listening: The Sound of Absorption in Classical Cinema*. Oxford: Oxford University Press, 2016.

Birdsall, Carolyn. *Nazi Soundscapes: Sound, Technology, and Urban Space in Germany, 1933–1945*. Amsterdam: Amsterdam University Press, 2012.

Bribitzer-Stull, Matthew. *Understanding the Leitmotif: From Wagner to Hollywood Film Music*. Cambridge: Cambridge University Press, 2015.

Brinkema, Eugenie. *Life-Destroying Diagrams*. Durham, NC: Duke University Press, 2022.

Brinkmann, Reinhold. "Tannhäusers Lied." In *Das Drama Richard Wagners als musikalisches Kunstwerk*, edited by Carl Dahlhaus. Regensburg: G. Bosse, 1970.

Brooks, Peter. *The Melodramatic Imagination: Balzac, Henry James, Melodrama, and the Mode of Excess*. New Haven, CT: Yale University Press, 1976.

Brown, Royal S. "How Not to Think Film Music." *Music and the Moving Image* 1, no. 1 (2008): 2–18.

Buhler, James, and David Neumeyer. *The Oxford Handbook of Film Music Studies*. Oxford: Oxford University Press, 2014.

Bush, George W. "Remarks by the President upon Arrival at Barksdale Air Force Base." September 11, 2001. https://georgewbush-whitehouse.archives.gov/news/releases/2001/09/20010911-1.html.

Butler, Judith. "Imitation and Gender Insubordination." In *The Lesbian and Gay Studies Reader*, edited by Henry Abelove, Michèle Aina Barale, and David M. Halperin. New York: Routledge, 1993.

Butler, Judith. "Performative Acts and Gender Constitution: An Essay in Phenomenology and Feminist Theory." *Theatre Journal* 40, no. 4 (1988): 519–31.

Canguilhem, Georges. *The Normal and the Pathological*. Dordrecht: D. Reidel, 1978.

Castanheira, José Cláudio Siqueira. "Timeline Philosophy: Technological Hedonism and Formal Aspects of Films and Music Videos." In *Music/Video: Histories, Aesthetics, Media*, edited by Gina Arnold, Daniel Cookney, Kirsty Fairclough, and Michael N. Goddard. London: Bloomsbury, 2017.

Cave, Terence. *Recognitions: A Study in Poetics*. Oxford: Clarendon Press, 1990.

Cavell, Stanley. "Knowing and Acknowledging." In *Must We Mean What We Say? A Book of Essays*. Cambridge: Cambridge University Press, 2015.

Cavell, Stanley. "Performative and Passionate Utterance." In *Philosophy the Day After Tomorrow*, 155–91. Cambridge, MA: Belknap Press of Harvard University Press, 2005.
Cavell, Stanley. *Pursuits of Happiness: The Hollywood Comedy of Remarriage*. Cambridge, MA: Harvard University Press, 1981.
Cavell, Stanley. *The World Viewed: Reflections on the Ontology of Film*. Cambridge, MA: Harvard University Press, 1979.
Chakrabarty, Dipesh. *Provincializing Europe: Postcolonial Thought and Historical Difference*. Princeton, NJ: Princeton University Press, 2000.
Chandler, James. *An Archaeology of Sympathy: The Sentimental Mode in Literature and Cinema*. Chicago: University of Chicago Press, 2013.
Chion, Michel. *Music in Cinema*. Edited and translated by Claudia Gorbman. New York: Columbia University Press, 2021.
Chuh, Kandice. *The Difference Aesthetics Makes: On the Humanities "After Man."* Durham, NC: Duke University Press, 2019.
Clausen, Jennifer Ann. "Addicted to 'The Big Book': Language, Identity and Discourse in the Literacy Practices of Alcoholics Anonymous." PhD diss., Arizona State University, 2013.
Collet-Serra, Jaume, dir. *Non-Stop*. DVD. Universal City, CA: Universal Studios, 2014.
Culler, Jonathan. *Theory of the Lyric*. Cambridge, MA: Harvard University Press, 2015.
Curtis, Richard, dir. *Love Actually*. DVD. Universal City, CA: Universal Pictures Home Entertainment, 2014.
Cvetkovich, Ann. *Depression: A Public Feeling*. Durham, NC: Duke University Press, 2012.
Deleuze, Gilles, and Félix Guattari. "What Is a Minor Literature?" Translated by Robert Brinkley. *Mississippi Review* 11, no. 3 (1983): 13–33.
Derrida, Jacques. "The Rhetoric of Drugs." In *Points . . . : Interviews, 1974–1994*, edited by Elisabeth Weber. Stanford, CA: Stanford University Press, 1995.
duCille, Ann. *The Coupling Convention: Sex, Text, and Tradition in Black Women's Fiction*. Oxford: Oxford University Press, 1993.
Duggan, Lisa. *The Twilight of Equality? Neoliberalism, Cultural Politics, and the Attack on Democracy*. Boston: Beacon Press, 2003.
DuVall, Clea, dir. *Happiest Season*. Hulu. Culver City, CA: TriStar Pictures, 2020.
Edelman, Lee. *No Future: Queer Theory and the Death Drive*. Durham, NC: Duke University Press, 2004.
Ephron, Nora, dir. *You've Got Mail*. DVD. 1998; Burbank, CA: Warner Home Video, 1999.
Famuyiwa, Rick, dir. *Brown Sugar*. DVD. 2002; Los Angeles: Searchlight Pictures, 2003.
Flinn, Caryl. *Strains of Utopia: Gender, Nostalgia, and Hollywood Film Music*. Princeton, NJ: Princeton University Press, 1992.
Ford, Tom, dir. *A Single Man*. DVD. Culver City, CA: Sony Pictures, 2010.
Fosse, Bob, dir. *Cabaret*. DVD. 1972; Universal City, CA: Universal Pictures Home Entertainment, 2013.
Foucault, Michel. *The History of Sexuality*. Vol. 1, *An Introduction*. Translated by Robert Hurley. New York: Pantheon Books, 1978.

Foucault, Michel. *The Order of Things: An Archaeology of the Human Sciences*. New York: Vintage Books, 1970.
Freud, Sigmund. "The Economic Problem of Masochism." In *The Standard Edition of the Complete Psychological Works of Sigmund Freud*, vol. 19. Translated by James Strachey. London: Hogarth Press, 1961.
Frye, Northrop. *Anatomy of Criticism*. Princeton, NJ: Princeton University Press, 2000.
Garcia, Desirée J. "'What's Happened to Chorus Girls?' Domesticity and the Postwar Backstage Musical." *Cinema Journal* 61, no. 5 (2021): 31–58.
Gelbart, Matthew. *Musical Genre and Romantic Ideology: Belonging in the Age of Originality*. Oxford: Oxford University Press, 2022.
Gervais, Ricky, and Stephen Merchant, creators. *The Office: The Complete Series*. DVD. Adapted by Greg Daniels. Universal City, CA: Universal Pictures Home Entertainment, 2018.
Gledhill, Christine. *Home Is Where the Heart Is: Studies in Melodrama and the Woman's Film*. London: BFI Books, 1987.
Goehr, Lydia. *The Imaginary Museum of Musical Works: As Essay in the Philosophy of Music*. Oxford: Oxford University Press, 2007.
Goldfried, Marvin R. *From Cognitive-Behavior Therapy to Psychotherapy Integration: An Evolving View*. New York: Springer, 1995.
Gorbman, Claudia. *Unheard Melodies: Narrative Film Music*. London: BFI, 1987.
Grzanka, Patrick R. "Queer Survey Research and the Ontological Dimensions of Heterosexism." *WSQ: Women's Studies Quarterly* 44, nos. 3–4 (2016): 131–49.
Gumbrecht, Hans Ulrich. *Production of Presence: What Meaning Cannot Convey*. Stanford, CA: Stanford University Press, 2004.
Gupta, Hemangini. "Modern Love." In *Gender: Love*, edited by Jennifer C. Nash. Farmington Hills, MI: Macmillan Reference USA, 2017.
Halperin, David M. "Queer Love." *Critical Inquiry* 45 (Winter 2019): 398–419.
Hart, Sam. "Box Office Breakup." February 14, 2023. https://www.reuters.com/graphics/USA-FILM/akveqmlarvr/.
Hayot, Eric. *The Hypothetical Mandarin: Sympathy, Modernity, and Chinese Pain*. Oxford: Oxford University Press, 2009.
Hedva, Johanna. "Sick Woman Theory." Accessed October 12, 2022. https://johannahedva.com/SickWomanTheory_Hedva_2020.pdf.
Herzog, Amy. *Dreams of Difference, Songs of the Same: The Musical Moment in Film*. Minneapolis: University of Minnesota Press, 2010.
Hitchcock, Alfred. "Why I Make Melodramas." *Film and Stars* (1937). Accessed October 15, 2022. https://the.hitchcock.zone/wiki/Film_and_Stars_(1937)_-_Why_I_Make_Melodramas.
Hoeckner, Berthold. *Film, Music, Memory*. Chicago: University of Chicago Press, 2022.
Hoeckner, Berthold. "Transport and Transportation in Audiovisual Memory." In *Beyond the Soundtrack: Representing Music in Cinema*, edited by Daniel Ira Goldmark, Lawrence Kramer, and Richard Leppert. Berkeley: University of California Press, 2007.
hooks, bell. *All About Love: New Visions*. New York: William Morrow, 2000.
Hooper, Tom, dir. *The King's Speech*. DVD. United Kingdom: UK Film Council, See-Saw Films, Bedlam Productions, 2010.

Hudson, Michael. *Super Imperialism: The Origin and Fundamentals of U.S. World Dominance*. London: Pluto Press, 2015.
Illouz, Eva. *Consuming the Romantic Utopia: Love and the Cultural Contradictions of Capitalism*. Berkeley: University of California Press, 1997.
Isherwood, Christopher. *A Single Man*. London: Methuen, 1964.
James, William. "What Is an Emotion?" *Mind* 9, no. 34 (1884): 188–205.
Jameson, Fredric. *The Political Unconscious: Narrative as a Socially Symbolic Act*. Ithaca, NY: Cornell University Press, 1981.
Jameson, Fredric. "Realism and Utopia in *The Wire*." *Criticism* 52, nos. 3–4 (2010): 367–68.
Johnson, Barbara. "The Frame of Reference: Poe, Lacan, Derrida." *Yale French Studies* 55–56 (1977): 457–505.
Jong, Tien-Tien and Dan Wang. *Watching Film*. Podcast audio. October 9, 2023. https://open.spotify.com/show/3U99UNB78X28wsCeILBsy1?si=27f5a71694744482.
July, Miranda, dir. *Kajillionaire*. DVD. Universal City, CA: Universal Pictures Home Entertainment, 2020.
Kallberg, Jeffrey. *Chopin at the Boundaries: Sex, History, and Musical Genre*. Cambridge, MA: Harvard University Press, 1996.
Kant, Immanuel. *The Metaphysics of Morals*. Cambridge: Cambridge University Press, 1991.
Kay, Jonathan. *Among the Truthers: A Journey Through America's Growing Conspiracist Underground*. New York: Harper, 2011.
Keane, Helen. "Smoking, Addiction, and the Making of Time." In *High Anxieties: Cultural Studies in Addiction*, edited by Janet Brodie and Marc Redfield. Berkeley: University of California Press, 2002.
Khúc, Mimi. "The Revolution Is in the Heart." TEDxUMD. University of Maryland. February 18, 2017. Video of lecture, 17:10. https://www.mimikhuc.com/projects/the-revolution-is-in-the-heart.
Kurtz, Ernest. *Not-God: A History of Alcoholics Anonymous*. Center City, MN: Hazelden, 1979.
LaPierre, Wayne. "NRA: Full Statement by Wayne LaPierre in Response to Newtown Shootings." *The Guardian*, December 21, 2012. https://www.theguardian.com/world/2012/dec/21/nra-full-statement-lapierre-newtown.
Leonard, Robert Z., dir. *In the Good Old Summertime*. DVD. 1949; Burbank, CA: Warner Archive Collection, 2017.
Lubitsch, Ernst, dir. *The Shop Around the Corner* DVD. 1940; Burbank, CA: Warner Home Video, 2002.
MacIntyre, Alasdair. "Liberalism Turned into a Tradition." In *Whose Justice? Which Rationality?* Notre Dame, IN: University of Notre Dame Press, 1988.
Mahmood, Saba. *Politics of Piety: The Islamic Revival and the Feminist Subject*. Princeton, NJ: Princeton University Press, 2005.
Majithia, Sheetal. "Rethinking Postcolonial Melodrama and Affect." *Modern Drama* 58, no. 1 (2015): 1–23.
Marder, Elissa. "Trauma, Addiction, and Temporal Bulimia in *Madame Bovary*." *Diacritics* 27, no. 3 (1997): 49–64.
Markel, Howard. "The D.S.M. Gets Addiction Right." *The New York Times*, June 5, 2012. https://www.nytimes.com/2012/06/06/opinion/the-dsm-gets-addiction-right.html.

Mason, Jeff. "Attacking Anti-Vaccine Movement, Biden Mandates Widespread COVID Shots, Tests." September 10, 2021. https://www.reuters.com/world/us/biden-deliver-six-step-plan-covid-19-pandemic-2021-09-09/.

Massumi, Brian. "The Future Birth of the Affective Fact: The Political Ontology of Threat." In *The Affect Theory Reader*, edited by Melissa Gregg and Gregory J. Seigworth. Durham, NC: Duke University Press, 2010.

Maté, Gabor. *In the Realm of Hungry Ghosts: Close Encounters with Addiction*. Berkeley: North Atlantic Books, 2008.

McDonald, Tamar Jeffers. "Homme-Com: Engendering Change in Contemporary Romantic Comedy." In *Falling in Love Again: Romantic Comedy in Contemporary Cinema*, edited by Stacey Abbott and Deborah Jermyn. London: I. B. Tauris, 2009.

Metzl, Jonathan, and Anna Kirkland. *Against Health: How Health Became the New Morality*. New York: NYU Press, 2010.

Michell, Roger, dir. *Notting Hill*. DVD. 1999; Universal City, CA: Universal Pictures Home Entertainment, 2007.

Miller, D. A. "Secret Subjects, Open Secrets." *Dickens Studies Annual* 14 (1985): 17–38.

Morel, Pierre, dir. *Taken*. DVD. Century City, CA: 20th Century Fox, 2008.

Newitz, Annalee. *Pretend We're Dead: Capitalist Monsters in American Popular Culture*. Durham, NC: Duke University Press, 2006.

Ngai, Sianne. *Theory of the Gimmick: Aesthetic Judgment and Capitalist Form*. Cambridge, MA: Harvard University Press, 2020.

Nowotny, Helga. *Time: The Modern and Postmodern Experience*. Translated by Neville Plaice. Cambridge: Polity, 1994.

Pence, Mike. "Vice President Remarks at NRA's Annual Leadership Forum." May 4, 2018. https://www.c-span.org/video/?444682-101/vice-president-pence-addresses-nras-annual-leadership-forum.

Peritz, Jessica Gabriel. *The Lyric Myth of Voice: Civilizing Song in Enlightenment Italy*. Oakland: University of California Press, 2022.

Povinelli, Elizabeth. *The Empire of Love: Toward a Theory of Intimacy, Genealogy, and Carnality*. Durham, NC: Duke University Press, 2006.

Rancière, Jacques. *The Politics of Aesthetics: The Distribution of the Sensible*. Translated by Gabriel Rockhill. London: Continuum, 2004.

Reddy, Chandan. *Freedom with Violence: Race, Sexuality, and the U.S. State*. Durham, NC: Duke University Press, 2011.

Rivera, Takeo. *Model Minority Masochism: Performing the Cultural Politics of Asian American Masculinity*. Oxford: Oxford University Press, 2022.

Robbins, Allison. "Doubled Selves: Eleanor Powell and the MGM Backstage Musical, 1935–37." *Journal of the Society for American Music* 7, no. 1 (2013): 65–93.

Roberts, Soraya. "RomCon: Our Failure to See Black Romantic Comedies." November 9, 2018. https://longreads.com/2018/11/09/romcon-our-failure-to-see-black-romantic-comedies/.

Saturday Night Live. "Weekend Update: Romantic Comedy Expert—Saturday Night Live." YouTube video. 3:37. October 26, 2014. https://www.youtube.com/watch?v=YxruI7Y7kww.

Schuyler, Susan. "Reality Television, Melodrama, and the Great Recession." *Studies in Popular Culture* 37, no. 2 (2015): 43–65.

Sedgwick, Eve Kosofsky. "Epidemics of the Will." In *Tendencies*. London: Routledge, 1994.

Sedgwick, Eve Kosofsky. *Epistemology of the Closet.* Berkeley: University of California Press, 2008.

Sedgwick, Eve Kosofsky. "Privilege of Unknowing: Diderot's *The Nun*." In *Tendencies.* London: Routledge, 1994.

Seigel, Reva B. "'The Rule of Love': Wife Beating as Prerogative and Privacy." 1996. Faculty Scholarship Series, Paper 1092. http://digitalcommons.law.yale.edu/fss_papers/1092.

Sherman, Rachel. *Uneasy Street: The Anxieties of Affluence.* Princeton, NJ: Princeton University Press, 2017.

Shyamalan, M. Night, dir. *The Happening.* DVD. Century City, CA: 20th Century Fox, 2008.

Sims, David. "Bartlet for America, Forever." *The Atlantic*, May 10, 2016. https://www.theatlantic.com/entertainment/archive/2016/05/west-wing-nostalgia/482022/.

Smith, Dean. "The 365 Day Proposal." YouTube video. 15:44. January 18, 2015. https://www.youtube.com/watch?v=ECRqF4BHkGk&t=183s.

Snorton, C. Riley. *Nobody Is Supposed to Know: Black Sexuality on the Down Low.* Minneapolis: University of Minnesota Press, 2014.

Snorton, C. Riley. "On the Question of 'Who's Out in Hip Hop.'" *Souls* 16, nos. 3–4 (2014): 283–302.

Sorkin, Aaron, creator. *The West Wing: The Complete Series.* DVD. Burbank, CA: Warner Home Video, 2021.

Spielberg, Steven, dir. *A.I. Artificial Intelligence.* DVD. 2001; Hollywood, CA: Paramount Home Media Distribution, 2015.

Spillers, Hortense. "Mama's Baby, Papa's Maybe: An American Grammar Book." *Diacritics* 17, no. 2 (1987): 65–81.

Spivak, Gayatri Chakravorty. "Time and Timing: Law and History." In *Chronotopes: The Construction of Time*, edited by John Bender and David E. Wellbery. Stanford, CA: Stanford University Press, 1991.

Stilwell, Robynn J. "The Fantastical Gap Between Diegetic and Nondiegetic." In *Beyond the Soundtrack: Representing Music in Cinema*, edited by Daniel Ira Goldmark, Lawrence Kramer, and Richard Leppert. Berkeley: University of California Press, 2007.

The American Journal of Bioethics 24, no. 1 (2024).

Thomas, Tony. *Music for the Movies.* South Brunswick, NJ: A. S. Barnes, 1973.

Trump, Donald. "Remarks at the National Rifle Association Institute for Legislative Action Leadership Forum in Indianapolis, Indiana." *GovInfo*, April 26, 2019. https://www.govinfo.gov/content/pkg/DCPD-201900243/html/DCPD-201900243.htm.

US Congress. House. *Homeland Security Act of 2002.* HR 5005. 107th Congress. Introduced in House November 22, 2002. https://www.dhs.gov/sites/default/files/publications/hr_5005_enr.pdf.

Valverde, Mariana. *Diseases of the Will: Alcohol and the Dilemmas of Freedom.* Cambridge: Cambridge University Press, 1998.

Wagner, Richard. *Tannhäuser: In Full Score.* New York: Dover, 1984.

Walker, Tim. 2011. "Colin Firth Was the Third Choice to Play George VI in *The King's Speech*." January 20, 2011. Accessed August 25, 2016. https://www.telegraph.co.uk/news/celebritynews/8269816/Colin-Firth-was-the-third-choice-to-play-George-VI-in-The-Kings-Speech.html.

Wally, Maxine. "WTV Club: Watching The West Wing to Escape From 2020 Politics." *W Magazine*, August 22, 2020. https://www.wmagazine.com/culture/the-west-wing-season-one-w-tv-club-quarantine-binge-watch.

Wang, Dan. "☺ [What Is an Asian American Style?]." In *The Routledge Companion to Gender and Affect*, edited by Todd Reeser. London: Routledge, 2022.

Warren, Mary Ann. "On the Moral and Legal Status of Abortion." *The Monist* 57, no. 1 (1973): 43–61.

Weheliye, Alexander. "After Man." *American Literary History* 20, nos. 1–2 (2008): 321–36.

White, Hayden. *Metahistory: The Historical Imagination in Nineteenth-Century Europe*. Baltimore, MD: Johns Hopkins University Press, 1973.

Whittall, Arnold. "Leitmotif." In *Grove Music Online*, 2001. https://www-oxfordmusiconline-com.pitt.idm.oclc.org/grovemusic/view/10.1093/gmo/9781561592630.001.0001/omo-9781561592630-e-0000016360.

Williams, Linda. "Melodrama Revised." In *Refiguring American Film Genres: History and Theory*, edited by Nick Browne, 42–88. Berkeley: University of California Press, 1998.

Williams, Linda. *Playing the Race Card: Melodramas of Black and White from Uncle Tom to O. J. Simpson*. Princeton, NJ: Princeton University Press, 2001.

Woodward, Kathleen M. *Statistical Panic: Cultural Politics and Poetics of the Emotions*. Durham, NC: Duke University Press, 2009.

Wu, Alice, dir. *Saving Face*. DVD. Culver City, CA: Sony Pictures Home Entertainment, 2005.

Wynter, Sylvia. "Unsettling the Coloniality of Being/Power/Truth/Freedom: Towards the Human, After Man, Its Overrepresentation—An Argument." *The New Centennial Review* 3, no. 3 (2003): 257–337.

Yan, Yunxiang. *Private Life Under Socialism: Love, Intimacy, and Family Change in a Small Chinese Village, 1949–1999*. Stanford, CA: Stanford University Press, 2003.

Žižek, Slavoj. "Madness and Habit in German Idealism: Discipline Between the Two Freedoms." Accessed May 3, 2024. https://www.lacan.com/zizdazedandconfused.html.

Index

Page numbers in italics refer to figures.

Abbate, Carolyn, 21, 103–4, 111–12, 115–19, 126
absence, 7–8, 14, 113, 168; absent presence, 164–65; "silent" orchestra, 115–22; in terrorism films, 133, 135
academic scholarship: affective turn, 12, 16–18; and credentialization, 22–23; essay form, 21, 125–26. *See also* music analysis
addiction, 21, 97–127; attachment drama, 100–101; compulsion texts, 97–100; as disease of both body and mind, 100–101, 110; and event of thought, 108–15; freedom and compulsion, claims of, 101–2; historical frame, 99, 126–27; medical and diagnostic reading of, 101, 126; metarhythm of, 113–15; pedagogy of, 95, 109–10; projections, compulsive, 106–7, 111–12; reversal of moral order of, 114–15; subjectivity effects, 113–15; temporal qualities, 107, 112–13; as term, 126–27; totalities of, 125, *126*; what could have been, 103, 105, 108. *See also* self-determination; therapy
Adorno, Theodor, 92, 119, 125, 126
aesthetic form, 4, 7; circular, 38, 66; historically contingent, 19; lowbrow, 9; and problem of the whole, 122–27; relation between content and form, 12–13

affect, 178n16; asymmetry with time, 62–63; and knowledge, 12, 16–18; of theory, 95–96; of therapeutic "story," 122
affect theory, 8–9, 99, 178n14. *See also* theory
Against Health (Metzl and Kirkland), 95–96
Ahmed, Sara, 38
A.I. Artificial Intelligence (2001), 171–74
Alcoholics Anonymous (AA), 108–10, 153
Althusser, Louis, 179n26
amateur videos, 68–75, 77
ambivalence, 15, 18–19, 41, 127, 130; of present, 111; toward clarity, 18–29
anachronism, 8, 11, 77, 79, 127
Anker, Elisabeth R., 129
aria or number form, 90. *See also* opera
"art" or "experimental" film, 135
assurance effects, 142
audience: as "after" and "outside" the text, 105; character, formal symmetry with, 70–71, 74; confession to, 38–39; crossover into space of fiction, 118–19; epistemic tension of, 13–15; formed into collective, 30, 36, 38, 153; interpellated by recognizable music, 37; mood of modulated by epistemic conventions, 48; narratorial vantage, 71–72; overhearing by, 87–88; passive spectatorial position, 103, 105; and

audience (*Cont.*)
  racism, 160–61; shift to "inside" of opera, 118–20; social recognition by, 38–39, 84; in triangulated love relationship, 71, 75; unsuspension of disbelief, 63–64
audiovisual medium: aesthetics and problem of the whole, 122–27; characters' inability to hear music, 48, 51, 54, 56–57, 118; everydayness/ordinariness imagined in, 128–29; hearing and not-hearing, 111, 115–22, 125, 128; personhood, formulation of, 6–7, 12; required in romantic comedy, 15–16; sound mix, 29, 64, 128–29
Austin, J. L., 8
autobiography, 34, 41, 163

backstage musical, 133
Baldwin, James, 47
Bayer, Vanessa, 50–54
BBC classical music broadcasts, 38
Beethoven, Ludwig van, Seventh Symphony, 35, 37
Behind Office Doors (1931), 13–15
Bergson, Henri, 30
Berlant, Lauren, 5, 8, 31, 49–50, 99, 169, 173; on privacy, 75, 76–77
Bernstein, Leonard, 1–4
Biancorosso, Giorgio, 53
Big Book (Alcoholics Anonymous), 108–10
bioethics, 5, 177n8
Branigan, Edward, 120
Bribitzer-Stull, Matthew, 185n18
Bridget Jones's Diary (2001), 78–79
Brinkema, Eugenie, 49
Brinkmann, Reinhold, 104
broadcasting, 38
brown herring trope, 161–62, *162*
Brown Sugar (2002), 57–62
Buhler, James, 13, 15–16
Bush, George W., 163
Butler, Judith, 182n2

Cabaret (1972), 97–99
camera: affective sense of "something out there" created by, 85–86; agnosticism of, 81; horror film shots, 85, 92; as instrument of romantic confirmation, 79; operatic techniques compared with, 118–19; visual style of, 35–36; as witness, 80; zoom-out and fade-in, 128–31
Cavell, Stanley, 5, 8, 44, 52, 184n35
celebrity, 62–64
Chakrabarty, Dipesh, 182n2
Chandler, James, 31
character: audience, formal symmetry with, 70–71, 74; as both protagonist and editor, 90–91; as "causal system," 120; doubled self, 90; parallelism with critic, 117; reader as, 121; separation of plot and metatext, 63; stripping away of fiction of, 63
Che, Michael, 50–54
child, figure of, 1–4, 67; in epistemic position of parent, 172–73
chorale, as public-domain genre, 111
chronicles, 72–73
Citizen: An American Lyric (Rankine), 11
citizenship, 142, 145, 148, 188n14; allure of being close to power, 132; informed/concerned dyad, 138; ordinariness of, 134–35; protective notion of shattered, 156; shifts in symbolic status of, 159–63; training of reader-citizen, 137–38
clarity, 42, 168–69; ambivalence toward, 18, 29; of epiphanic moments, 95–96, 99, 105–8, 124; as factor of distance, 46; pleasure of, 29; repetition of, 168–69; retrospection within present, 70; search for, 1–4, 15, 18. *See also* thought
cliché, 21, 129, 131; brown herring trope, 161–62, *162*; originality demanded, 154–55; and personhood, 148–56; political phrase as, 149–51; repetition of, 149–50, 167; in romantic comedy, 46, 50–51, 62
Climate Lyricism (Song), 11
common sense, 12–13, 48, 114, 150
Composing for the Films (Adorno and Eisler), 119
concealment: brought out by plot, 81–83; of Hollywood production

mode, 91; of knowledge, 70–71; photographic, 81–82; of "something out there," 85–86. *See also* secrecy

confession: to audience, 38–39; as central formal event of romantic closure, 30; in melodrama, 22; of secret, 60–61; and social dimension of language, 28; social order healed by, 34; structure of disclosure, 61; in terrorism film, 153, 163

consciousness, 100; "public," 37–38

conspiracy genre and theorists, 130, 131, 156–60

conventionality, 149, 168–69, 171

COVID-19 pandemic, 130, 156–57

Culler, Jonathan, 10, 180n2

Derrida, Jacques, 114

desire and sexuality, 13–15; absence of in romantic comedies of 1990s, 76; love as entry into representation, 50; reach of law expanded by, 49, 76; shift from internal to external matter, 29. *See also* heterosexuality

Desplat, Alexandre, 33, 35, 37

diegesis: operatic, 118, 120; romantic comedy, 54–57. *See also* nondiegetic score

difference: and anxiety about public life, 153–54; categorization of, 92–94; knowledge as erotics of, 66; similarity as mark of, 3

disappearance: dimming of aural world, 53–55, 67–68, 111; of forms, 18–19, 184n35; of nation and history, 47; privacy, eradication of, 61

"diversity," rhetoric of, 66, 75

Do the Right Thing (1989), 170

documentary footage in film, 28, 65

double entendre, device of, 56–58, 68

"D.S.M. Gets Addiction Right, The" (Markel), 100–101

Ducille, Ann, 78

Duggan, Lisa, 75

duration, 30, 164

Eisler, Hans, 119

Enlightenment, 5, 10, 110; and addiction, 99, 110, 114

Ephron, Nora, 50, 79–80, 87, 90. *See also You've Got Mail* (1998)

epilogue, 169–71

epiphanies, 117; clarity of, 95–96, 99, 105–8, 124; failure of, 108, 111–12

event, 135–36, 139, 143, 145–48

everydayness/ordinariness: as aesthetic and aural form, 131; as ahistorical, 77; attempts at distancing from, 166; audiovisual imagination of, 128–29; as genre, 69; genre operating in background of, 91–92; intensified awareness of final day, 172; of labor, 133; in musical montage, 74–75, 77, 81; national, 132, 168; performance of, 172; as protected from damaging effects of history, 21, 131, 135–36, 144–45, 156–57, 168; reading the room, 9; relocated from health to illness, 100; sounds of, 166–67; time shift after event, 147–48

expertise, 22–23, 122–23, 138–39

feeling: continuity of, 49, 52; flow of, 34–36, 38; italicized for emphasis, 16–17; knowledge, convergence with, 17, 99, 102; and political hope, 31–32; sentiment, 31–32, 34, 134–35, 172

film music: aural figure of the world dimming, 53, 55, 67–68; characters' inability to hear, 48, 51, 54, 56–57; cliché in, 152–55; co-constitutive relation with love and sexuality, 15–16; diegetic and nondiegetic registers, 57; glossiness of soundtrack, 92; indistinct, 128–29; interpretive role of, 13–15; motivic threads in, 29–30, 88–90; recognizable music vs. score written for film, 37; return to ordinary time from, 42; separation of foreground and background, 15–16, 55–56; shared past of collective listening, 37–38; teaching of, 13–15, 123; technical sources of, 164; transportive effects, 43–44; work of to not be noticed, 119. *See also* nondiegetic score; underscore, musical

Firth, Colin, 20, 24–45

Ford, Tom, 41. See also *Single Man, A* (2009)
Foucault, Michel, 10, 12, 60
Frances Ha (2012), 52–54, 55, 57
freedom, 101–2, 124, 126
future, 48; future-omniscient narratorial position, 69–70, 72; musical montage indicated by, 68; pregnancy as signifier of, 64, 160; "someday," 169. *See also* time

Garland, Judy, 82–84
gaze, 31–32, 36–37, 44
generality, 62, 139, 143, 145, 153, 163, 167, 168
genre, 4, 184n35; and affect theory, 8; in background of ordinariness, 91–92; chorale, as public-domain, 111; conspiracy, 130, 131, 156–60; of the everyday, 69; formal effects of categorization and difference, 45, 92–94; gaps in application of, 148–51, 155–56; heist movie, 165–66; horror, 82, 85, 145; lyric as poetic, 10, 179n22; movement across, 25, 45; musicals, 83–84; and pleasure, 174; post-9/11 terrorist film, 131, 135–48; protagonists as fans of, 93–94; racialized knowledge of, 78–79; synchronic and diachronic models of, 25; zombie, 189n30
good and evil, 151, 155, 163, 184n41
Gorbman, Claudia, 119, 125
Grant, Hugh, 32, 63–64
Griswold v. Connecticut, 76
Gumbrecht, Hans Ulrich, 42
Gupta, Hemangini, 46–47

Halperin, David M., 78
Happening, The (2008), 131, 135–48, *140, 143, 147*; citizenship in, 134–35, 137–38; directorial consciousness present in, 139–41, 143; dispersed aesthetic effect, 139; epistemic anxiety addressed by music, 154–55; explanation withheld, 136, 138–39; generality referenced in, 139, 143, 167
Happiest Season (2020), 60–62

health, ideology of, 20; affective experience of, 98; awareness, intimate and moral practice of, 100–101; capacity to work equated with, 95; and concepts of tragedy, 100–107; moralizing essentialisms about, 95–96; normativity of, 95–96, 101–2; as site of capitalist extraction, 95; subject as implicitly ill, 98–99. *See also* addiction; mental health; therapy
heist movie, 165–66
heterosexuality: as exemption to reach of the law, 49, 76; and musical montage, 67–75; as musical structure, 74. *See also* desire and sexuality
Hitchcock, Alfred, 141
hold music, 164–67
hooks, bell, 49
Hooper, Tom, 32, 35–36. See also *King's Speech, The* (2010)
hope, 31–32, 111
horror genre, 82, 85, 145
human/subhuman distinction, 6

I Hate Music! (Bernstein), 1–4
Illouz, Eva, 49
In the Good Old Summertime (1949), 79, 82–84
individual, singularity attributed to, 10–11
indoctrination, 95–97
interpretation, 148; discomfort with lack of, 13–15; leitmotivic analysis, 104–5; reading the room, 9; through soundtrack, 14–15. *See also* music analysis

Jameson, Fredric, 8, 22, 92, 184n41
July, Miranda, 131. See also *Kajillionaire* (2020)

Kajillionaire (2020), 131, 163–67; "Mr. Lonely" as underscore, 164
Kant, Immanuel, 4–5
Kay, Jonathan, 159
Keane, Helen, 112–13, 114
Khúc, Mimi, 95

King's Speech, The (2010), 20, 24, 32–41; Beethoven's Seventh Symphony in, 35, 37; empire produced as audience, 38; movement from failed speech to successful one, 34, 36; national crisis event in, 27, 32; superhero film structure, 35; talk-therapy plot, 33–34; thematic continuities with *Love Actually*, 32–33, 38–39; visual style, 35–36

Kirkland, Anna, 95–96

knowledge, 46–48; and affect, 12, 16–18; as affective anchor, 110, 124; assurance effects, 142; concealment of, 70–71; epistemic clarity, search for, 1–4, 15, 18; as erotics of difference, 66; expertise, 22–23, 138–39; feeling, convergence with, 17, 99, 102; figures of, 138–39; obvious, 3, 6, 19, 47, 86, 116, 123; of otherness, 155; "political" as a kind of content, 12–16; problem of not knowing, 14–15; racialized knowledge of genre, 78–79; of virtue, 151; withheld in form of puzzle, 104. *See also* thought

Kunst, Ernest, 109

lament, genre of, 42–43

LaPierre, Wayne, 149, 150

leitmotif, 104–5, 112, 185n18; proto-leitmotif, 104, 115

liberalism, 5, 29–31, 35, 49, 78, 81–82, 161

literary romance, 92–93

love, romantic, 174; as aesthetic configuration of the world, 57; audiovisual component required in film, 15–16, 20, 48–49; confirmed by camera, 79; as "cultural" property, 16; description of avoided, 46, 48; embodiment exfoliated by, 49, 80; formal and rhythmic components of, 20; and historical context, 48–49, 77; inversion, 28; liberal, 49, 81–82; "little did I know" as pleasurable, 65–66; modern and "Western," 46–47; as pedagogy of personhood, 68; personhood granted by, 64; as political event, 81; presentness as goal of, 52–54; promise of, 18, 28, 48–49; and representation, 50, 72; revisions of, 78; sense of meeting someone already known, 62–63; transmission of norms, 47–48. *See also* romantic comedy

Love Actually (2003), 20, 24–32, 36; audience formed into collective, 30, 36, 38; closed visual loop of couple, 31, *31*, 36–37; national crisis event in, 27–28; presentness in, 24–25, 27; running scene, 28–29; thematic continuities with *The King's Speech*, 32–33, 38–39

Love & Basketball (2000), 78

Loving v. Virginia, 78

lyricism, 10–12, 24, 36, 45, 179n22; and epistemic difference, 173–74; lyrical time, 11, 83–84, 90

MacIntyre, Alasdair, 29

Marder, Elissa, 21, 107

Markel, Howard, 100–101

Marxist critique, 8, 152, 181n3, 189n28

Maté, Gabor, 113–15

"Maybe This Time" (*Cabaret*), 97–99

McDonald, Soraya Nadia, 78

McDonald, Tamar Jeffers, 183n29

melodrama, 8, 21–22, 181n4, 182n23, 184n41; confessional self-revelation, 22, 38–39; early twenty-first-century resurgence, 148–49, 156; formula of good and bad guys, 151; generality required for, 163; inadequacy of to process threats to US, 129–30; mode, 25–26; national crisis events in, 27–28, 32; newspaper as site of, *140*, 141–42; as response to terrorism, 143, 156

mental health: "if only" idiom, 103–4, 108; self-noticing required, 108; therapeutic discourses, 100. *See also* health, ideology of

"Metempsychotic Wagner" (Abbate), 103–4

Metzl, Jonathan M., 95–96

middle distance, 21, 129, 131, 167

Middle East, as vague "over there," 130

Miller, D. A., 60–61

Minelli, Liza, 97–98
mode, 25–26
modernity: and addict, 21; collective story transformed into individual, 121; modern love, 46–47; music and felt historical transition into, 125; world's indifference, 93
momentum/movement, 11, 31, 44; running in romantic comedy, 28–29
montage, musical, 67–75, 77, 81; amateur, 69–75, 77; character as protagonist and editor, 90–91; as Enlightenment propaganda, 110–11; everyday portrayed in, 74–75, 77, 81; lip-synching in, 73–74, 73
"moral community," 5–6, 177n8
music: as evidence, 116; and representation, 84; retrospective grasp of, 88. *See also* film music
music analysis, 122–26, 153; analyst in role of compulsive subject, 125; and essay form, 21, 125–26; totality by addition and by addiction, 125–26, 126. *See also* Abbate, Carolyn; academic scholarship; interpretation
"Music and the Ontology of the Sound Film" (Buhler and Neumeyer), 13, 15–16
"Music in the Background" (Adorno), 125
musicals: backstage, 133; survival of in nonmusical film, 83–84

narrative: chronicle vs., 72–73; epilogue, 169–71; fantasy centered on, 112; lament about, 42–43; talk therapy as storytelling profession, 120–21
National Rifle Association, 149
nationality/national belonging, 130, 181n6; affective experience of, 20–21, 26–27; circular sense of coherence, 38; national crisis event, 27–28, 32; production of, 133; and sentiment, 31, 34; stammering as emblem of, 32–33, 34
Neeson, Liam, 150, 158–59, 163
Neumeyer, David, 13, 15–16
Newitz, Annalee, 171–72
news, 59–60, 64, 147–48

Nilsson, Harry, 88–89
9/11. *See* September 11, 2001
nondiegetic score, 13–15, 36, 51–57; diegetic source of, 164; elements of in opera, 104–5, 120; imperceptibility of to characters, 51, 54, 56–57, 84. *See also* diegesis; film music
Non-Stop (2014), 150–56, 158–63
normativity, 9, 19; antinormative critical reading, 171–72; child as channel for, 67; chronicle and history within, 73; of health, 95–96, 101–2; lifelong absorption of, 68; as obvious, 47–48; positional or spatial fantasy of, 169; uneven responses to nonheteronormative couples, 64–65
Notting Hill (1999), 57–60, 62–64, 63; Costello song in, 64, 67

Office, The (TV series), 133
"On Being White . . . and Other Lies" (Baldwin), 47
opera, 20–21; aria or number form inherited from, 90; audience shift to "inside" of, 118–20; diegesis of, 118, 120; multiple perspectives portrayed in, 111; recitative, 43, 83; as referent in *Tannhäuser*, 112, 115. *See also Tannhäuser* (Wagner)
optimism, 99, 112
ordinary language philosophy, 8–9. *See also* everydayness/ordinariness
otherness: in film's audiovisual apparatus, 15; knowledge of, 155; as predetermined, 3–4
"Over the Rainbow" (Nilsson), 88–90
Oxford Handbook of Film Music Studies, The, 123–24

pain: movement from trauma to transformation, 35–36; and narrative movement, 31–32, 34; political, 5, 75–76
particularity, 26, 61–62, 78–79, 96, 152–53
pedagogy, 137–38; in personhood, 68; political, 95–96, 99
"perfect day," 42–43

performance: of adult in relation to child, 11, 172; bad acting, 1, 139, 167; being put on the spot, 14–15; of character with imperfect knowledge, 173; of obviousness, 47–48; of ordinariness, 172; performativity of speech, 44, 54–55; referents, 1, 4, 14–15, 47, 63, 74; "unperformed" music, 111; of words marked as words, 54. *See also* audience

Peritz, Jessica Gabriel, 10

personhood/subjectivity, 2–9, 21, 177n8; aesthetic continuousness to the imagination of, 19; appearances of to experiencing subject, 7–8; audiovisual formulation of, 6–7, 12; and cliché, 148–56; comforts of, 169–70; contemporary subject of health, 20; desire as material for, 29; as effect of a rhythm, 113–15; as effect of secrecy, 61; eighteenth-century formations of, 10–11; formal sameness of, 2–3, 45; gendered national, 181n6; granted by romantic love, 64; historical context, 6, 8–9, 48–49; and intimate registers, 15; intramural and intermural functions of, 127; originality demanded by, 154–55, 168–69; as political aspiration, 2–4, 6, 29; retroactive liberal redefinition of, 78; romantic love as pedagogy of, 68; and voice, 32, 39–40. *See also* subject

photographic image, 79–81

politics: cliché, political phrase as, 149–51; empathic, sentimental scene of, 135; "equality" or "diversity" discourse, 66, 75; feeling and political hope, 31–32; love as political event, 81; 1990s as decade of privatization, 75–77; personhood as political aspiration, 2–4, 6, 29; political hope, 31–32; political pain, 5, 75–76; political pedagogy, 95–96, 99; of representation, 12–13; theory, 12, 26; "of true feeling," 75; "voicelessness" as absence of power, 40

Povinelli, Elizabeth A., 31, 49, 81

present: ambivalence of, 111; "little did I know," 65–66; retrospection within, 70; stuckness as failure of knowledge, 66. *See also* time

presentness, 19–20, 24–25, 27; attempt to reproduce, 42–44, 172–74; as goal of romantic love, 52–54; as trope in romantic comedy, 51–52

press conference, architecture of, 58–60, 61

privacy, 61, 115

privatization, 75

Production of Presence (Gumbrecht), 42

public, 36–37; anxiety about in post-9/11 US, 153–54; Black, as semi-private public, 67; chorale as public-domain genre, 111; dance floor as surveilled space, 54; and interview format, 57–60; love, 57–60, 64; "public consciousness," 37–38; representation of, 30; and terrorism, 146; voice amplified by, 33

race: after "postracial" terrorist film, 156–63, *162*; brown herring trope, 161–62, *162*; ordinary life of racism, 11; racialization of genre, 78–79; racialization of will, 110; racial/sexual public, 66; as replacement for nonsecular binaries, 6

Rankine, Claudia, 11

realist style, 141

Rear Window (1954), 170

reciprocity, 31–32

recitative, 42, 83. *See also* opera

recognition, 22, 32; by audience, 38–39, 84; reconciliation of, 91–93; uneven for nonheteronormative couples, 64–65

Reddy, Chandan, 78, 188n9

repetition, 97–98; of clarity, 168–69; of clichés, 149–50, 167; of D-A figure in *Tannhäuser*, 103–5; and event of thought, 109; leitmotif, 104–5; temporality of addiction, 112–13

representation, 12–16, 45, 130, 147; and epilogue, 170; musical score as technique of, 15, 84; of public, 30; and romantic love, 50, 72; of social world, 32, 39; and therapy, 120

respect, 4–5
responsiveness: as epistemic mystery, 14; and social world, 32, 39; temporal lag in, 5, 39, 44
Roberts, Julia, 63–64
Rocky (1976), 74
romantic comedy, 24–32, 46–94, 168; Black film, 78–79; celebrity's function in, 62–64; child image in, 67; cliché in, 46, 50–51, 62; codas, 64; comedy's function in, 39, 50–54; couple as closed visual loop, 31, *31*, 36–37; and liberalism, 31, 39, 81–82; meet-cutes, 54–55; musical love theme, 29–30; partition of inside and outside sound within diegesis, 54–57; presentness as trope in, 51–52; proposal video, 20, 68–75, *70*, *77*, *85*, *90*; protagonists as experts and fans of the genre, 93–94; secrecy as component of, 57, 60–62, 66, 68, 81–83; self-transformation as most essential component, 52–53; spatial distance in, 28–29; uneven recognition for nonheteronormative couples, 64–65; whiteness of as presumed, 78–79. *See also* love, romantic; *Love Actually* (2003)
Rush, Geoffrey, 34

Sandy Hook Elementary School shooting, 149–50
Satie, Erik, 167
Saturday Night Live, "Weekend Update," 50–54, 57
Saving Face (2004), 54–57, 64–65; coda, 64–65; image of child in, 67
science, 10, 137–39, 158
secrecy, 57, 60–62, 66, 68, 79; as marker of present, 86; photographic concealment, 81–82. *See also* concealment
Sedgwick, Eve Kosofsky, 8, 61, 101, 102, 157
self-determination: as attempt to resist compulsive damage, 102; "believe it and it will happen," 99, 107; Enlightenment frame, 99–100; link between will and transformative potential, 99, 107; thought-event of, 107, 108–15. *See also* addiction
sentiment, 31–32, 172; national, 31, 34, 134–35
September 11, 2001, 27–28, 129–30
Shop Around the Corner, The (1940), 79–80, *80*
Shyamalan, M. Night, 131. *See also Happening, The* (2008)
silence, 115–22; analytic relevance of word, 122; audience shift to "inside" of opera, 118–20; displacement of sound, 117–18, 186n35; parallelism between critic and character, 117; reading of in passage of orchestral sound, 115–17, *116*, *117*; unheard melody, aesthetic of, 125, 135
Single Man, A (2009), 24, 41–45; *45*; national crisis event in, 27, 41
Single Man, A (Isherwood), 182n23
Sleepless in Seattle (1993), 76
Smith, Dean, 68–75. *See also* "365 Day Proposal, The" (2015)
social, the: ambivalence toward, 41; pain as birth of, 35; as place where nothing happens, 129; as space of pure transaction, 166; as texture, 128–29
solutions, 96, 99
Song, Min Hyoung, 11
sound mix, 29, 64, 128–29
Souriau, Étienne, 120
spatiality, 28–30, 182n21; external, 42; and musical analysis, 123–24; and subjectivity, 114–15; terrorist attack's agnosticism of, 148
speech: birth of, 39, 44; "coming out," act of, 61; indistinct, in sound mix, 128–29; performativity of, 44; press conference, architecture of, 58–60, 61; Q&A interview, 57–60; uninvited, 54–55, 179n30; words marked as words, 54. *See also* voice
Spielberg, Steven, 171–72. *See also A.I. Artificial Intelligence* (2001)
Spillers, Hortense, 3
Steiner, Max, 15
"Structures of Feeling" (Williams), 178n14

subject: compulsive, 21, 107, 114–15, 124–26; effect of political pedagogy on, 95–96; as implicitly ill, 98–99; impulse for legible selfhood, 96; as interpretive field, 120; of love, 48; minoritized, 130, 143–44, 188n15; unmarked, 19, 77, 100, 130–31, 177n8; Western American, 130; white male revivified by terrorism, 158–61. *See also* personhood/subjectivity

surprise, 23, 55, 62, 70–71, 90, 174

Taken (2008), 135–36, 158–59, 163

Tannhäuser (Wagner), 20–21, 98–99; D-A (perfect fifth) figure repeated, 103–5, 112; epiphany in, 105–7, 111, 117; form of life, 111, 117, 122; hearing and not-hearing in, 111, 115–22, 125; historical newness of soundscape, 115–16; "I should" mode in, 105, 107; leitmotif, 104–5, 112, 115, 185–86n18; modes of tragedy in, 102–4; operatic idiom as referent in, 112, 115; Pilgrims' Chorus, 106, 111, 115, 116–18, 120–21; proto-leitmotif, 104, 115; silence and world in, 115–22; stage directions, 106, 117–18, 186n35

terrorism, 135–48; affective experience of, 130; agnosticism of time and space, 148; as attack on identity, 143–44, 156; brown herring trope, 161–62, *162*; as brown threat, 158–61; epistemic assaults of, 137–38, 143; indifference toward target, 143–44, 148, 156; and knowledge of the other, 155; melodrama as response to, 143, 156; modification of the terrorist figure between 2008 and 2014, 156–60; population itself as target, 145–46, 148; right to everydayness interrupted by, 21, 135–36

terrorism films, Western, 21; American ordinariness as central to, 129; conspiracy genre, 130, 131; race after "postracial" terrorist film, 156–63, *162*; white male subject revivified, 158–61. See also *Happening, The* (2008)

theory, 99, 137, 143; aspirational achievement of, 171; comforts of, 169; of difference, 2, 152–53; fervencies for, 175; as frantic interpretive activity, 148; political, 12, 26; saturated writing on romantic love, 46; as sensory-affective experience, 95–96; sonic, 55. *See also* affect theory

therapy, 20, 50; immanence of past in present, 121; talk therapy as storytelling profession, 120–21; talk-therapy plot, 33–34; used to differentiate West from symptomatic rest of the world, 127. *See also* addiction; health, ideology of

thought, 168; event of, 108–15; metaphysical, 4–5; thought-projection, 112; "will power" and "self-knowledge" uncoupled from, 109. *See also* clarity; knowledge

"365 Day Proposal, The" (2015), 68–75, *70*, 77, 85, 90; lip-synching in, 73–74, *73*; reconciliation of recognition, 93

time, 188n10; and addiction, 107, 112–13; asymmetry with affect, 62–63; "best day of your life" idiom, 69–70; duration, 30, 164; edit, temporal register of, 74; eventness, 135–36, 146; "every moment of every day" idiom, 69–70, 72–73; external, 42; extraction of, 163; linear, 21, 84, 97, 101, 113, 147–48, 188n10; lyrical, 11, 83–84, 90; "maybe this time" idiom, 97–99, 110, 121–22; phased out at end of romantic comedy, 68; sequential, 97–98; subjunctive mood, 103, 105, 108, 172. *See also* presentness

tragedy, classical and modern concepts of, 100–107

transparency, 6–7, 12, 151

Trump, Donald, 149–50, 153

2001: A Space Odyssey (1968), 67

underscore, musical, 21, 190n37; audience awareness of, 119–20; and cliché, 151–52; hold music, 164–67; musical backgrounds of modernity, 125; nondiegetic, 13–15, 36, 51, 54, 55,

underscore, musical (*Cont.*)
  83–84; recognizable by public, 37; unheard melody, aesthetic of, 125, 135; voice tied to, 30; zoom-out distinct from, 128–29. *See also* film music
Unheard Melodies (Gorbman), 119
United States: affective experience of vulnerability, 130; "America" as obvious, 47; antistate position and institutional authority, 156–58; January 6, 2021, attack on Capitol, 157; liberal aesthetic mode, 161; ordinariness, audiovisual imagination of, 129; terrorism discourse, 129; Western American subject, 130

Valverde, Mariana, 110
virtue, as knowable, 151
voice, 10, 182n17; abstraction of, 44–45; birth of speech, 39, 44; disembodiment of, 27; as metonym for promised self-realizations, 19–20; and personhood, 32, 39–40; public amplification of, 33; shift from intimate to public, 36–37; singularity of, 40–41; sound of underscore tied to, 30. *See also* speech
voice-over, 24, 42, 65
vulnerability, affective experience of, 130

Wagner, Richard, 20–21, 98; *Gesamtkunstwerk*, 124, 126, 187n42; leitmotivic practice, 104–5. *See also Tannhäuser* (Wagner)
Warner, Michael, 49
Warren, Mary Ann, 177n8
"West": as an identity and an object, 130–31; loss of meaningfulness, 18–19; "Western love," 46–47
West Wing, The (TV series), 128, 131, 132–35, 148; as antidote for political depression, 134; figure of president as History, 133–35; patriarchal symbolic in, 135; terrorism in, 159, 160
White, Hayden, 72–73
Whittall, Arnold, 185n18
Williams, Raymond, 178n14
witness: audience as, 38–39; camera as, 80
Wu, Alice, 54. *See also Saving Face* (2004)
Wynter, Sylvia, 6

X-Files, The (TV series), 158

You've Got Mail (1998), 50, 79–93, 84, 89; musical motifs in, 88–90; "Over the Rainbow" theme in, 88–90, 92

www.ingramcontent.com/pod-product-compliance
Lightning Source LLC
Chambersburg PA
CBHW022055290426
44109CB00014B/1112